THE PRIDE AND THE PRESSURE

THE
PRIDE
AND THE
PRESSURE

A SEASON INSIDE THE
NEW YORK YANKEE
FISHBOWL

MICHAEL MORRISSEY

PHOTOS COURTESY OF ANTHONY J. CAUSI

DOUBLEDAY
NEW YORK   LONDON   TORONTO   SYDNEY   AUCKLAND

PUBLISHED BY DOUBLEDAY

Copyright © 2007 by Michael Morrissey

All Rights Reserved

Published in the United States by Doubleday, an imprint of The Doubleday Broadway
Publishing Group, a division of Random House, Inc., New York.
www.doubleday.com

DOUBLEDAY and the portrayal of an anchor with a dolphin are
registered trademarks of Random House, Inc.

Insert photographs courtesy of Anthony J. Causi, except for
the Torre/Cashman photo, © Steve Nesius / Reuters / Corbis.

Book design by Tina Henderson

Library of Congress Cataloging-in-Publication Data
Morrissey, Michael, 1972–
The pride and the pressure : a season inside the New York Yankee fishbowl/
Michael Morrissey. — 1st ed.
p. cm.
1. New York Yankees (Baseball team) I. Title.
GV875.N4M66 2007
796.357097471—dc22
2007000825

ISBN 978-0-385-52086-7

PRINTED IN THE UNITED STATES OF AMERICA

1 3 5 7 9 10 8 6 4 2

First Edition

To Mom and Dad, the cornerstones of my life.
And to Alena, the inspiration of it.

"We're a different club this year."

JOE TORRE, APRIL 7, 2006

CONTENTS

ACKNOWLEDGMENTS

I'd like to thank everyone at the Yankees who helped make this book possible. It was an enjoyable journey, despite the abrupt finality of the season. Brian Cashman, Joe Torre, and Randy Levine deserve special thanks for allowing me to repeatedly draw upon their considerable expertise.

Other interviews included Bobby Abreu, T. J. Beam, Larry Bowa, Brian Bruney, Robinson Cano, Melky Cabrera, David Cone, Bubba Crosby, Johnny Damon, Billy Eppler, Sal Fasano, Kyle Farnsworth, Jason Giambi, Goose Gossage, Ron Guidry, Reggie Jackson, Derek Jeter, Jeff Karstens, Joe Kerrigan, Cory Lidle, Jim Leyritz, Hideki Matsui, Don Mattingly, Lee Mazzilli, Bobby Murcer, Mike Mussina, Mike Myers, Andy Phillips, Jorge Posada, Scott Proctor, Mariano Rivera, Alex Rodriguez, Gary Sheffield, Matt Smith, Darryl Strawberry, Ron Villone, Suzyn Waldman, Chien-Ming Wang, Bernie Williams, and Jaret Wright. Additional information was obtained through other sources who wished to remain anonymous. Randy Johnson declined an interview, and George Steinbrenner refused repeated written inquiries.

I am indebted to those who provided the day-to-day coverage of the most scrutinized team in North America. Their coverage is without peer, and this book is better because of it. Wherever possible, I attempted to attribute quotes that were exclusive to a given news organization. The writers at MLB.com, the *Hartford Courant, Newark Star-Ledger, Bergen Record*, Westchester *Journal News, Newsday, New York Times*, New York

Daily News, and *New York Post* do their jobs in the most professional manner possible, and it's been a privilege to work with and get to know many of them well. Peter Abraham, Jack Curry, Ken Davidoff, Jennifer Royle, and Anthony McCarron are just a few people who have made the clubhouse more enjoyable.

Scott Waxman of the Waxman Literary Agency deserves my deepest gratitude for taking a chance on someone he met through a cold-call e-mail and honing my proposal into something worth reading.

Doubleday's Jason Kaufman, simply one of the best editors in the business (*The Da Vinci Code* is atop his résumé), deserves great thanks for working with a first-time author and answering my many questions and concerns. The people at Doubleday are top-notch.

My thanks to *New York Post* sports editor Greg Gallo for allowing me to pursue this project, and assistant sports editor Dick Klayman deserves credit for juggling my schedule. I am indebted to Mike Vaccaro for always providing sound wisdom. The *Post*'s baseball people—Joel Sherman, George King, and Mark Hale—are invaluable to the newspaper. I'm thankful to have learned so much from them. Other *Post* colleagues who have become friends include Brian Costello, Steve Serby, and Dan Martin. Matt Romanoski deserves infinite gratitude for hiring me for *New York Post Sportsweek,* and for remaining a friend I can I count on to this day.

At the University of Massachusetts, former journalism heads Howard Ziff and Norm Sims deserve special thanks. In Amherst, I made lifelong friendships with exceptional people like Dan Wetzel, Andrew Bryce, Matt Vautour, Art Stapleton, Tracy Monahan, Caleb Cochran, Emily Marino, and Kelly and Andrew Ferguson.

Along my journalism journey, Pat Turley, Greg Smith, and Mike Clark deserve credit for seeing some talent and nurturing it. And I don't think I would've remained in the industry without friends like Matt Youmans and Steve Hanlon.

Finally, I'd like to thank Helen Pandelios, who so warmly welcomed me into her life (and her home on the Greek island of Kefalonia, where a portion of the book was written); and Peter and Sophie Jemas and the entire Jemas clan, whose zeal over this project is matched only by the enthusiasm with which they've welcomed me into their lives.

To my loving sister, Pamela, brother-in-law, Dan, and nephew, Andrew, I wholeheartedly agree: life makes the best story of all.

THE PRIDE AND THE PRESSURE

CHAPTER ONE

HOME OPENER

APRIL 11, 2006

B rian Cashman fiddled with his World Series ring. Twisted it, turned it, slid it off his ring finger, and put it back on. It was a glorious spring day in New York City, and the Yankees were about ninety minutes from their home opener against Kansas City, which, for millions of fans who live and die with the team, meant renewed hope and anxious expectation.

As Cashman stood on the lush grass just wide of the first-base line at Yankee Stadium, he intermittently (and subconsciously) toyed with the bauble while discussing, among other things, how badly he wanted to win another. And how immense the challenge would be. And how lucky the Yankees were to have the ones they owned. The diamond-encrusted ring was, obviously, gorgeous; it was a talisman that signified the triumphant moment men spend their lives toiling to attain. Having been in the Yankees organization since he was an intern in 1986—and having been the GM since 1998—Cashman had his pick of rings.

But he always gravitated toward the one from 2000.

"It was the toughest one to get," he said.

It was also the twenty-sixth, and last, the Yankees had earned.

Just a few moments earlier, Cashman had shared a moment with Johnny Damon, the newest hired gun in the Yankees' mercenary arsenal. The two joked around and gave each other gentle pats on the back after batting practice, and then Damon went into the clubhouse to prepare for the game. Damon's improbable, clandestine departure from Boston over the winter was the stuff of legend, a late-night coup that enraged Boston fans. Even some Yankees fans had a tough time initially swallowing the move, which once and for all bumped the beloved Bernie Williams out of a position he had owned since 1993. In essence, it was a real-life defection with as much suspense as a Tom Clancy novel. Damon was the Yankees' *Red October*.

So when Cashman was asked whether it would take time for Damon to completely win over Yankee Stadium, the GM paused for four seconds. The answer was one he would rather not acknowledge.

"Probably," he finally responded. "Some people are already on board, some people are die-hard Red Sox haters. Roger Clemens took a while for people to adjust [to] when he got here. And I'm sure for some people it took a while for Wade Boggs to adjust to when he got here. So some people are going to embrace it right off the bat. Some people are still going to have some of those memories of the damage that Johnny did against us over the years."

Cashman was right on target, judging from the boos Damon received that day. But it was nothing like the nasty reception the Yankee center fielder would receive when he returned to Boston in early May.

Not only was it bizarre that the Yankees had an "idiot" Boston immigrant patrolling center field, but Cashman's return in 2006 was something that was far less than a certainty. When the Yankees lost to the Angels in Game 5 of the ALDS in October 2005, he cried in the bowels of Angel Stadium. His contract was up, and many baseball observers thought the episode was proof he was mentally and emotionally moving on. (Coincidentally, it was only a few days earlier that Damon had broken down in the Fenway clubhouse, mourning a season and his own potential exodus.) For years, Cashman had uncomfortably wiggled under The Boss' thumb, honored to be in such a lofty position at such a young age but constantly thwarted by the backstabbing and machinations of others in the Yankee Fishbowl.

The rogue Tampa faction was especially insidious, since it operated where Steinbrenner, looking feebler every year, now made his home year-round. In the end, Cashman knew his best chance of winning came in New York. And he couldn't cut the cord to a team he himself had built.

"The challenges would've been anywhere," Cashman said. "If I went somewhere else, I would've been in the same mind-set. But I have a lot invested. It's not just as simple as you sit down at a table in the winter with an agent, or you sit across the table from a player."

Cashman felt the obligation to players such as Alex Rodriguez, who had agitated for a trade from Texas after the 2003 season even though he had just won the MVP there and was the game's highest-paid player, with a $252 million contract. When a deal with Boston fell through before the 2004 season, Rodriguez offered to change positions and become a third baseman. Jason Giambi was another established All-Star who had followed to the place where Tino Martinez, Paul O'Neill, and other Steinbrenner "warriors" had once beaten all comers. Giambi exited Oakland after the 2001 season, even though the California native was a frat-house king with the A's. Of course, the money was way better in New York (seven years, $120 million), but Giambi toned down his personality and polished his image in order to conform to what he hoped were world-championship standards.

"I mean, there's so many examples," Cashman said. "And it's not BS. These guys are sincere."

Cashman cited another: Mike Mussina, who prior to the 2001 season had left the Baltimore organization he grew up in, alienating a fan base with which he had an excellent relationship, to sign with a hated division rival. Back on November 30, 2000, the day Mussina signed a six-year contract, you never in your life would've guessed that he wouldn't win at least one World Series with the Yankees—who had won four of the previous five at that time. Mussina, who was now thirty-seven, was in his final season with the Yankees unless the team exercised a club option. Late in 2005, his pitching elbow began bothering him for the first time, and he missed twenty-one games.

"Who knows how much longer he's pitching?" Cashman said. "He's been great for us so far, and he's been a great free-agent sign. In his first year, we got to the World Series. And in his third year, we got to the World Series. But we didn't complete it. You don't want to be that close."

Essentially, Cashman conceded that the pressure to win a title had grown greater. The Yankee Fishbowl had grown smaller, and every year there were bigger fish swimming in it. Whereas the Yankees had once relied on a mixture of homegrown talent and veterans such as Scott Brosius, Martinez, and O'Neill, who seemed to be better than their stats when crunch time came, they had now accumulated immense talent and big personalities—some would say at the expense of chemistry. And yet the GM chose not to think of the title drought in terms of pressure.

Instead, Cashman took a proactive approach, trying to cultivate a culture where being a Yankee meant being accountable to the exacting standards of perfection. That's why he insisted, when he signed his new contract with Steinbrenner, on a separate agreement acknowledging that he'd have full authority over the personnel of the club. (Whether the famously impatient and temperamental Steinbrenner would adhere to such a guarantee was another story.)

When the dust settled on the 2006 season, Cashman said, he wanted to be able to look in the mirror and know he had done everything he could to try to attain a championship. He believed in setting a goal, and establishing a plan to achieve the goal. But at the same time, he understood that it was a sport played by fallible people. He recognized that there were other teams in other cities trying to accomplish the same goal.

"If somebody's better than you, you can live with it," he said. "You just don't want to miss opportunities, you don't want to look back and say, 'I wish I did it differently,' or 'I wish I would've worked a little harder,' or 'I wish I would've planned a little bit better.' You just don't want any of those. Because I can live with doing everything possible, checking off everything and tip your hat if someone was better. But you don't want to look back and say, 'That should've been ours.'"

The Yankees hadn't even returned to the Fall Classic since 2003, where they lost to an upstart Florida bunch after holding a two-games-to-one lead in the series.

"I know people are worried about how we haven't won a World Series in five years," Cashman said. "It's supposed to be some sort of insult, I guess. But it's not. I recognized even when we were winning how difficult [it was]. You can look in the archives and pull it out. We said at that time, 'People better pay attention to what they're witnessing right now, because this stuff doesn't happen like this very often.' And it doesn't, runs like that.

"And obviously we're operating in the shadows of the '96, '98, '99, 2000 championship clubs. And people keep saying, because we haven't done that, we're failures. That is so special. It's hard to win one, let alone [four out of five] and being in the World Series two years after that. It was such a great, successful run. We still feel like we're capable. But we've got to prove it. I know how difficult it is, I know how hard our guys try. And it's all I can ask of anybody, and all that these guys ask of themselves."

Once again, the Yankees outspent the competition. Their Opening Day payroll was about $194 million, which was actually down $14 million from the year before. But the former boy-wonder GM knows that everybody from The Boss, George Steinbrenner, on down is restless. The fact that the team opened 2-4 on the road did nothing but raise the alert level a notch.

"There's definitely an urgency here," Cashman said.

For Cashman, the human toll of wins and losses is all too real. It really bothered him, for instance, that Tom Gordon came to New York for the 2004 season and left without winning a world championship. Gordon, an accomplished former starter who'd switched to being a closer in the latter stages of his career, had his choice of Boston, Oakland, and Tampa Bay that particular winter. He probably would've closed with either the Devil Rays or A's, as it turned out, but he instead became Mariano Rivera's eighth-inning setup guy.

"And he came here—because he wanted the ring," the GM said. "And it bothers . . ." Cashman's voice trailed off. "It's just kind of a wake-up call for the rest of us here, that you know what, we're on the clock," he said.

In the midst of this discussion, Cashman began fiddling with the 2000 World Series ring again. He'd transported himself back to a February day in Tampa when Joe Torre gave perhaps his best speech as a Yankee manager and Cashman followed with a soliloquy about missed opportunities. Torre, who considers himself an introvert, has never been totally comfortable addressing groups, but his impassioned speech about the unacceptability of anything less than a world championship was punctuated with a determination that left even the veteran players impressed and inspired. Cashman, in his turn, challenged the clubhouse full of superstars, appealing to them at their most human level.

The message Cashman was describing during this April conversation was the exact message he had given the players a few weeks earlier.

"I'm here to try to win," Cashman had told the players that day. "I've won before, but it's not like that's satisfying. You're here to try to do something together here now."

Cashman, whose slight, balding exterior is juxtaposed with the tenacity of a junkyard dog and the deal-making skills of a Beltway lobbyist, actually began singling players out. He wasn't calling them out, but rather bringing attention to their status. By pointing fingers, Cashman was hoping he'd unite the team. It was a calculated attempt to foster chemistry, and Cashman hammered his message home.

"Guys, Moose [Mussina] is at the end of his contract," Cashman began. Then he turned to Jason Giambi and Gary Sheffield. "Giambi, you've got two years left. Sheff, you've got this year and most likely next year.

"Johnny Damon, all right, you've just signed on for four years. And A-Rod, you've been here for two. But we're all on the clock: to try to win.

"I don't want to feel like I did this winter, when Tommy left us to join the Phillies. You know what? He had a great time. But all he has is memories. We're here to try to do more than just that."

A-Rod, for one, took the message to heart and parroted Cashman's phrase that "we're all on the clock" during the spring.

"We've got guys who came here for a reason that haven't been able to complete that purpose yet," Cashman said. "And you focus on those things."

In the home opener against Kansas City, Williams, the longest-tenured Yankee, received the warmest ovation of anyone. But he made a baserunning gaffe in the fourth inning that killed momentum, and the Yanks lost an early lead and trailed 7-4 heading into the eighth.

Damon heard boos in his first at-bat and whiffed feebly on three pitches in the eighth in a potential go-ahead situation, and the disappointed crowd collectively groaned. But Derek Jeter followed with a go-ahead three-run homer that saved Damon's bacon, helped the Yanks to a 9-7 victory, and served as the first hint that it might be a particularly special year for the team's captain. Damon was relieved that he wasn't the goat in a loss. Cashman, ultimately, felt the fans would rally behind his biggest acquisition in the off-season.

"Johnny? They're going to like him," Cashman had said confidently hours earlier. "They will."

That wouldn't be an issue in 2006. Damon's return to Boston was a much bigger story. And as it turned out, Boston fans weren't ever going to feel the same way about him again.

CHAPTER TWO

DAMON

The irony was almost too unbelievable to be true, but it was seemingly lost on everyone in the media swarm that gathered at Fenway Park on a nastily cold afternoon on May 1. Exactly a year earlier, Johnny Damon had vowed this day would never happen. To Red Sox fans, that was the shame of it all.

On May 1, 2005, before a Sunday game in Arlington, Texas, Damon told MLB.com, "There's no way I can go play for the Yankees, but I know they are going to come after me hard." He went on, "It's definitely not the most important thing to go out there for the top dollar, which the Yankees are going to offer me. It's not what I need."

Yet here he was, exactly a year later, dressed in a navy blue pullover with the NY crest on his chest, sitting down in an afternoon press conference as an enemy. About seventy-five media members crammed into a small, windowless room that had the look of a classroom and listened to the new Yankee center fielder say all the right things for about seventeen minutes. Much of the questioning had to do with how Damon felt he'd be received.

"Most of the fans that I have seen on the streets have said, 'Thank you, we wish you were here. We kind of understand what you had to do,'" he said, adding later, "I think I just had a fan ask me, 'Was it worth it?' and I told him, 'So far, so good.'"

Since Damon was introduced as a Yankee on December 23, he had been answering the same questions as to whether the Red Sox fans would cheer him for bringing an improbable world championship to Beantown during his four wonderful years there or boo him for defecting to the enemy. After all, this was a rivalry that in various accounts had been called a "hundred-year war," a "blood feud," and even a dispute that rivaled the one in *Star Wars*. Or the Cold War, if you happen to believe CEO Larry Lucchino was calling the Yankees Commies when he referred to them as the "evil empire" a few years earlier.

Damon said he would understand if fans booed him, but he called his time there "magical," the 2004 team "very special," and the Red Sox "a class organization." He even claimed the return of backup catcher Doug Mirabelli, in a trade that day, was a bigger story than his own return.

"Boston was just incredible to me," he said. "For four years, going to Fenway Park every day was a treat. Going to the house today was nice. It definitely is a lot bigger than a condo in Manhattan."

He liked to portray himself as an idiot, but the reality was that Damon combined his many childlike traits with a shrewdness and grasp of nuance that made him far more intelligent than many major leaguers. In trying to deflect the possibility of widespread boos, Damon noted that ballplayers get booed everywhere they go, even at home. At the same time, though, he pointed out—in his own docile way—that he didn't agree with the approach.

"That's the unfortunate part of this," he noted. "I know I'm going to have some boos. And I can get on with my life, I can move forward. I think that's just the kind of person I am. . . .

"I've never been to a sporting event, concert, walking down the street, I've never booed anyone. And I commend my parents for being so great in teaching me how life is. Unfortunately, we did not grow up in an area that was passionate about baseball like Boston, like New York, St. Louis. We kind of just grew up in Happy Land, close to Disney World."

Damon clearly was no dummy, having prevented his wife, Michelle, from coming to what was scheduled as a two-game series (the May 2 game was rained out). Michelle Damon had once reportedly gotten into an altercation with Curt Schilling's wife, Shonda, during the 2004 ALCS, apparently over whether or not to wear "good-luck scarves." She had gone on record in the *Boston Globe* to address her reputation as a home wrecker (Damon's first wife reportedly called her that) and a former stripper (she said she wasn't). Imagine how such a woman, unafraid of verbal combat, might tear into your average Jim from Abington with a "Benedict Damon" sign.

"She wanted to be here to support me, but things can get crazy," he said. "She stands out; that's the bottom line. People say things, and she's very defensive of me.

"Whenever she hears something about me, she doesn't want to hear it. I told her, 'Now's not a good time to be here.' I'm sure there will be cheers, but I'm sure they're also going to be saying things about me. I'm OK with that. Here I am."

Damon ended his press conference with his signature gesture, giving peace signs with both hands. Hours later, the Fenway fans would reject that offering. But when Damon left the media throng behind to prepare for the game, something spontaneous—something wonderful—happened. As he walked through the Fenway Park underground concourse from the first-base side to the third-base side, concession employees began clapping and waving.

"Hey, Johnny," a young woman called out.

"Thank you," another woman said.

The culmination was a group of about twenty Red Sox employees who were stationed along the third-base side, where the visiting clubhouse is. They were all wearing the team colors. Some wore authentic fire-red Red Sox jackets.

"Welcome back, Johnny," most of them shouted, clapping with their hands above their heads.

A woman in her fifties stopped Johnny, asked him to come over, and told him how cute he was and how she wished he hadn't had to shave and cut his hair.

A short, world-worn fellow in his sixties then caught Damon's attention and simply said, "Thank you," and gave him a thumbs-up. It was one of those rare moments when a person can touch another on the most basic human level, when title or status doesn't matter. From the look in the man's watery eyes, you could tell he was referring to the 2004 World Series, and he was able to thank one of the people responsible for ending a lifetime of heartbreak in New England. Damon acknowledged the sentiment with a smile and went in to prepare for that night's game, went in to prepare for the hatred that would follow such a wonderful exchange.

As 5 P.M. rolled around, fans waited outside Gate A on Yawkey Way to pour into the majors' oldest ballpark, and more than a few wore T-shirts dissing Damon or carried signs pointing out what they felt was his betrayal. Across the street from the ballpark, inside a souvenir store, a sign declared, "All Damon Shirts $10." A helpful employee noted that it was still possible to buy an authentic number 18 Red Sox jersey, although "it's now a Dustan Mohr jersey."

The gates opened, and fans streamed through the turnstiles. Don Coburn, a twenty-five-year-old who had driven down from Vermont, was wearing a black "No Hair No Beard No Soul" T-shirt with his camouflage Boston hat. The way Coburn saw it, Damon had gone back on his word. Regardless of the disparity of the offers, the center fielder was a traitor for going to what Coburn called "the worst team in baseball." He told one reporter that he'd even considered bringing his formerly treasured copy of the Jimmy Fallon/Drew Barrymore movie *Fever Pitch*—which was a fictional account of a Red Sox fan's ride through the 2004 season—and tossing it on the field.

"When the Yankees came and offered him a little bit more, he decided to go to the retirement home and go over to play in New York," Coburn said. "Oh, I hate 'em."

Daryl Conant drove down from Kennebunk, Maine, and carried a life-size torso of Damon in a Red Sox uniform that was defaced. On the torso were the phrases "Benedict Damon," "I Like Men," and "I Sold Out." The Red Sox logo on the uniform was scratched out and replaced with "I Am a Loser." The *B* on Damon's cap became an *L*.

Conant, thirty-seven, will never forget when he heard the news of Damon's departure. He was in his office at the health club he owns, and the event shook him to his core. He was so "pissed," he said, it took him about a month to get over it. But clearly he was still holding on to some strong feelings.

In the dead of winter, Sox fans look forward to spring training the way a child looks forward to Christmas. While Damon was preparing for his season in the warm climes of his Orlando home, Boston fans agonized over the turn of events in the depressing dreariness of a New England winter. This night, they reasoned, was their chance at revenge, their chance at redirecting their hurt.

"He sold out," Conant said. "He's making plenty of money. He knows how much it hurts the Red Sox Nation to go to the Yankees."

In assessing Damon's financial value, both the Red Sox and Yankees had to take into consideration how productive he'd be three and four seasons down the road. The Yankees offered $12 million more. Conant was unwavering in his analysis of Damon circa 2009.

"I think he's going to be a bum," he said.

Not everyone shared that sort of vitriol. Dana Calnan, a forty-two-year-old from Portland, Maine, said he would cheer Damon once and then boo him. "I don't blame him," Calnan said. "Hey, he went for the money. But I'm a Red Sox fan."

New Yorker Steve Tillim attended the game with his date, Jody Kipnis, from Boston. Tillim wore a Yankees T-shirt with Damon's name and number along with his Yankees cap, while Kipnis was sporting a red "Real Women Don't Date Yankee Fans" T-shirt. Tillim predicted he'd be treated almost as rudely as Damon but said he could handle it "as long as the crowd does not throw too much stuff at me."

"He had his shirt Scotchgarded," Kipnis cheerfully noted.

Inside the park, the posters that many fans sported were unflinchingly harsh. One had a sign that said "Johnny Demon," with an "NY" on the forehead of a picture of Damon. Others read, "Hey New York—Your Village Has Our Idiot," "Anywhere but There," "Johnny, You Truly Are an Idiot," "Damon Looks Like Jesus, Acts Like Judas, Throws Like Mary," "Damon Has an Arm Like a Foot," "WWJD? Betray?" The anger cut across gender lines. One young lady wore a Damon jersey with the number crossed out. Another woman, with two kids in tow, carried a sign that read, "Johnny Who?"

The Fenway crowd was merciless. Damon was heckled when he took batting practice, booed when he warmed up in the outfield, jeered during the lineup announcement, and then given the coldest possible reception when he stepped in the batter's box.

As Damon prepared to dig into the dirt around home plate with his Puma cleats, boos rained down not only from Fenway but also from virtually everywhere in Red Sox Nation. If you looked through your mind's eye during the thirty-second boofest, you could almost envision a senior

citizen in Kittery, Maine, or a six-year-old in Clinton, Connecticut, screaming at the TV at the exact same time. New England, birthplace of the town
meeting, had voted democratically and resoundingly. The nays had it.
Damon was no longer welcome or even held in esteem in the community,
a modern-day Hester Prynne. "Suck it, Johnny," one leatherlung belted
out from the outfield seats.

The upbeat outfielder was undaunted, however. He acknowledged his
former teammates in the home dugout on the first-base line, pointing to
them. He even took off his helmet in tribute to Red Sox fans and in honor
of what he'd been able to help accomplish: namely, the 2004 World Series.

And something happened, if you listened closely enough. The minority cheers in the crowd continued, at least around the stands behind home
plate. Damon certainly heard them. Eventually, the fans who wanted to
thank Damon had their brief say, growing louder as the bass sound of
boos dimmed. Finally, the left-handed hitter got down to the business of
batting. He flied out to right, part of an 0-for-4 game.

"Regardless of the reaction, I felt a lot of fans wanted to see it," Damon
said of his tipping of the helmet. "I heard more cheers than jeers, so I was
going to do it regardless."

In the bottom of the first, Damon listened to chants of "Johnny Sucks"
and "Traitor!" from his old, familiar spot on the Fenway Park lawn. Fans
tossed both real and fake money on the warning track. In the ninth, with
Boston's 7-3 victory well in hand, he was serenaded with derisive "Johnny"
taunts. Damon's old Boston teammates were livid but not surprised. As
Kevin Youkilis told reporters, "It was kind of sad. He acknowledged the
crowd and they didn't want any part of it."

Actually, Damon said he'd prepared for the vitriol before the game with
his teammates: "I told them to start calling me every name in the book."

Joe Torre, always a thoughtful man, provided perhaps the best perspective.

"Well, Johnny Damon, there's a lot to him. I was a little disappointed
in the reaction by the fans. I guess we should feel proud," Torre said. "Evidently, wearing a Yankee uniform overrides winning a World Series and
busting your tail for four years. Without Johnny here, they might have
been working on eighty-nine or ninety years. It's too bad they don't appreciate that more so than they dislike the fact that he's wearing our uniform."

Although Damon said nearly all the right things, he was stung. Privately, his animosity was directed toward Boston management, which had

encouraged him to come to Beantown in December for charity work but kept him at arm's length the entire time, saying they didn't want to deal with his contract and would rather focus on signing Kevin Millwood. Although their best, last offer was a four-year, $40 million pact, Damon was insulted by their initial three-year, $27 million proposal. Former Boston pitcher Luis Tiant said the Red Sox ran Damon out of town on their cable network, NESN; the comment pleased Damon.

"I think they're just upset that I'm not out there for them," he said the next day. "They knew all along how I wanted to be here for the rest of my career. And now I bought a huge house that is sitting empty.

"It's just unfortunate. In the game of sports, guys are free agents. And it's hardly ever good."

Truth is, Damon was liberated from Boston—he said his final season there was excruciating. The Red Sox, who'd come back from a three-games-to-none deficit in the 2004 ALCS, were swept by Chicago in the five-game ALDS the next year. He felt the winds shifting in Boston, and not necessarily for the better. Instead of Red Sox Nation expecting a summer swoon, as had happened uncountable times, now nothing but a world championship would suffice.

"I think the players of the past, it was tough for," he said about Boston. "Because they didn't have anyone who just [said], 'Big deal, who cares about the Curse? We weren't alive when it started.' But I think just a group of guys, we really didn't give a shit.

"Last year was tougher because everybody expected us to do well. And when you don't have a healthy Schilling, when you don't have a healthy [Keith] Foulke, when you're fiddling around with who's closing. You've got [Jonathan] Papelbon in the minors and it's, 'Hey, let's do something.' When is [Kevin] Millar and a lot of guys going to start hitting again?

"So we were dealing with a lot of problems that made the year miserable when all was said and done. When we lost, we didn't feel like we had much going in, especially after we got drilled that first game [Game 1 of the ALDS versus Chicago]."

During a candid discussion in late May, Damon explained the differences between the Boston and New York organizations. Since he came up as a member of the Kansas City Royals, he'd always admired George Steinbrenner and the Yankees from afar. Damon noticed that Steinbrenner understood that if he spent the money, a winning team would be worth more. More fans would come out, and the value of the franchise would increase. It's something that Kansas City, which drafted Damon thirty-fifth overall in the 1992 draft, has failed to realize more than twenty years after its last World Series win.

Year after year, Damon also noticed, the best players gravitated toward the Bronx. Mussina. Giambi. Sheffield. A-Rod. Randy Johnson. All of them knew that this was a consistent chance to make the playoffs and strive for a world championship—something that can't be said in Milwaukee or Cincinnati or Tampa Bay or many other places.

"Obviously the money drove me here, but also the winning tradition," Damon said.

Just as Boston fans might never feel the same way about Damon, he seemed to take a hard-line view of the Red Sox organization. It couldn't compare, at least in the front office, with how the Yankees operated.

"There's not many teams who fail to pursue their most popular player, or one of their better players," he said in Boston on May 2. "I know the Yankees would never be like that.

"Derek Jeter is going to get 'em. Bernie Williams, they're going to keep him. It's obvious these people are real upset, but it's year after year, me, Millar, [Bill] Mueller, Pedro [Martinez], one of the game's greatest pitchers of all time. He's always going to be looked at as a Red Sox.

"But there's a line to the way you feel you should be treated, and other things happen."

At the end of May, when he had totally digested the rude return, Damon expanded on the difference between his old organization and his new one.

"The way they run business, it's night and day," he said. "If you do well in Boston, you're always going to be up in free agency. You're going to have that option to leave.

"It wasn't just me, but Pedro left. Derek Lowe, Mo Vaughn, everybody. So in here, when you're a free agent, you know you're going to get top dollar as a Yankee player. And if you've done a good job for them, if you're one of their guys, they're going to be around.

"And all the other guys, they've pretty much retired as a Yankee or if they left, they always wanted to come back because of how this organization is run."

Damon wasn't able to bond for very long with all the Yankees during spring training, because he spent a good portion of that time at the World Baseball Classic with Derek Jeter and Alex Rodriguez. However, that might have been a benefit, because he could pick the brains of two of the most important superstars in the Yankee universe. Damon, who grew up in the Orlando area, met Rodriguez—who was raised in Miami—when the two were touted teenagers on the way to fortune and fame. He said it was especially nice to get A-Rod's counsel about the trials and travails of coming into New York a made man.

"It seems like we haven't skipped a beat since we were fifteen and sixteen," Damon said.

Damon's loosey-goosey attitude penetrated the pinstripes in a way that hadn't happened in years, probably since the last championship run. Hitting coach Don Mattingly told ESPN's Peter Gammons that Damon's acquisition was a critical move in transforming the clubhouse, and the younger players especially felt that Damon brought some levity to the often frosty environs.

For example, one afternoon in May, Damon loudly asked Rodriguez if he'd like to go "free-balling" during a game in a show of solidarity. On the street, that means wearing pants without underwear. Rodriguez, who found the notion hilarious, pointed out that he needed to wear a protective cup, considering he plays a position known as the hot corner. Instead, he offered to hike his uniform pants to show his socks in unity.

Less than two months in, Damon already felt like he was accustomed to New York. He wasn't as healthy as he'd like to be, though. He suffered some tendinitis in his shoulder during the WBC, which put him out for a time. A small stress fracture in one of the sesamoid bones in his right foot hampered him, but he was getting intermittent rest (three days off in late May) and was taping two toes together. Although his right elbow locked up in June, he wouldn't take time off. Damon had played in at least 145 games in each of the last ten years, and he'd be damned if this season would be any different.

So other than the fact that his Ferrari wasn't street legal in New York, he was a man at peace in New York.

"It's definitely much better than I anticipated, and I'm glad," Damon said. "I'm glad that I'm a player who can go into a very tough situation and feel like a person who belonged here all the time.

"I have to give a lot of credit to the players, the fans, the coaches. Everybody knew what to expect of me. They know if there's a bad game, there's still going to be that smile on my face—and always rooting on other teammates.

"This feels like home already."

CHAPTER THREE

CASHMAN

A few years ago, Cashman would've driven himself crazy over a soggy Sunday morning in New York. By 2006, he said he had become one with the rain. Call it Zen and the Yankee GM.

The city was drenched by rainfall for virtually an entire weekend in late April, putting a pair of games in jeopardy. The Yankees were close to canceling their game with the Orioles the day before. They didn't, simply because they didn't want a never-ending string of games in August without an off day.

In recent years, team officials believe, the Major League Baseball schedule makers have done them no favors. A season-opening West Coast trip to Oakland and Anaheim was preceded by two exhibition contests in Arizona (which the Yankees scheduled as a contingency of the Randy Johnson trade made before the 2005 season). Then they returned home for only three games against Kansas City (which they swept) before departing to Minnesota and then Toronto. They were besieged by five off days in the first twenty-two days of their season, and manager Joe Torre didn't know whether to call it a blessing or a curse. After all, they'd get only two off days in August and September, when the games ran on and on like the decimal places of pi. And those final two months are where playoff berths are almost always earned.

So just as Noah searched for higher ground in the family RV, the Yankees were hoping to get in the series finale with Baltimore as scheduled.

Cashman was a picture of serenity about this situation as he greeted a visitor in his office. He admitted this easygoing disposition had come to him in a shazam moment, and he wasn't talking about getting struck by lightning. But if he had been, you wouldn't have been surprised.

"In '98, '99, I used to stress out over the rain. 'Do we play? Do we not play?'" he said. "I used to run down, I'd stand out in the rain, I'd feel the water. I'd come back up.

"And they'd tell you, 'Hey, it's raining out.' All right, let me check the field. 'Yup, it's raining out.' It's like, what are you doing? What are you doing?"

Cashman, who holds perhaps the most stressful front-office position in professional sports, was saying things like, "What will be, will be" about the day's game.

As proof, the GM's Yankee-blue drapes were almost completely drawn. While his office has the best view in New York—that of the Yankee Stadium field—he was facing in the opposite direction and looked out only when he got the occasional phone call about the weather.

"I've gotten some peace knowing that since I can't control the rain, I shouldn't let it consume me," Cashman said. "We'll make the best of it.

"I've gotten comfortable in making the best decisions with the facts at hand . . . rather than really fucking stress about stuff that's out of my control. I've gotten a chance to take a step back and say, 'Why are you freaking out over this?' But it's taken time and experience to allow that to come through."

Overall, Cashman said, his job in 2006 was less stressful than it had been even five years before, when he hadn't been as certain about his qualifications and tried to prove himself at every turn. He was coming off three consecutive World Series titles at that point, it's worth noting.

The thirty-eight-year-old said now that he had a "pretty strong lay of the land," which helped him within and outside the organization. But the truth is, the job was less stressful than it had been the previous year. The 2005 season was grueling for everyone involved in the franchise. The team started 11-19, and Steinbrenner and Torre weren't communicating. More-over, the media buzz was that certain higher-ups were using the home-owned YES Network to torture Torre with postgame questions about strategy, and the tactic infuriated the manager.

The whole six-month campaign felt like a sports reenactment of the Bataan Death March. The Yankees earned an AL East crown in the 161st game but fell to the Angels in the Division Series in October. At the end of that month, Cashman had his opportunity to walk away from the grind. In recent years, The Boss had allowed certain factions around him to procure more and more players, which was ostensibly Cashman's main job duty.

So when Cashman broke down in tears at Angel Stadium, it was because he legitimately felt he might be walking away from an employer he'd spent twenty years with. He had been running an executive's mara-thon, which isn't much different from what a lab rat does on a treadmill. With his contract expiring, it was his chance to get off.

"I don't think certain other GMs would care to be in the pressure cooker I'm sitting in," he told me back in 2000, during the team's last championship season. "This is the New York Yankees. I'm not saying it's not serious business everywhere, but New York is a big-market, high-pressure situation, and it's not for everybody."

Much soul-searching ensued, both for the former Yankee intern and for his employers. Philadelphia needed a new GM at the time, and the speculation was that Cashman might bolt there or head to Washington once the new Nationals' ownership picture was resolved.

But the Yankees were what he knew, what he loved, and he decided to stay if he could insist upon more power and responsibility. Steve Swindal, Steinbrenner's son-in-law, took the lead on the negotiations, but president Randy Levine and chief operating officer Lonn Trost were also involved. Proposals were exchanged in writing and plenty of discussions took place among the brain trust.

"We came up with a concept, which was basically to give the general manager the entire baseball operations," Levine said. "What do I mean by that? I mean he's in charge of putting together the major-league roster, he's in charge of player development, scouting, the whole Tampa faction will report to him.

"And we all thought that was absolutely right. George agreed with that wholeheartedly."

Although the job responsibilities were not a binding part of the new three-year, $5.5 million contract, Cashman reportedly was given a personal letter from Steinbrenner that laid out his new responsibilities.

"I wouldn't be here without them," Cashman said now, as the rain continued to fall. "He's given me a lot of opportunities here, but for me to continue, this job is so demanding, and over the years, especially when things weren't going right, you'd see, 'It's in Joe Torre's hands and Brian Cashman's hands.'

"If I'm accountable for this as the front man for the organization, then I need to be allowed to do the job. And so it was vital for me in terms of staying."

Cashman argued that it was equally important for Steinbrenner to draw the line in the sand. During the struggles of April 2005 and through other periods of adversity, Cashman remembers having conversations with the owner and looking for culpability.

But because there were "so many hands in the pot," as Cashman put it, he was left asking The Boss, "Who are you going to blame?"

Or as Levine put it, "Clearly, it wasn't working. People's roles weren't clarified."

"If I'm going to be responsible for ten players on this roster, and somebody else in the Tampa office has got seven of the players and somebody else outside the organization has got two of the players and Joe Torre has a few of the players . . . that's not a big puzzle that's going to fit together rather neatly," Cashman explained. "It's going to be a lot of different philosophies involved, and they kind of bang up against each other. And you wind up with something that can't be the best it should be able to be."

Cashman is not his own island, however. When it comes to his budget, he reports to Levine, Swindal, and Steinbrenner in the off-season. They decide how much money to spend, filtering revenue sharing and luxury tax against revenues—the big picture. Cashman and his baseball operations staff decide on the players and come back to the head honchos on how much to offer and how to structure the contract.

As the Yankees failed year after year to reach the summit, the pressure mounted and things spiraled out of control in the organization. In 2002, an ALDS loss to the Angels was shocking. The Bombers reached the World Series in 2003 but were upset by a younger team from Florida. And although the club was one victory away from a World Series appearance in 2004 before a historic choke in the ALCS against Boston, that group consisted of unlikable players such as Kevin Brown and Kenny Lofton.

Torre called the 2005 season his toughest in New York, and Cashman wasn't happy, either. One of his mentors, Gene "Stick" Michael, was completely elbowed out of the loop. And it was believed that Bill Emslie, a former traveling secretary, wielded tremendous influence because of his Tampa-based friendship with Steinbrenner.

Crazy? You bet. So when did the schizophrenia set in?

"I think everyone wants to be part of a winner," Cashman said. "I think when we lost to the Diamondbacks in 2001, that stung the organization pretty tough. And it reacted in a way where other people, 'Oh, we should've done this, rather than that.' Or 'I think this will help.' Or the desire 'Well, that can't happen again.'

"And the next thing you know, a lot of different people threw their opinions in. And over time, those opinions became more weighted—for whatever reason. And I think ownership looked at that World Series loss as somehow a failure on behalf of the decision makers."

The words were coming quickly out of Cashman's mouth.

"It was just kind of a mess," he concluded.

In 2006, Cashman saw his job as putting together a championship-caliber team, but he knew he couldn't make it win a World Series. He knew that a lot of it is luck, who gets the breaks at the right time of year. Both in 2001 and two years later, Cashman felt, he did his job.

"But this is a human sport, these are human beings, man, and actually will it get done during that week?" he said. "You have to play the game.

"And unfortunately, things didn't work out in 2003 or 2001—although our team was, I think, stronger on paper than both teams we played. It just didn't happen."

The Yankees are derided as the U.S. Steel of baseball, a bunch of soulless corporate types. Wearing a baby blue zip-up sweater and designer blue jeans on this particular day, Cashman was the antithesis of a pencil-pushing suit. That doesn't mean he takes a casual approach to his job, however. In fact, his office was a model of well-organized information overload.

Three-ring binders were on the rug against a wall, and different folders were arranged on his desk. One folder mentioned Japan. Cashman sat in a black leather executive swivel chair. On his left was a tote board listing every player in the American League, with their names in yellow, red, or blue. On his right was the same board with National League players. On the AL wall, there was a domestic scouting map of where every Yankee scout was currently located, and there was a Caribbean map below that.

In back of him to his left was a greaseboard with a crude drawing of a baseball field, where the Yankees' starters and backups were listed. From time to time, his office phone and cell rang, but most inquiries were about the weather.

"Now I'm in charge of everything, baseball-wise, top to bottom," he said decisively. "[The goal] is just do everything you can to run the most effective organization possible, and to secure, right now, a 27th championship."

On Cashman's desk, within grasp of his left hand, was a hardcover copy of *Finding the Winning Edge* by Bill Walsh. The former 49ers head coach and front-office executive was hailed as a "genius" for his innovations, particularly his intricate perfection of what is now called the "West Coast offense."

"Smart guy," Cashman said. "You just read things and you shake your head, saying, 'He's right,' how he described people's roles and organization and philosophy and how to be successful in the industry of sports, to run a professional franchise. And it was a helluva book."

Cashman's corporate-speak wasn't just bluster. He'd done everything from hiring a rules interpretation consultant and conducting spring training clinics on rules to creating a new analysts' department on the model of Wall Street firms' research analysts. Mike Fishman, a Yale graduate and actuary, was hired in 2005 and soon began assisting at the major-league level, to the point of constructing lineups to give to Joe Torre. Just don't call Fishman a sabermetrician (for reasons unknown even to himself, Cashman hates the term).

"My attitude is, we're the New York Yankees," he said. "And because of what George Steinbrenner provides, we aspire to be the best at everything—not just on the playing field.

"We shouldn't stop at getting the top-shelf player. That's why this winter, Larry Bowa was available. And Luis Sojo has been a great Yankee, but I had a chance to get Larry Bowa, who most consider the best third-base coach in baseball. We got him.

"Tony Peña, who a couple years ago was the American League manager of the year, as you know. We lost Gary Tuck to the Marlins, who was a great, effective catching instructor. I got Tony Peña to coach first base here with obviously his influence as a Dominican, Latin American, as an effective baseball leader on our staff.

"It turns out we ended up getting four former major-league managers on our coaching staff—and a former major-league manager at Triple A in Dave Miley. So that's five guys with those type of experiences to, again, help the individuals. So to go back to the original question, the mind-set is to make sure we have all bases covered."

In the winter of 2005, after re-signing Hideki Matsui to a four-year, $52 million contract, Cashman set his priorities on a limited number of areas: center field and the bullpen. He acquired lefty Ron Villone from Florida in a trade and signed righties Kyle Farnsworth, a former closer in Atlanta and Detroit, and Octavio Dotel, a former closer in Houston who was recovering from Tommy John surgery.

The bullpen had become slipshod since the days when Mariano Rivera, Mike Stanton, and Jeff Nelson were setup men, which not coincidentally was the last time the Yankees won the World Series.

Center field was a problem area in 2005. Bernie Williams had never been universally regarded as a great center fielder even when he earned four consecutive Gold Gloves from 1997 to 2000. Over the last few seasons his defense had declined as fast as *The Sopranos*. His poor instinct in tracking fly balls was now a serious liability when combined with his loss of speed. Williams also became a free agent after the 2005 season.

In 2005, Cashman tried to replace him with Matsui, who'd played center in Japan but was now a corner outfielder (and a declining one, some would argue). Melky Cabrera, a youngster the Yanks liked, was rushed to the big leagues during the summer and flopped both offensively and defensively. Even Tony Womack, a dismal signing at second base that characterized the front office's formerly dysfunctional hierarchy, was given a brief stint in the outfield. Nothing worked, and by Game 5 of the 2005 ALDS, Bubba Crosby was the starting center fielder. Cashman made loud proclamations in the winter of 2005 that he was perfectly happy with Crosby starting on Opening Day, but in reality he was the proverbial duck on the pond—calm on the surface, but paddling furiously under the surface.

Scott Boras, known for being uncanny at extracting every last penny from even the most penurious owners, had boasted that his client, Johnny Damon, was worth $84 million over seven seasons. It was a sales pitch that Cashman had no use for, and he initially treated Boras like an unwanted vacuum cleaner salesman, slamming the door in his face. He barely spoke to Boras and didn't meet with him during the GM meetings, which are the precursor to the winter meetings. Boras brushed it off, but it was an unmistakable—and calculated—snub.

During the winter meetings in Dallas, Boston made a four-year, $40 million offer to Damon, a follow-up to a three-year, $27 million offer that the player found insulting.

Cashman's options that particular winter were unappealing. Brian Giles, a corner outfielder who loved the West Coast, was masquerading as a center fielder in the free-agent market to drive his price up. Giles eventually re-signed with San Diego for three years and $30 million. Juan Encarnación and Jacque Jones were other free-agent outfielders who couldn't really play center, and Cashman didn't think Juan Pierre, who was on the trading block, was a true center fielder anymore, either. (Pierre wound up traded to the Cubs.)

But as Boston continued to procrastinate with Damon, Cashman was having no luck finding a new center fielder.

"It was a very thin market," Cashman said. "This team is built, it's an older team, it's built to try to win now. There's a major hole in center field."

According to a Yankee executive, the farm system didn't have enough prospects that could be used to acquire Coco Crisp, then with Cleveland, or Tampa Bay's Joey Gathright, or Jason Michaels, who at the time was in Philly.

"So you look at when you have a need, you analyze our team, it's an older team that's built to try to win now," Cashman said. "And those opportunities can go by you. So Johnny was available on the market."

Cashman talked to his scouts and evaluators, and they liked Damon. Joe Torre had always respected the hard-charging leadoff hitter, both because of his hustle and because of his overall offensive game. He could steal a base, or he could hit a homer—or two, as he did in Game 7 of the ALCS to pull off a miraculous comeback against the Yankees. Fishman and the analysts approved of the decision, projecting that he would have a positive impact on the lineup.

All the questions were answered. Was he an upgrade in center? Well, his arm wasn't very strong after years of shoulder problems, but he could track down the ball better than Crosby. Offensively, he was a gigantic upgrade. Damon's legs and baserunning savvy greatly improved the team speed. In 2005, the Yankees' slow, station-to-station vets resembled the early-bird patrons at a Boca Raton buffet.

After that, it was decided that Damon's loose, "idiot" persona would liven up the buttoned-down clubhouse. If the Yankees were senior citizens on the bases, then they often resembled corpses in the frigid clubhouse. Oh, there was one more consideration that factored into the four-year, $52 million pact that Damon received.

"Does it hurt our opponent? Yes," Cashman noted. "I mean, Boston was forced to take their farm system and to replace him—significantly.

"They lost a guy, Guillermo Mota, who was a power arm in their bullpen. They were forced to take Andy Marté, who was a big trade chip or the future third baseman there that everybody believes is going to be an impact player in the big leagues for some time. And so all those things hurt them. It hurt us in draft picks alone. And money.

"We felt that based on the choices this winter, if Johnny was willing—which, eventually he was, and we paid for him to be willing—it made enough sense to do so."

When asked whether the deal would make sense in three or four years, Cashman said he hoped so. But he acknowledged the risk of injury, saying, "Look at A. J. Burnett. Look at Carl Pavano. You just don't know what's going to happen, but based on all the information in front of us at the point we made the decision, [I'm] very comfortable with it."

But there's a dark side to the Damon signing, one that critics believe is a critical flaw in the current Yankee structure. In the exuberance of the "win now" philosophy, Crosby was never given a chance to flourish. Although publicly Crosby said all the right things, who could blame him if he felt pushed to the side?

Williams earned his job in 1993, two seasons after his major-league debut and after more shuttling back and forth to the minors than Delta. Now his replacement was plucked off the high end of the free-agent market. To some, it seems almost counterproductive if you want to build a championship team. Cashman doesn't see it like that, and said he'd love to have as much young talent as possible "if it's ready to help us win."

"But the championship years, we incorporated a player a year [from the farm system], it seemed like," he said. "Some years it was a little bit more. But one or two guys having an impact every year on a frontline basis. I'm not saying it's a rule of thumb.

"In '98, Jeter had his impact for the first time. Rivera had come up in '95. [Andy] Pettitte came up in '95 and had his big impact in '96. Jeter was '98. In '99, Jeter and Shane Spencer late in the year that year also. And then Ricky Ledee started having an impact somewhere around '99.

"We tried to get frontline guys. [Ramiro] Mendoza obviously was in the mix. It's hard to look back now, but there was a guy or two every year that we tried to incorporate from the system. Tried to, because they put themselves in a position to allow that to happen.

"Obviously, [Alfonso] Soriano was a guy in 2001 wound up playing a significant role for us. It carried over, but then it stopped because our system ran dry. We had some poor drafts."

Ultimately, is it possible for someone homegrown to become the next Derek Jeter?

"Oh, sure, just not in the next few years," he said. "But we don't have anyone who's capable of doing that, anyway.

"I don't have a third baseman in the next three years that would be challenging [Rodriguez]. And I don't have a shortstop. I have some quality, high-end young guys. But maybe in year four, year five, but we'll see."

Late April isn't the time to explore trades. In baseball, the length of the season allows teams to come out of early funks—or teams that start out strong to fall into one. Cashman was using the period to evaluate the major-league roster, before he began heating up the phone lines. It was all about defining roles.

"Is Jaret Wright a fifth starter?" Cashman asked rhetorically. "Right now for us, Joe continues to give him a chance. Or do you go with Aaron Small when he comes back or Carl Pavano whenever he's going to be ready?

"Do you move [Scott] Proctor in? Is [Tanyon] Sturtze an eighth-inning guy, or is he more of a sixth-inning long man? What is Villone, and how does he fit in? How far away is Dotel?

"Andy Phillips is going to play again today. We need to find out," Cashman said, clapping his hands together for emphasis, "can he play? And so we're trying to find out what we don't have. And then what we do have, get them in the right spots before we decide to go into the marketplace looking for anything else to shore up. Because we've got to make sure the answers aren't right here in front of us first."

Finding the winning edge, for Cashman, also meant delving into the mind. In 2005, Cashman hired Chad Bohling as the team's director of optimal performance. Cashman was quick to point out that he's not a sports psychologist. Although the GM claimed there's no stigma attached, good luck finding Bohling in the media guide. Or getting an interview—as terms of his employment, Bohling can't do them. Cashman reasoned that there is some proprietary material that other teams might pick up on, for example, by reading this book. Cashman isn't too proud to steal from other teams, but he doesn't want anyone stealing from him.

Bohling's job is to assist with the mental side of the game, and to do it on the down-low. His résumé includes work at the IMG Academies in Bradenton, Florida, which churn out world-class athletes every year.

Cashman knows the players are the company's assets, and he wants to make sure he can help put them in the best position possible to succeed. Bohling is able to assist them with motivation, the importance of routines and communicating with managers, trainers, and the press. It's part of the process of leaving no stone unturned. Carl Pavano and Scott Proctor were two of the major leaguers who had dealt with him in 2006.

"When a player, whether he's a minor leaguer or a major leaguer, when he enters the organization and then eventually leaves, whether he retires, gets traded, is released, what have you, he can say there was every avenue available to him to reach his peak performance levels," Cashman said.

The issue of pressure is always the elephant in the room, be it the clubhouse downstairs or the executive offices. During the home opener, Cashman tried to play the notion off. But the history of the Yankee Fishbowl is unmistakable. Randy Johnson accosted a cameraman before he ever officially donned pinstripes. After coming over via a late-season trade in 2005, Matt Lawton turned to steroids after a 3-for-38 start with the Yankees. These were well-trained athletes melting down like the Wicked Witch of the West.

"For me, the pressure is to try to find a way to allow these players— these great athletes—to reach their maximum potential," Cashman said. "And if you have talent, and you combine that with hard work and with programs that allow that to happen, then good things should happen.

"There's no doubt there's pressure. It is impossible to predict beforehand if a guy is going to perform despite the pressure. Some years they do, some years they don't.

"That's the tough thing. Somebody might be in a situation, bases loaded, Game 7 of the World Series, and they might get the job done. Same person five years later might not. That's what baseball's about."

The inescapable truth is that there's no personality template that would predetermine success, especially success in New York. Some people are loudmouths and hogs for the spotlight, like David Wells, who earned a ring in 1998; others are quiet as a church mouse, like Jimmy Key, but still thrive. Some people are quiet, and it eats them up, as it did to Kenny Rogers.

Sometimes a player has overwhelming talent but his lack of dedication or work ethic derails him. Sometimes a personal crisis prevents success, and it's an issue the press and the public never find out about. Other times players triumph through the adversity. Jason Giambi and Gary Sheffield were two players who thrived despite the steroid scarlet letter that has been attached to them.

Cashman, in particular, said that he has seen a gradual shift in the media coverage since ESPN and *SportsCenter* have come to dominate the sports world.

"ESPN has really turned up the lights on the sport," Cashman allowed. "And there's good things. That's good, but it also brings added negatives at the same time. But overall, it's a positive."

Torre, in particular, has been disdainful of the network since it repeatedly aired Roger Clemens' beaning of Mike Piazza in the 2000 season, and for a time he wouldn't answer questions from the network. ESPN, in turn, resorted to sticking a microphone without its logo in his face. Torre wasn't fooled, and said so at least once.

The GM understands the tabloid wars are as fierce as the American League playoffs, albeit played on a different field. Writers from eight daily newspapers travel with the team to all eighty-one road games, as does a sports reporter from WFAN radio. Add to that the proliferation of Web sites and chat rooms.

"The one thing I've noticed: it's not just the game," Cashman said. "Like, it's not as simple as just covering what's on the field.

"Sometimes it gets personal, sometimes family [or] off-the-field stuff gets pulled into it. And again, it's all because of competition. People need to differentiate their paper's stories for selling, et cetera.

"It creates that type of environment, that competition creates a thirst of coming up with something different and something new, whether it's covering a player and his family issues—or his family, period, or who they're dating, or what problems they might have in their lives.

"And sometimes, that's a burden. It is a burden for anyone who has to work in this environment to deal with.

"In most cases, it's not personal. As long as you understand the dynamic of the *New York Post,* the *Daily News,* the *New York Times, Newsday.* Especially those four, plus everybody else. And the fierce competition that takes place on our field every day is no different from what's going on in their boardrooms and their editors demanding . . . or, obviously, tearing to shreds a beat writer for getting [scooped], 'Why didn't you have this story?'

"You start looking at it that way, you understand it more. It doesn't make it easier . . . well, it does make it easier. You just understand it more, that's all. It's a by-product of where we're playing, that's all."

In 2006, Cashman gave the team a speech about being on the clock. But some years he talks about dealing with the press. In 2003, George Steinbrenner criticized Derek Jeter for partying too much, thinking that the frequent sightings of Jeter on the gossip pages meant the star shortstop was suddenly a dilettante. Naturally, the Yankee players defended their teammate, and the press ate up the story like a hot-fudge sundae. Every day, someone from one of the papers would ask a teammate for his take on Steinbrenner versus Jeter. One day it was Andy Pettitte, the next it was David Wells. Cashman was fuming, and so was The Boss.

"So I had a fucking meeting with everybody, and I said, 'Shut the fuck up,'" Cashman said. "'He's getting pummeled just because we have sixty-three guys in camp and every day the fuckin' writers are going to each player and getting opinions. So this story will not die for the next sixty days if you guys keep opening your fuckin' mouths!'"

Cashman must tell incoming players there are no secrets in the organization. Results of medical tests are usually disclosed immediately, which is something that takes some players some getting used to. When Chris Hammond came on board in 2003, he lied about a physical issue even though the club revealed results of an MRI. Media members, who resented it, couldn't wait to pounce on the reliever whenever he struggled, and his tenure in New York lasted one year before he was dealt to Oakland for two minor leaguers. Naturally, he ripped New York when he got to Oakland.

"Some people just don't know, because other places: (a) stuff doesn't seem to leak out and (b) they're not used to this, or (c) they're afraid, 'Well, I don't know if they want people to know,'" Cashman said. "So yeah, there's a getting-to-know-you for everybody and what goes on here."

Although Randy Johnson was the biggest media target in 2005, Carl Pavano was a close second. Cashman chafed at every pot shot that New

York columnists took at the right-handed pitcher, who signed a four-year, $39.95 million contract before the 2005 season. In his inaugural season, Pavano seemed openly disdainful of the media, even though he grew up in nearby Southington, Connecticut. When he couldn't or wouldn't pitch through shoulder problems in 2005, some media members perpetuated the rumor that fellow starters Jaret Wright and Chien-Ming Wang gutted out worse injuries.

"Carl Pavano has been labeled as a guy who can't win in New York," Cashman said. "If you have a physical problem, you get a pass. Dr. [James] Andrews found something in his arm. Dr. [Robert] Watkins found something in his back."

The GM went so far as to say that if Pavano could overcome his latest setback, he would succeed in New York. If he turned out to be right, a lot of media members would eat crow. If not, Cashman would come off as an overly optimistic Pollyanna, blindly defending a misguided signing to the bitter end. There wasn't any way of knowing whether Pavano—or, especially, the next Pavano—would succeed in New York, and Cashman concluded that the amount of psychological information you'd need to know beforehand probably wouldn't even be available.

"You'd make a lot of money if you can unlock that," he said.

CHAPTER FOUR

MUSSINA

Mike Mussina graciously offered up a clubhouse folding chair for a visitor, but he couldn't start the conversation just yet. The front of *USA Today* caught his eye, the tease of new puzzles too tough to resist. Mussina began thumbing through the paper to see if there was something in there to challenge his remarkable intellect.

Mussina is a crossword puzzle player extraordinaire, even starring in a feature film, *Wordplay,* about the subject. He first began working on crosswords as an undergrad at Stanford, during some of his "less exciting" classes, as he put it. Mussina, though, finished his economics degree in three and a half years, lest one think he spent his days in Palo Alto killing time until practice.

Although Sudoku had taken over the Yankee clubhouse (Damon is the clubhouse savant, able to finish a tough puzzle in twenty minutes), Mussina hadn't caught the bug.

"I just don't get into it, I guess," he said. "Growing up, I was always better with numbers. Maybe if I just did them, I'd get into them. But I've just done crosswords so long."

Similarly, the gimmick-filled puzzles that USA Today had to offer didn't pique his interest, and he tossed the paper back into his locker.

To Mussina, who loves the analytical aspect of the game, life with the Yankees is something of a puzzle. And it's one that certain players never solve.

"It's always interesting, at least for me, to watch the new guys come in and see how they deal with what goes on here," Mussina said. "Between the media coverage, the high expectations, the fans—all the stuff that goes with being able to go out on that field and play the game at the best of your ability.

"And if those players can deal with all that stuff and still play well, then you know they're going to be players for this team. If they struggle for a little while and they're criticized, or the expectations are higher than they're putting out there and they can't handle what people say or they take it too much to heart or let it affect them, then you're skeptical as to whether that person is going to be able to do it here."

When the thirty-seven-year-old came to the Bronx prior to the 2001 season, the same questions surrounded him. That 2001 team had won the last three World Series, and Roger Clemens and Andy Pettitte were the cornerstones of the pitching staff. Mussina, who has never won a Cy Young or twenty games in a season, comfortably fit into their shadow after being Baltimore's ace. One of his final regular-season starts in Boston that first season summed up his career. In Boston on September 2, Mussina was one strike away from a perfect game when pinch hitter Carl Everett lined a single.

He went 17-11 with a 3.15 ERA in his first season and hasn't lost more than 10 games with the Bombers ever since. His career ERA in 288 starts with Baltimore was 3.53. It was 3.80 as a Yankee as of June 27, 2006, which meant his overall career mark had only elevated .10 after five and a half seasons in New York. When ESPN's Buster Olney wrote an article a few seasons ago assessing whether various Yankees had "earned their pin-stripes," Mussina was one of the few without a World Series ring who had, he judged. After an adjustment period, he's one of the guys who have handled New York.

Mussina thought that some players (Jeff Weaver, Javier Vázquez, Jose

Contreras, Kenny Lofton, Tony Womack) came up Mini-Me small in the Big Apple for a couple of reasons. As the veteran righty noted, the coverage of the Yankees in their home city was unlike that of any other team. Although he's quick to say he never played in Boston, Philadelphia, or Los Angeles, three major markets with plenty of critical coverage, Mussina can't imagine that the daily dissection of those teams is anything like that of the Mets and Yankees. The tabloids cover the Yankees the way *Roll Call* covers Congress.

"And because of that, the constant barrage of questions," Mussina said, "the barrage of, 'Why didn't you get three hits? You only got two. Why didn't you get three? Why didn't you pitch the eighth inning? You pitched seven good. You could've pitched the eighth.' The constant analysis.

"If you can't let it go—people constantly analyzing whether we did it right or wrong or did it well or not well—then it really bothers you."

Moreover, here's the rub: Other than Bernie Williams, Mariano Rivera, Derek Jeter, and Jorge Posada, the rest of the team wasn't born into this. This isn't how it was for Mussina in Baltimore, or Randy Johnson in Montreal or Seattle, or Jason Giambi in Oakland. In those cities, the coverage is far tamer and baseball players are more often treated as icons than as disappointments. They've had tremendous success over the course of their lifetimes, so being challenged by ink-stained wretches and harangued by fans is often a shock to the system.

"So to play for a long time, and be successful . . . then you come here, and if you don't do well for the first month, everybody wants to talk to you because they want to know why you struggled," Mussina said. "When you're all of a sudden criticized *every* time you don't do well, not just when you get into a 1-for-22 slump . . .

"In other places, you go 1 for 22, *then* they'll wonder why you're slumping. Around here, if you in one three-game series go 1 for 12, or you go 0 for 4 and leave five guys on base in one day, they're after you. It's just, it's a different animal here than everywhere else."

It took time for Mussina to get acclimated, and he admitted he was probably too sensitive. That first year, that near-perfect game? The day after, he groused to a swarm of reporters who wanted to follow up on his astonishing performance that he hadn't hurled a perfect game, so what'd they want to talk to him for?

He reached the World Series twice, in 2001 and 2003, and his best season as a Yankee came in '03, although it resulted in another frustrating near miss. Mussina went 17-8 with a 3.40 ERA in the '03 regular season, but he really earned his pay at the end of October. In the clinching game in the ALCS against Boston, he worked three shutout innings, allowing Aaron Boone to become a hero with his extra-inning walk-off homer.

Earlier in that postseason, Mussina struggled, but he capped the play-offs with a Game 3 victory that put the Bombers up two games to one against Florida. He would've thrown Game 7 of the World Series that year, but Josh Beckett tossed a shutout in the Game 6 clincher at the Stadium.

One of the pitchers who crossed paths with Mussina from that Florida team, Carl Pavano, took his World Series ring to the Bronx and signed a four-year, $39.95 million contract after the 2004 season. From June 2005 until May 2006, Pavano was on the shelf without ever undergoing surgery. He was initially shut down with rotator cuff tendinitis in the summer of 2005, and he began the next spring experiencing back woes. He developed a sore butt during a spring training appearance, and then triceps stiffness occurred right before he was scheduled to return in May. Finally, a bone chip was removed from his elbow. By that point, Pavano had become a pariah in the clubhouse.

Mussina was one of his leading critics, according to sources, and Pavano was hurt and discouraged by the snickering and whispering. During a May Q-and-A with the New York Post's Steve Serby, Mussina revealed that the toughest thing about playing in New York was "realizing that every-body else's expectations aren't as high as my own." When given a chance to elaborate on the disappointment of playing with unmotivated Yankees, Mussina explained that he hears his own clock ticking.

"I guess I'm coming towards the end of my career," he said. "I haven't had a chance to win a championship. I've been close a couple times. . . . It would be nice to have before I stopped playing.

"Other guys, for whatever reason—and I don't know how these guys think—but you see other people, and it just doesn't seem like not winning bothers them as much. And I'm not in these guys' heads—I don't know what they think or what they feel—and I guess it's tough for me."

On a certain level, it seems amazing that a player can reach the height of success in the major leagues, come to the Yankees, and then shy away from the spotlight. Or flinch when duty calls. It seems counterintuitive that somebody can have misplaced values, an unremarkable work ethic, or a total unwillingness to pitch in pain at this level of sport. But in the final analysis, it's no different from the MTA worker who falls asleep in the toll collector's booth. As Mussina was essentially trying to explain, stealing money is stealing money.

"It doesn't matter," Mussina argued. "It doesn't change who you are. The makeup of the player, I think, is really brought out when you play for this team.

"When you play in this situation where we play in, you find out the guys who want to be involved and want to be out there. And you find out the guys who just prefer to not be put in that situation all the time. It's always going to be that way. You can tell sometimes."

Mussina's locker was right next to that of Tanyon Sturtze, a well-liked reliever who blew out his rotator cuff in May 2006 after refusing to tell manager Joe Torre he was hurt. Sturtze also refused to confess to a tired shoulder the year before when Torre overworked him, and the manager insisted that he not do it again. Sturtze was another Yankee who would convey, in conversations with people, his displeasure with Pavano. The two men were initially scheduled to have their surgeries the same day in Birmingham, Alabama, by noted orthopedic surgeon James Andrews, but Pavano rescheduled his to later in the week so as to avoid a confrontation with Sturtze.

Sturtze hadn't been around the clubhouse recently, and memos and fantasy league standings were piled up on his chair. Although many media members thought Sturtze's case was a classic example of unchecked bravado, Mussina said the journeyman reliever commanded respect.

"I guess the thing is for baseball players, that's what you expect out of someone," he said. "Look, we have a chance to play this for a given amount of time . . . whether that period of time is five years, whether it's ten years, whether it's two years.

"But you want to give everything you have for that period of time, however long it is. And the guys who don't seem to exude that affect the ones who are doing it—who want to go out there, even if they're in discomfort, even if they're hurt. They want to be involved in it.

"You're always going to have both sides. You're always going to have those who don't have the same makeup."

Remarkably, there remained some members of the media in New York who questioned Mussina's makeup in 2006. During his first season or two, his aloofness turned off some reporters. His frowning disapproval to many questions, brow always furrowed and hands usually on his hips, was a stop sign to those who wished to tap into Mussina's intellect and expertise.

But Mussina had softened and mellowed by 2006, becoming totally comfortable with his Yankee routine. In the first half of the season, he was enjoying something of a renaissance, and a June 5 victory over Boston was his eighth in nine decisions.

Even with Mussina 8-1, though, the *New York Times* columnist Murray Chass chose to harp on Mussina's shortcomings, calling him "a whiner" at one point and mentioning that he had often come close to, but never attained, 20 victories in a season. Chass dug deeper later in his column, questioning Mussina's leadership qualities and claiming he needed to do better because of Randy Johnson's struggles.

Chass also described Mussina waving away Torre in the ninth inning on May 21 in Detroit, when the pitcher wanted to save the bullpen, as a brazen act by a veteran throwing his weight around.

It seemed illogical that Mussina could somehow be smeared by Johnson's disappointing first season. The Yankees could have also benefited, say, if Johnson had won 22 games and looked anything like the consistent ace the Bombers thought they were importing.

The truth was, Mussina did take a more active role as a leader of the staff in 2005, becoming more vocal once he noticed Johnson struggling. He voiced his opinion more in scouting meetings and took Sturtze and Jaret Wright under his wing, giving Wright pointers about his curveball and generally providing on- and off-field advice. In 2006, he took a shine to Scott Proctor and helped him in the same way.

Chass' wasn't the lone voice in the wilderness, as there were some who pointed to Mussina's inconsistent showing in the postseason. For example, in 2005 he earned a victory in Game 1 with 5⅔ shutout innings against the Angels, but was shelled in Game 5, allowing five earned runs over 2⅔ innings. To be fair, though, a collision between Bubba Crosby and Gary Sheffield changed the game entirely.

Naturally, the pitcher was aware that his harshest critics didn't deem him a leader. "I don't bring my pom-poms?" he asked with a smirk.

Ultimately, Mussina conceded, anybody can view it through any prism they'd like. He felt that starting pitchers really can't be leaders because they don't play every day, unless they have something like a decade of service. That's not to say Mussina wasn't sensitive to the issue. As long as his teammates felt they could come to him with questions, though, he believed he was doing his job.

Although Mussina realized that he had been in New York longer than anyone besides Mariano Rivera, he was not brought to town as the pitcher who would lead the franchise. He was never the alpha dog.

"I'm sitting there, I'm pitching with Roger Clemens, Andy Pettitte, Randy Johnson. I'm not on the top of the totem pole," he said in a pleading tone.

The mentality of those like Chass clouds the bigger picture. Unlike Weaver, Vázquez, and Contreras, Mussina made it here. He continued to pitch consistently, continued to give his team at least a puncher's chance most nights for almost six seasons.

That's a sharp contrast to Kevin Brown, who famously broke his hand smashing a wall and torpedoed the end of the 2004 season.

"Punching a wall?" Mussina said. "It's tough to be a leader when you're punching a wall and putting yourself out for six weeks.

"And it's tough to do it if you're struggling. Like someone like Randy, it's tough for him to go out there and be a leader when he's got his own problems."

Derek Jeter, the captain of the team, put it like this in late June: "Moose is kind of quiet, he keeps to himself. But on the field, he's taken on a leadership role in terms of just going out there and pitching well, wanting the ball. He takes a lot of pressure off the rest of the pitching staff with how he's performing. I think he's adapted well, he's adjusted well to New York. He's pitching as well as he ever has. And Moose is a big reason for why we are where we are right now."

Mussina is conscientious, saying that he sometimes spends too much time thinking about his teammates and their problems and not enough about himself. He knows, though, that his work is first and foremost. The reality is that major-league baseball players, unlike soldiers, don't walk over to somebody and offer advice. They don't intrude on another man's problems unless someone seeks help. Always aware of his setting, he tried to make an analogy.

"It's like somebody telling you how to write, instead of you going and asking them, 'What do you think?'" Mussina said.

Ultimately, the Yankees' excellent coaching staff is expected to tutor and counsel those in need, and Mussina noted that his locker is right next to the corridor to the coaches' room. A player cannot head over there without coming by his locker first. He vowed to help anyone who came to him. Presumably that included even Pavano.

"If they want me to be a coach . . . I've still got to go pitch," Mussina said.

Mussina gears himself up for thirty-four days in the season—thirty-four starts. If on the day he pitches the team plays flat, he doesn't get another chance for four or five days. A regular player can shake off an 0-for-4, but Mussina can't afford one.

"I've come to this point in my career where now playing the season and getting to the postseason, it's all important to me—because I'm certainly not on the first half of the ride," he said. "The ride might be making the last, the last . . . coming down the last hill. And I'm getting a little close here pretty soon.

"So I'd like to get one more thrill out of it."

Mussina felt there was a better vibe in the clubhouse in 2006 than there had been in 2004 or even 2005, when there were many of the same people. Instead of needing to frantically catch up to Boston and Baltimore, which they did in '05, the Yanks held a 35-26 record on the afternoon of June 13. That night, Chien-Ming Wang would prevail in a 1-0 victory over Cleveland, and the injury-ravaged Yanks tied Boston for first place.

"The first two months of this year, almost to the first half of this year, we've been beat up and banged up and guys out," he said. "And still we're finding ways to go out and get it done.

"No, we're not having as great a year as we could. But we're one game out of first—with a team that's nowhere near what we anticipated when we started.

"So whoever's doing the leading around here is doing a pretty decent job."

CHAPTER FIVE

OLD-TIMERS

A s Reggie Jackson strode through the Yankee clubhouse that he once dominated, he let out a loud fart by Jorge Posada's empty locker. The clubbies gathered nearby thought it was hilarious. Never let it be said that Mr. October minds being the center of attention.

It was June 23, the day before the franchise's sixtieth annual Old-Timers' Day, and Jackson quickly moved to Alex Rodriguez' locker. He was rifling through A-Rod's collection of shoes, looking for something he could wear to batting practice later that afternoon.

For three decades, Jackson has been a Big Apple icon, from his namesake candy bar to his guest TV spot with Archie Bunker to his TV commercials fusing him into the collective consciousness of the American public. Although he wasn't universally loved even by Yankee fans during his playing days, even those who hated his arrogance grew to admire him for his clutch performances, if nothing else.

He hit three home runs in the culminating game of the 1977 World Series, including a shot into the black backdrop in center field. Unless someone homers every time up in the Fall Classic someday, consider it the closest batting equivalent to Don Larsen's perfect game that we'll ever see.

Jackson departed after the 1981 season for the California Angels and played only five of his twenty-one seasons in New York, but his Hall of Fame plaque in Cooperstown bears an interlocking "NY" on it. Perhaps the foremost Yankee authority on grace under pressure, he was asked if the Bronx Zoo was tougher than the Yankee Fishbowl.

"It depends on who you are. No doubt about that," he bellowed mischievously. "In 2006, it's tougher if you're Alex Rodriguez. In 2006, it's tougher if you're Randy Johnson.

"If you were me, it was tougher to play in '77. I didn't run from it, either."

By the time he came to the Yankees for the 1977 season with a five-year, $2.93 million contract (fat for the time) in hand, Jackson had already won three World Series with the A's from 1972 to 1974. He was both league MVP and Fall Classic MVP in that middle year. He said he "brought his own star here," a comment that got him "torched" by the media even though it was 100 percent accurate. (A-Rod and Johnson have also carried their own stars to the Big Apple, although sometimes it seems like they're still lugging them around like a sofabed.)

There were many other comments like that from Jackson over the years that were as cocksure as they were true, from "the magnitude of me" to the "straw that stirs the drink." When Jackson said that Yankee captain Thurman Munson could only stir the drink badly, it infuriated many of his teammates.

Jackson's tenure was made tougher because of his combustible relationship with on-again, off-again manager Billy Martin. After Martin removed Jackson for defense during the 1977 season, the two nearly came to blows in the visiting dugout at Fenway Park. In praising Joe Torre, Jackson made it clear that the bitterness of the Martin era still resides inside him.

"This manager is interested in an even keel and doesn't promote," Jackson said of Torre. "He's interested in the gold ring. He's not worried about his star or his mountain. His legacy.

"It makes it different. It makes it better."

Goose Gossage, the mustachioed reliever who joined the team in 1978, concurred with Jackson. In some ways Gossage was the pitching equivalent of Jackson, in that he signed a six-year, $2.75 million contract and was expected to replace the 1977 AL Cy Young Award winner, Sparky Lyle, as the closer and immediately lead the Yankees to another World Series.

In those days, Steinbrenner was constantly meddling, and Martin didn't believe in the Torre school of managing, where brush fires are extinguished and trust is built. The constant bickering between Steinbrenner and Martin became a circus act, and hence Gossage said it was "way tougher" for him and his teammates than for the 2006 Yanks. Gossage actually told Torre, "I wish we could've had you as a manager."

"We would've won some more world championships, because he's a great buffer," Gossage said during Old-Timers' Day. "Billy was not a buffer.

"[Martin and Steinbrenner] were fire and gasoline. That's how it was when we were here. There was no buffer. There was always some kind of dissension or some kind of bullshit."

Although Gossage still thinks it's very difficult to play for the Yankees and said the scrutiny and "fight for the story" are off the charts, he's put his money behind the good old days, when everything was tougher or better.

Sadly, Gossage has become increasingly defensive of his era with every year that he's left out of the Hall of Fame.

Jackson doesn't hold quite the same defensiveness about the difference in eras. He allows that the scrutiny of the game and the media attention and intensity are much greater than when he played.

"But do you get barbecued any quicker today than when I played?" he asked. "I don't think so. Is the bonfire bigger today? Yes."

Officially, Jackson is a member of Steinbrenner's "special advisory group," and he's a clubhouse regular when he's in town. Although Jackson is interested in buying another team, his love of the Yankees runs deep. He's always willing to dispense advice to anyone, from A-Rod to Gary Sheffield, and even pitchers such as Jaret Wright and Carl Pavano got a hello and a kind word from him on this particular day. In his time in the clubhouse on a Friday afternoon, he did the nearly impossible: he made Johnson smile *and* laugh.

Whereas taking BP now makes the sixty-year-old slugger sore, he's still the same thoughtful, provocative interview that he was in his heyday. When asked if it was tougher to be on the Yankees than on the Kansas City Royals, he replied, "That's an editorial; that's not a one-word answer."

Jackson knows there are plenty of successful players who could come to New York and cope with the unique pressures and pleasures, but he emphasized that you have to be a special player to succeed here. Therein lies the distinction.

"This is not for everybody," he said. "The ordinary player doesn't play here. There is a uniqueness to the personality and the character that is here. It has to be different."

In the world of sports, an athlete can hone his skills with repetition and lift weights to build muscles. But how does someone strengthen his mind?

"Have success and good people around you giving you some input," he answered.

It's as simple as that?

"It's not simple," Jackson interjected angrily, his eyes momentarily fiery. "None of it here is as simple as that. Nothing in New York is as simple as that.

"That's what it is. It's a handful. Your cup runneth over here with situations to manage and deal with."

Ultimately, Jackson doesn't think it's intelligence that carries a player through. He was careful to say he doesn't think he's smarter than anybody else. But, not surprisingly, he stressed how important self-confidence is. When he played, he rationalized that he was going to get paid better in New York, but he was probably not going to play any better. He was a player of a certain talent level before he arrived, and he would probably produce numbers similar—but not superior—to those he put up before.

"This is how it is, this is who I am, this is what I am," he described it. "And finally when I got comfortable here with my surroundings because of who I was and realized I couldn't do things that I didn't have the ability to do, I could only do what I could do, once I got comfortable with that . . ."

He didn't need to finish the sentence.

For David Cone and Darryl Strawberry, the perspective is a bit different. Cone and Strawberry first played in New York with the Mets in the late 1980s. Strawberry was a cornerstone of the 1986 world champions, Cone a key member of the 1988 NL East champs. They reunited as teammates in 1995, to great success.

Strawberry won three World Series in pinstripes, while Cone stayed through the 2000 season and won four. In 2006, both returned to Yankee Stadium for Old-Timers' Day, although the game itself was rained out.

"The beauty of the Yankees is connecting the generations," Cone said.

To him, this was no lip service. One of the reasons he came to an Old-Timers' Day so soon after retiring (Cone hung up his spikes during the 2003 season with the Mets) was that this year, the franchise was honoring the 1956 champs, with Larsen as the centerpiece because of his perfecto in the World Series against the Dodgers.

Cone threw his perfect game with the Yankees on July 18, 1999, when Larsen was in attendance for Yogi Berra Day and tossed out the first pitch.

As the baby-faced right-hander looked at the pressures facing the 1996 and 2006 Yanks, he saw two sets of separate and distinct difficulties. In 1996, the long dry spell between championships had Steinbrenner on edge and the city holding its breath. The Bombers had been considered a favorite to reach the Fall Classic before the strike ended the 1994 season, and the 1995 season had gone down in flames after a two-games-to-none lead in the brand-new Division Series against upstart Seattle. But the '96 team was considered weaker, and it was managed by Torre, who had never won before.

"It was somewhat of a breakthrough just to be able to win in '96," Cone said, "whereas now there's tremendous scrutiny on individual players to make it very difficult for individuals to thrive here."

As Cone saw it, the '06 Yanks were "caught in between." There was a core group in Bernie Williams, Mariano Rivera, Derek Jeter, and Jorge Posada that owned plenty of championship experience, but there were plenty of new superstar faces since the twenty-sixth title in 2000. Although the Yankees' string of eight division titles was still alive in 2006, Cone resided in the camp that believed the Yankee dynasty of 1996–2000 was over.

"It's tough to continue a dynasty when you're kind of in a position to start your own," he said. "I know A-Rod would like to be part of championship teams. And it's kind of a different dynasty for him if they can get something going. For several guys.

"What was done back in the nineties is history. I'm here [at Old-Timers' Day] to prove that. It's ten years ago."

Strawberry, from the generation in between Jackson and Rodriguez, could relate to the highs of one and the lows of the other. He won the Series with the Mets in '86 when they owned the city (elderly baseball fans will tell you New York is a National League town) and then bottomed out because of drug addiction there.

Strawberry knew the ecstasy of delivering in the clutch when everyone in the ballpark expected the big hit, and he also knew the crushing disappointment of being booed out of a home ballpark. He disappointed millions of fans with a coke addiction and personal failings that sapped him of a Hall of Fame career, but he also earned four world championships in the Big Apple.

"You have to get used to the fact that New York fans, they mean well," he said. "When they boo you, they're saying, 'Hey, you're special. You've got to do special things.'

"That kind of like motivated me. They looked at my talent and said, 'OK, we're not going to let you get away without performing like you're capable of performing.' Other places, it's not like that.

"But if you look at that as a negative, it's going to affect your play."

Strawberry sees a lot of himself in Rodriguez. Neither player could hide from the masses. Both had imposing size and the corresponding offensive advantage. Both had the same remarkable gifts that gave them the potential to be the best sluggers in the majors. Although Strawberry rarely came to New York in 2006, he was aware the fans were riding Rodriguez hard.

"They did it to me when I played with the Mets," Strawberry said. "I got booed, I was like, 'OK, I need to hit two today to show them who the man is.'

"But see, that's the kind of game I played. I don't know if he [Rodriguez] has it. That's what I had down inside of me."

Maybe coincidentally, maybe not, Strawberry began talking about Jeter after being asked if he was close with A-Rod. Strawberry was a teammate of the Yankee shortstop for parts of five seasons, and he leveled with him about his own cautionary tale in the Tampa clubhouse one spring. As one might expect, Jeter was respectful but didn't need the well-intentioned lecture.

"See, Jeter's a gift," Strawberry said. "This is natural. He knows this is nothing to him. He knows how to fit in. He knows how to do his thing. He always did, when he came up. He was born to do this."

Whereas Jackson considered himself a true-blue Yankee, Strawberry viewed himself as a Met, even though his time there ended as poorly as possible. He spent the 2006 spring training in the Mets' camp working with minor-league talent, and he tried to impart his wisdom to them.

"A lot of people . . . say they'd love to play in New York," Strawberry said. "But don't say that if you don't know the expectations and what you have to deal with.

"There's more to it than just saying it. You're going to have to have confidence in yourself. Nobody else.

"Me, I had to not worry, I had to block out what everybody thought of me. You've gotta win. You've gotta win. It's not just about going through a great season."

Strawberry conceded that the expectations are greater in the present day, but he noted that the '96 team won with guys who weren't getting paid as much and weren't, on paper, nearly as gifted as the most recent club.

"Our talent was nowhere close to the talent of the 2006 team," he said.

Clichéd as it may sound, Strawberry praised the heart of his former teammates, including Cone and Andy Pettitte, for not buckling under the pressure and expectations. Although he was far from the model teammate in his own career (he once fought Keith Hernandez during team photo day in spring training), he said part of the winning formula is having teammates who like each other.

"I'm not saying that they don't this year, but you can't have it where it's about one particular guy," Strawberry said.

Jim Leyritz used to think it was all about him. At least that's what his critics said. Leyritz was not well liked in the Yankee organization in the 1990s by those who set the rules and/or those that followed them. He was a benchwarmer who would be "King," which was a nickname Don Mattingly gave him because of Leyritz's ceaseless self-promotion.

With all that said, the club wouldn't have earned the '96 ring without Leyritz. His seminal shot off Atlanta's Mark Wohlers in Game 4 of the World Series earned him endless gratitude from Yankee fans waiting out a championship drought since 1978. Moreover, it basically catapulted him into pinstripe perpetuity.

Looking around the auxiliary clubhouse where former Yankees dressed on Old-Timers' Day, there were far more accomplished players. None had been more vital to the actual earning of a given championship. Leyritz's three-run bomb in the eighth inning off Wohlers erased a 6-3 deficit and changed the course of Yankee history.

If anybody knows about pressure, it was the backup catcher, and he didn't need a barometer to know what happened after the Yankees' string of championships ended after 2000.

"They have more pressure, because they're expected to win a World Series," Leyritz said. "To me, that's the most highly pressurized part of it. Because you come in here, you have a great season like A-Rod had, and if you don't go into the postseason and you don't win, that's what they remember. They don't remember the great year, the MVP year. That's a prime example of it. . . .

"That's a hard thing, knowing early in the season you could have as great a season as you want, and if you don't win the World Series, people consider it a failure."

Although people such as Torre, Cashman, and Jeter have cautioned observers that it wasn't as easy as it looked, fans and media didn't realize it until the mass production of World Series rings stopped cold. In the past, the Yankees could earn a World Series berth by owning the best record in the American League. In 1969, the ALCS began. In 1995, another round of playoffs was introduced, meaning that a team needed 11 victories to emerge as the world champion. More than anything else, it's a grueling march after a marathon season, a war of attrition.

"The one thing most people have to realize, no matter how much money you put on the field, it doesn't necessarily bring you a winner," Leyritz said. "A lot of it has to do with luck. Timing.

"I'm from Miami, so I just had a chance to be with Wade and Shaq and [the NBA champion Miami Heat]. And they said the same thing: 'You know what? We don't know if we were as good as Detroit or as good as Dallas, but we clicked at the right time.' Sometimes that's what it's all about."

Without the right personalities, though, it's impossible. Leyritz cited Kenny Rogers as someone who joined the Yanks in 1996 and flopped miserably. The Mets brought him back to town in 1999 and he walked in the winning run in the NLCS. Leyritz caught him enough to know that "this guy could beat anybody." Fair or not, Rogers' epitaph in a New York cemetery would be "Couldn't make it here." Rogers' later meltdown with a harmless cameraman in Texas in 2005 revealed him to be a total jackass, at least regarding the media.

Leyritz, a gregarious sort who never turned away from a microphone as a player, is—not surprisingly—working for MLB.com. Players who don't know how to take the media criticism or take the booing in stride will never play to their best capabilities, he said. Even though Yankee uniforms come with an invisible bull's eye on the back that every opponent takes aim at, the off-field stuff is the hardest thing about playing in New York.

"You cannot be weak to play in the city," he said. "It's a mental grind.

It's all on your personality. Some people can do it, some people can't. It doesn't make them any less of a person, it's just a different place to play."

Nobody would ever confuse Leyritz with Reggie, but both played their best when the lights were brightest. There were a couple of reasons for that, Leyritz thought. Most important, his father was his biggest critic growing up. Even when he went 3 for 4, Leyritz recalled, his dad was never satisfied. Why hadn't Jim gone 4 for 4? he'd ask.

There was something else at stake, too. Leyritz could never shake the utility man label, could never get off the bench for more than a few games at a time. He was always considered a backup, and he knew if he didn't play well on a given day, his name wouldn't be in the lineup the next.

"Everybody said, 'How did you come up in moments and not feel the pressure?'" Leyritz said. "I was kind of in the World Series every day. So that's why I think it made it easier for me to be calm in those situations."

For the past few seasons, fans and media alike had demeaned the most recent Yankee clubs as inferior, always pointing out why and how they differed from the 1996, '98, '99, and 2000 clubs. And in June, nobody was sizing up the present-day Yanks for rings. They were in second place for most of the year, fighting injury after injury.

Leyritz, though, saw some similarities between the 2006 team and the '96 squad, which wasn't as talented as future editions.

In 2006, Leyritz saw a different kind of camaraderie from the previous few years, perhaps brought to bear by the major injuries to Hideki Matsui and Gary Sheffield. Leyritz presumed, correctly, that Torre had circled the wagons and instructed his men that nothing had changed, that the expectations hadn't been lowered.

"That's what Joe did in '96 so successfully. The way Joe handled that was one of the reasons we were successful. We should've never been on the same field with the Atlanta Braves, but we were."

CHAPTER SIX

BERNIE

There is something deep inside Bernie Williams that has allowed him to succeed in New York for so long. Good luck finding it.

Williams, one of the most enigmatic figures to wear pinstripes since his center field forefather Joe DiMaggio, is a jazz guitarist, a former teen international track success, and an intellectual who studied biology in college. He released an album called *The Journey Within*, but he hasn't made many people privy to his own personal odyssey.

"We don't know what makes Bernie tick. We've been trying to figure that out for fifteen years," bench coach Lee Mazzilli said. "I'm not too sure Bernie knows."

Joe Torre, who has managed his center fielder since 1996, loves telling stories about Williams almost as much as he reveres the switch-hitting Puerto Rico native. One of the manager's favorite tales came from the 1999 Division Series, when a line drive off Chuck Knoblauch's checked swing nailed then bench coach Don Zimmer in the left side of the head in the fifth inning of Game 1 against Texas. He was knocked off the bench, and blood gushed from his ear and jaw. Although Yankee Stadium and many other ballparks now have mandatory screens on the dugout steps that protect game-day personnel, that wasn't the case a few years ago.

Most famously, Zimmer began donning an old Army helmet with a Yankees logo soon after the inadvertent beaning, but the tangential consequence to the incident was far more fascinating. Williams, a soft-spoken man who doesn't try to hide his humanity, came up to Zimmer and asked, "Are you all right?"

What Torre saw next was astonishing. Williams had his bat in his hands, and Torre saw his player grip it as hard as humanly possible, as if he was trying to wring sawdust out of the ash. Williams' eyes became glassy with fury, and he went to the plate a few batters later against Aaron Sele. He ripped a two-run double off the center-field fence to give the Yanks a 3-0 lead. The next inning, he came up again and smashed a three-run homer to right that helped make the game an 8-0 laugher. He finished 3 for 5 that night with a postseason career high of six RBIs.

As Torre recounted the tale, he noted that it was obvious, even to Williams, that nobody hit Zimmer on purpose. Knoblauch, after all, was a Yankee teammate.

"But it was just something that lit the fire," Torre said.

To the Yankee manager, Williams is a lion with great heart, a ballplayer with elegance but also with fire in his belly.

"But sometimes you've gotta find the right button to push, because there are times he'll just seem to be floating along, and then something will make an impact," he summarized.

Unfortunately, there was someone early in Williams' career who made a negative impact, who constantly tried to push his buttons in order to break him. For those students coming late to the history of the franchise, there was a time when it looked like Williams might not even be a Yankee, never mind a cornerstone of the club. After making his major-league debut in 1991 and making the team the following spring, Williams was optioned back to Triple A on April 15, 1992, and wasn't recalled until July 31 of that year, after Danny Tartabull was placed on the disabled list.

The Yankees in those days were losers, literally and figuratively. Nobody personified that notion more than Mel Hall, a once-talented, destructive force. As best described in Joel Sherman's book *Birth of a Dynasty,* Hall would torment Williams on a regular basis. Hall, an outfielder who obviously saw the burgeoning Williams as a threat, once taped a sign reading

"Mr. Zero" atop Williams' locker, signifying his presumed worth to the team. According to Sherman's book, Hall one day nearly reduced the introverted Williams to tears.

"My experience starting off with the team wasn't a very pleasant one, I guess," Williams said in April 2006, the scars still evident after a decade and a half.

The reason Williams was not a sure thing with the Yankees back then was that he wasn't an instinctive baseball player, and that still came through in 2006. He'd been a teenage track sensation in Puerto Rico, and he came late to the game because of his other interests. Torre once told him, "You're more at home with a guitar in your hand." The manager always lamented that with his blazing speed, Williams should've been able to steal a lot more bases than he did in his prime, when he never swiped more than 20 in one season.

As the manager explained, something clicks within Derek Jeter or Alex Rodriguez or Gary Sheffield or Robinson Cano when a given situation occurs. They react without thinking. Bernie always needed to analyze first. Fortunately, his teammates grew to appreciate his misadventures in the outfield and on the basepaths, instead of making fun of them as Hall once did.

"Bernie makes a mistake, the players look at each other," Torre said. "It's not something that comes from being lazy; it comes from being Bernie.

"Guys accept it. They shake their head—and Bernie does, too. It's nothing we keep from him. He comes in, we talk about it."

Williams eventually became a perennial All-Star, batting champion, four-time Gold Glove winner, and one of the most prolific postseason hitters ever, but he remembered where he came from.

"I love the way he carries himself, the way he handles himself," Derek Jeter said in 2006.

When Williams went from the scared, shy rookie to the cornerstone in the corner locker, he made sure never to maliciously put anyone down.

"But that wasn't the case in the early nineties, '91, '92, when we had a lot of tough guys here," Williams said, gritting his teeth as he spoke. "So . . . If the priority of the people is not really winning, it's just being here and going about your job on a daily basis of 'This is my job, this is what I do, I'm just going to try to put up good numbers so I can have a better contract next year,' then you can run into situations like that. That's the only thing I can say about that.

"I wouldn't want to expound on that, because it happened such a long time ago, anyways. I would say this, though: once we started getting rid of those people, it was a completely different attitude in the team, and I think there was more excitement, not because we were the Yankees, but because we had a good team and we were competing."

When Williams talks of being a Yankee, he does so reverently, calling it his home. When he talks to teammates and peers about being in the Bronx, they tell him, "You don't want to get out of here. You do what you have to. You want to stay where you're at right now."

It was a minor miracle that in 2006, Williams was still a Yankee. Even he called it extraordinary and remarkable that in all his years in the major leagues, he'd been with only one team. In 2005, he'd stumbled badly in the field and at the plate, losing his starting job before Memorial Day. Torre was always especially protective of Williams and took great pains to shield him emotionally, though. When Steinbrenner ordered the signing of Kenny Lofton for the 2004 season, Torre—who normally vacations in Hawaii for a month in the off-season and is loath to do much official business—specifically called Williams to tell him that the best man at the end of spring training would earn the starting job.

Williams was waylaid by appendicitis that spring, but Torre brought Lofton and Williams into his office early that season to draw names from a hat. Only one player could be on the All-Star ballot, and Williams' name was the one picked out of the hat.

By early May 2005, not only was Williams not an All-Star candidate, but his hold on the regular job had slipped—even without a solid replacement lined up. He was never a strong thrower, and a right elbow injury began turning his starts into an embarrassment. With the Yankees trying desperately to make changes after an 11-19 start, they couldn't afford to give much leeway even to Williams.

During an 8-6 loss to Toronto on May 1, his flaws were glaringly visible. In the seventh, Eric Hinske tagged up and scored standing up on a fly ball that Williams came in for. Also, the lumbering Shea Hillenbrand tagged up from first on a fly ball that didn't even reach the warning track.

Torre, who was forced to relay the bad news, called the decision and aftereffects "two weeks of torture." At Shea Stadium, during one of the most anticipated series of the season from May 20 to 22, the manager said, "I just don't envision you as a regular center fielder, and we're going to do something different." According to the skipper, it took Williams nearly

Johnny Damon emerged as the center fielder and leadoff hitter the Yankees needed in 2006, but it took time for him to get over the sting of his abrupt exit from Boston. Damon provided some levity in the Yankees' businesslike clubhouse, goofing around and cracking jokes constantly. Damon provided solid defense in center, a dire need for the Yankees after Bernie Williams showed he could no longer play the position every day in 2005.

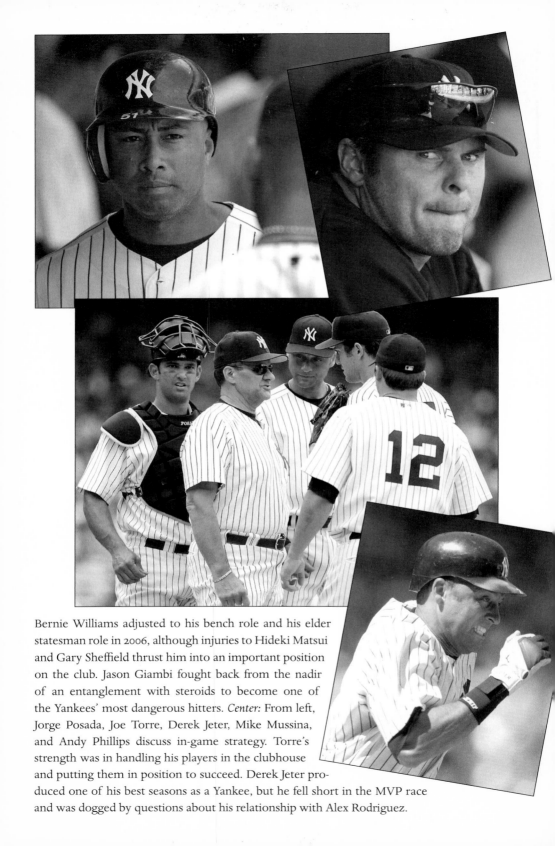

Bernie Williams adjusted to his bench role and his elder statesman role in 2006, although injuries to Hideki Matsui and Gary Sheffield thrust him into an important position on the club. Jason Giambi fought back from the nadir of an entanglement with steroids to become one of the Yankees' most dangerous hitters. *Center:* From left, Jorge Posada, Joe Torre, Derek Jeter, Mike Mussina, and Andy Phillips discuss in-game strategy. Torre's strength was in handling his players in the clubhouse and putting them in position to succeed. Derek Jeter produced one of his best seasons as a Yankee, but he fell short in the MVP race and was dogged by questions about his relationship with Alex Rodriguez.

For Alex Rodriguez, 2006 was one of the most tumultuous years of his career, a far cry from his MVP season in 2005. Although Mike Mussina continued to provide dependable value on the mound and grew into a staff leader, it wasn't enough to quiet his most vocal critics. Despite a quiet personality, Chien-Ming Wang emerged as the ace of the staff in 2006 on the basis of a deadly sinker. He also came out of his shell . . . a bit.

Robinson Cano celebrates with Jason Giambi and A-Rod. Cano (*center*), a second-year player, became an All-Star in 2006 and proved he could hang with the big boys.

Bobby Abreu was Yankee GM Brian Cashman's midseason masterstroke. Abreu was an on-base machine who forced the exit of Gary Sheffield.

Above: Once again in 2006, Mariano Rivera proved invaluable. But in the final three games of the Division Series, Rivera could only watch helplessly. *Right:* The season changed for good when Hideki Matsui broke his wrist in May, leading to the emergence of Melky Cabrera.

Melky Cabrera made a remarkable catch to rob Boston's Manny Ramirez of a home run on June 6 to preserve a 2-1 victory over the Red Sox. Alex Rodriguez and Derek Jeter share a moment of fun. The two superstars' relationship was scrutinized as never before in '06, when Jeter had a great year and A-Rod didn't. Gary Sheffield hurried back from a serious wrist injury to be ready for the playoffs, but he wasn't his old self. He took plenty of parting shots before being traded to Detroit.

Gary Sheffield said he was a sounding board for Alex Rodriguez and indicated things would get much worse for A-Rod in 2007 after he left.

Derek Jeter finished second in the MVP balloting to Minnesota's Justin Morneau, although the captain would say his primary focus was on a world championship. Joe Torre admired Jaret Wright's grit, but the Yankee starter often couldn't go more than six innings and produced a stinker in Game 4 of the Division Series.

Above: Joe Torre (left) and Brian Cashman chat during the beginning of spring training 2006, when the Yankees were brimming with optimism and purpose for a run at the franchise's twenty-seventh world championship. Before agreeing on a new contract, Cashman demanded control of baseball operations, which he received. He trusted and respected Torre's ability to lead the club on the field. *Below:* Don Mattingly, Derek Jeter, Joe Torre, and Ron Guidry look on helplessly in Detroit, where the Tigers turned the Yankees' season into a disappointment.

Alex Rodriguez in a preliminary champagne celebration from 2005. As Yankee fans and A-Rod know, the only bubbly that really matters is the stuff that flows after a World Series victory.

Alex Rodriguez unhappily looks on at the turn of events in Detroit, where the Tigers dispatched the Yankees. A-Rod's future as a Yankee became cloudy after a miserable season.

Cory Lidle loved being a Yankee and all that it entailed. His untimely death came just a few short days after the Bombers were abruptly dismissed in the playoffs.

two weeks to accept the situation, during which time he'd come into the manager's office and vent.

In August, it seemed as if his fate might have been sealed. White Sox center fielder Aaron Rowand enjoyed a tremendous defensive series, ranging from gap to gap as Chicago won two of three from the embattled Bombers. By contrast, in the series finale on August 10, Williams failed to get to a gapper from Juan Uribe and couldn't make a strong throw to prevent him from getting to third. Uribe scored the winning run in a 2-1 Yankee loss. You couldn't help but notice how far Williams had slipped from the days when he could outrun his bad reads on balls.

"Last year, I was expecting out of myself to be an everyday player," Williams said. "That's why I got so frustrated: because they sort of said, 'Well, you're not.'"

There was nobody, in good times or bad, who took more advantage of Torre's open-door policy over the years. As Torre would recount with a laugh, Williams wouldn't even look at the lineup but would rather stop in for a check of where he was hitting. If it was a bench player who always asked or a rookie, it might aggravate a manager to no end. Torre chalked it up to part of Williams' unique personality.

"I laugh at it, I make fun of it, but I love it," Torre said.

At the end of the year, Williams came into Torre's office and said, "I'd like to stay here next year."

The Yankees had tried everyone from Tony Womack to Melky Cabrera to Hideki Matsui to Bubba Crosby in center in 2005 but never found a steady replacement to their liking. Williams, meanwhile, finished with a .249 batting average, his worst since his rookie season in 1991. He had lost his bat after 2002, when he batted .333 with 19 homers and 102 RBIs. The next two years he batted .263 and .262 before another precipitous decline.

Brian Cashman loudly and repeatedly pronounced that the team's priority was improving its center field situation, and Williams was a free agent after earning $12,357,143 in the final year of his seven-year contract.

When the Yankees struck gold with Johnny Damon just before Christmas, it appeared for a few days that there'd be coal in Williams' stocking. Luckily, Williams made peace with his age and skills and decided to return on a one-year basis.

He didn't want to retire at thirty-seven, because he wanted to be sure he was at the end. He wasn't one of those guys who wanted to try to make a comeback in two or three years, when he was forty. He didn't want to be watching TV and say, "Dude, I know I can hit this guy!" He wanted to play out the string.

"Every other team that we talked to was basically offering the same thing that the Yankees were," he recounted. "If that was the case, it was basically a no-brainer in my decision making."

Williams, the longest-tenured Yankee, has seen subtle changes over the years. When he arrived in 1991, it always struck him as odd that the team's marketing campaign was to evoke the players of twenty, thirty, forty, or more years ago. Don Mattingly was the only present-day Yankee thought to have any marketability; the bulk of the strategy revolved around Babe Ruth and Mickey Mantle and Joe DiMaggio.

"Back then, that was the thing," Williams said, erupting in laughter. "The nineties Yankees, the front page [of the media guide or the yearbook] was Joe D. doing something. And I never understood what that was about.

"Now I do, obviously, after spending a whole career here. You want to be able to tap into greatness and tag along with those times. Just remind the fans about how great those times were and how proud the organization is to have guys like that and teams like that in those years."

Thinking of the Bambino still made him laugh, though.

"Dude, he played in the thirties, dog," he chuckled, very un-Williams-like. "Best player ever—but he played in the thirties. What happened to us?

"But then we obviously started adding to the legacy in a big way. Once you started getting one, two, three, four rings, you're part of a very exclusive group within the same organization—and basically considered part of the dynasty and things like that. And I am so proud to be part of that. It's a great feeling."

Similarly, Williams felt the media coverage shifted from being a voyeuristic view into a circus to being more serious-minded and results-oriented. Back in the nineties, it had been a he-said, she-said type of mentality, and Mattingly's feud with Steinbrenner over his hair was one such instance. It was so bad, it was parodied on an episode of *The Simpsons,* where Mattingly was ordered to shave his sideburns by the nefarious Mr. Burns.

The changes extended into the makeup of the clubhouse itself. Although he overstated it a bit, Williams remembered the teams in the mid-1990s boasting a great core of players developed within the organization. Although that might've been true in 1995, when the club bore the fruit of homegrown players Scott Kamieniecki, Sterling Hitchcock, and

Gerald Williams in addition to Derek Jeter, Andy Pettitte, Mariano Rivera, and himself, even then the Yankee front office was bringing in mercenaries such as David Cone (acquired during the 1995 season) and Darryl Strawberry.

Later in the run, stud pitchers such as David Wells, Orlando Hernández, and Hideki Irabu were brought in, but Williams is right about one key distinction. Whereas players such as Scott Brosius, Tino Martinez, and Paul O'Neill were brought to town to fill a role well, none was at the top of his profession. There was no imported "mega-superstar player," as Williams saw it, and that had a positive effect on the atmosphere in the clubhouse.

"We were creating a chemistry as we went," he said. "Obviously winning had a lot to do with it, but it was like everybody was creating the chemistry at the same time. . . . The success fed off the great camaraderie that we had, and vice versa."

Williams felt the Yankees played National League–style baseball in the dynasty era, running, bunting, and using the hit-and-run a lot, with some great defense mixed in. He also felt, with a bullpen that held the likes of Mike Stanton, Jeff Nelson, Jason Grimsley, and Mariano Rivera over the years, that the game was theirs if they held a lead after the seventh inning.

By the time the string of four world championships in five years was over, Williams reasoned, the word about the great clubhouse atmosphere in New York had spread around the majors. No longer was the Bronx home to malcontents and losers; Torre and company had instilled winning. Hence, Mike Mussina was signed as a free agent for the 2001 season, Jason Giambi for the 2002 season, Hideki Matsui for 2003. Alex Rodriguez and Gary Sheffield were brought in before 2004, and Randy Johnson was dealt to New York prior to '05. The mega-superstars had arrived, even if more championships hadn't.

Success was a magnet for these people, according to Williams, who believes that once you get past all the big-city distractions and curiosities, New York is a terrific place to play. Although Williams was fortunate to live in only one baseball town during his career, he had heard too many stories of teams that wanted to simply fill the seats, too many teams that only wanted to play a little better than .500.

"When you get into a stage of your career that you have made your money, you have made your fame, you're a prominent player, I think that sort of wears out a little bit, wears off a little bit," he said. "And you want to experience how it feels to be on a winning team or a team that has a chance to win day in and day out."

Yankee fans challenge players to perform at their best all the time, and nothing less than a world championship is expected. Williams said that you want to play for a team that has high expectations, and justifiably so.

"Realistic?" he asked. "That's another story."

Williams sees the New York press as a vital organ in selling George Steinbrenner's vision of an annual World Series title, but he acknowledged that the expectations were high because the club was the highest-paid team in baseball during the beginning of the twenty-first century. Players in the 1990s might not have made the most money and might've even been on the decline, he noted, but many of the current Yankees were "commanding big dollars" during their prime.

"When the owner wants to collect on his investment, he has every right in the world to do that," Williams said. "And you guys have every right in the world to talk about the expectations.

"We have high expectations here. But I don't think they're real, you know? To win the World Series every year? Every single year? And to see the season as nothing but a failure if that doesn't happen. I mean, come on.

"It's highly unrealistic. But the good thing about the game is it's not impossible. You always have that thing on your mind that you can actually do it with the team we have."

If 2005 was a surprisingly disappointing year for Williams, 2006 held the promise of a renaissance. Although GM Brian Cashman was hoping to integrate first baseman Andy Phillips into the starting lineup and move Jason Giambi to more of a full-time DH role, Torre found himself again and again going to Williams as the DH. It was a philosophical difference between the manager and the GM, one that went along predictable lines. Cashman was adamant about integrating young, homegrown talent into the parent club, in hopes of both raising the trade value of certain prospects and making the team stronger from within.

Torre, meanwhile, was simply leaning on one of his old reliables, a player who had come through for him time and again, especially in the postseason. After all, Williams held the records for most postseason homers (22), RBIs (83), and runs scored (83), and he was the 1996 ALCS MVP.

And then twin catastrophes struck the Yankees within a few days of each other. On April 29, Gary Sheffield collided with Toronto's Shea Hillenbrand down the first-base line, suffering a left wrist injury that placed him on the DL twice and kept him out from late May until September. And on May 11, Hideki Matsui broke his wrist charging a fly ball from Mark Loretta, an injury that also kept him out throughout the summer.

The Yankees immediately brought up their young outfield prospect, Cabrera, the player who had failed as Williams' successor the year before. But Williams was also thrust into a more active role, one he handled with aplomb.

Instead of patrolling center, a position that had taxed his weary legs too often in 2005, he was moved to right field. Mazzilli, who works with the outfielders, said he adjusted to the new position well, took the learning of the new angles seriously, and developed a comfort zone out there. His professionalism, especially after what he had accomplished in his career, was a quiet example to the younger players, the Yankee bench coach maintained.

After seventy-nine games, Williams had started in right thirty-six times, in center seven times, and in left six times. In addition to that, he was the starting DH fourteen times, meaning he had started all but sixteen of the games in the first half of the season. So much for being a part-time player, a spare part, or a fifth outfielder. Instead of finding places to play him, Torre said, he had to catch himself and find times to give Williams a day off.

As Mazzilli said, Williams is fresh when he plays three or four times a week, and he's a tremendous asset off the bench with his bat the rest of the time. His experience ("He's been through all the wars," Mazzilli said) was invaluable, and he was a beloved teammate.

"I was writing his name in automatically, which I had been doing for ten years," Torre said. "I've got to pay more attention."

Williams knew the reality: if he and the youngsters Phillips (playing every day because of the injury glut) and Cabrera didn't come through, the team was screwed. He had never seen a year when so many Yankees went down at the same time, which changed his own outlook. He had prepared since spring training to fill the role they'd said they wanted him to play. He'd come to terms with the fact he wasn't going to play every day. Now, by early July, he was on pace to play 130 games.

"It's very ironic," he said with a Mona Lisa smile.

Physically, Williams oscillated. Torre constantly had to caution himself not to overwork his former cornerstone. Williams held up his end. He was hitting .282 with six homers and 35 RBIs at the All-Star break. In early July, he was batting .342 from the right side.

"You get to be my age, some days you feel twenty-eight and some days you feel sixty-eight," he said in early June. "The most important thing for me right now is I'm approaching it from a different perspective mentally.

"I'm like, 'You know what? This is basically towards the end of my career. Why stress? I get to do this every day, get to come here and play for a great team. I get to go out there and do my thing. Why should I be frustrated? Why should I just stress about this?'

"That's the attitude I had from spring training. Let's just have fun with this. Forget about all the distractions."

CHAPTER SEVEN

TORRE

In the final hours before first pitch is where Joe Torre shines—engaging in the critical give-and-take with the local media, schmoozing with the VIPs who get field passes and demand autographs or just a brief word. Torre is in many ways the public face of the franchise, and he handles it all with aplomb—which is funny, because Torre thinks of himself as a shy, introverted sort.

There are certain managers who could never handle such an additional burden, but Torre makes it seem as light as a feather. Most skippers are chained to the batting cage for BP, insistent about watching how their stars and benchwarmers are handling the 70-something-mile-an-hour meatballs from the daily BP chucker. Torre delegates those responsibilities and doesn't even watch most of batting practice on most days, because of what are considered his more important duties.

Torre is no phony, although if you catch him on the way out to the dugout around 4:30 P.M. you might get a grunt instead of a hello. He knows his role, he knows how to handle it, and nobody in the modern age has ever been better. John McGraw couldn't hack this. Torre, who managed the Mets from 1977 to 1981, Atlanta from 1982 to 1984, and St. Louis from 1990 to 1995, said the extra responsibilities were nothing like this place.

When Torre stands next to one of his coaches or general manager Brian Cashman for a photo, it's almost the baseball equivalent of the Rat Pack, with Torre as a uniformed Sinatra. Most of the people who wangle passes before games are affiliated with charities, which strikes a chord with Torre. He's able to get these pictures or signed baseballs auctioned off for donations to help worthy causes.

Growing up in Brooklyn, Torre saw firsthand the destructive influence on his family of his father's verbal abuse of his mother. He was often too frightened by his father's hot temper to return to his household after school. When he achieved world championship success in New York, he established the Safe at Home Foundation with his wife, Ali.

Doing what he can, even thirty minutes before a game on some afternoons, is totally worthwhile.

"Whatever goodwill we can pass on, it just takes some time," Torre said. "It takes, what, fifteen minutes? But people will respond with, 'Wonderful time!' And it's such a little bit of my time to make them have a special time. . . .

"When people all of a sudden recognize you as something they think you are, you sort of have to understand if meeting me means that much to them, well, you don't try to reason with it. You just do it, basically."

Torre is still uncomfortable with the attention, but he realizes that by being in the sporting eye as a leader of men, he's a role model. One of the things that always makes him proud is when people from other cities come up to him and mention how professionally his players act. The manager detests how certain athletes—he singled out football players in an April conversation—misbehave. He's aghast that Major League Baseball would sanction a video game where a player slides into second base and punches somebody. And don't even get him started on ESPN. He's been livid at the network since 2000, when Roger Clemens' beaning of Mike Piazza was repeated ad nauseam before the Subway Series. Torre always felt that contributed to the bat-throwing incident between the two in Game 2 of the World Series. Torre's cooperation with the network is kept to a bare minimum, with teeth gritted.

Otherwise, Torre's job security has been helped by his genial dexterity with the press, but he also blew his top with the home-owned YES Network in 2005.

With his placid eyes and well-worn face, Torre is usually a picture of calm in a roiling sea. Even if the now-established skipper can't forge players into Yankees, he can take the heat off them. Yet when he became convinced that someone in the Yankee front office was feeding a YES reporter questions to publicly embarrass him after tough losses, even the manager with the famously long fuse became enraged.

The fallout for 2006? He refused to do the YES pregame and postgame shows, turning down a reported $300,000. Usually, the YES reporter—Kimberly Jones—would ask a series of questions to get the media interaction kicked off before and after games. But Torre's friends suspected that president Randy Levine, at the behest of Steinbrenner, was pushing certain questions down the chain.

"It's not an issue," Torre said in April. "If it was going to bother me, I wasn't going to do it.

"The most important thing for me—when you work for someone, you want to feel that everybody's working, pulling in the same direction. Because when you're talking, you're talking for the organization.

"Anytime you say, 'I want something to happen,' unless it's an isolated case on the field, this is the way we do it in this organization. And I think this organization deserves that, because it's so proud. It was more important for me to be comfortable."

Levine didn't deny tinkering with the broadcasts, saying it was "not a case of people planting questions, but in guiding a new network, observations were made to improve the broadcast.

"It was never intended to put Joe in a bad light," Levine said.

Although Yankees officials thought the issue was "totally overblown" by the media for pure titillation, the manager felt differently. As he assessed his future in the winter before the 2006 season, the sixty-five-year-old knew his professional problems went far beyond a television microphone.

The manager felt that all year long, owner George Steinbrenner was sniping from afar. His good friend, pitching coach Mel Stottlemyre, was pointedly criticized. Stottlemyre decided to step down as pitching coach and retire after the 2005 season, preferring peace and quiet to the alternative.

It took almost a week in October for Torre to officially announce he himself was returning, but he decided to honor his contract, which runs through 2007 and will pay him $13 million for those two years, after a key meeting with Levine during the airplane ride to Florida, and then with Steinbrenner himself.

The team president said it came down to the fact that 2005 was a very hard season that led to "a lot of problems." But Levine, who said he respected Torre's leadership and liked him personally, beseeched him to return.

"Joe, we need you back," Levine told him as the plane took off toward Tampa. "We want you back."

"He needed to know all of us were behind him," he said. "We all are human, we all need [positive reinforcement]."

When he arrived, Torre spoke with Steinbrenner. They cleared the air about the YES Network and other matters, and Torre promised not to let the lines of communication get cut on his end. He pledged himself that he would speak with Steinbrenner about once every ten days or so. Later, Levine and general partner Steve Swindal joined the discussion.

"I needed to find out if George wanted me back," Torre said. "It doesn't matter that I make a lot of money, and it doesn't matter that I've been the manager here when we went to six World Series.

"What mattered to me is if the guy who's paying me still wants me here. Because this is a game where unless you trust somebody with what you're doing, I mean, you can nitpick all day long and find something on a 162-game schedule that if you wanted reason to say, 'He's not doing his job,' you can find it.

"And I didn't want that to happen."

After an 11-19 start in 2005, Torre's troops picked themselves off the canvas and won the AL East on the second-to-last day of the season, when a few days before it had looked as if they might not even win the wild card. The hunger that his club finally showed in the final five months and the fight they exhibited made him prouder than at any other time as Yankee manager. He also conceded it was his toughest season as a manager.

"They had to take off the gloves and understand that they're going to have to get down in the foxhole here," he said. "And they had absolutely no regard for their own personal well-being."

Although the Yanks were bounced from the postseason by Anaheim in the Division Series, the players came to Tampa in the spring of 2006 with a certain pride in what they had accomplished. Grown men were excited about picking up where they left off, and that exhilarated Torre. He wasn't sure exactly why, but he was invigorated in the spring and having a lot of fun, even though his club trailed Boston virtually from Jump Street.

"I feel much more—I don't want to say relaxed, but I'm much more comfortable with the environment. Because relaxed is not something you want to say around George Steinbrenner," he said with a small smile. "There's a continuity here and there's a structure that seems to be very healthy.

"Because when there's all this turmoil—and that's why I didn't want to address anything from George last year, because I knew it would filter down to somebody going in there and wanting to get the players' take on whose side they were on. It wasn't fair. I couldn't have that happen."

In addition to the task of keeping Steinbrenner at bay, Torre's job has other challenges. He's watched a revolving door of newcomers in recent seasons, and the championship drought hasn't ended.

Although the latest edition of the Yankees was statistically superior to their predecessors (Gary Sheffield versus Paul O'Neill; Jason Giambi versus Tino Martinez), the sum was less than the parts. After four rings in five years, Torre had spent the previous five seasons unsuccessfully trying to reverse that trend.

When he addressed his team on February 22, at the beginning of spring training, it was with a renewed vigor and gusto. His challenge was unmistakable: the goal was a World Series title, and nothing less would be satisfactory.

"He let us know what time it is," Gary Sheffield told the *New York Post* that day. "This one was more intense. For whatever reason, you felt more conviction. We are going to do it this time. I felt it from him."

Interacting with the players is Torre's favorite part of the job. He quickly gained trust in the Yankee clubhouse in 1996, his first year, by building players up and extinguishing brush fires whenever possible. As a native New Yorker, Torre knew about all the attention, the criticism, and the pressure placed on the Yankees. He knew what the Bronx Zoo was like at its most chaotic.

"The one thing I noticed during those years was a lot of the news— supposedly newsworthy stories that were coming out of here—had nothing to do with baseball," he said. "And that was . . . something I was gonna have to address.

"Whatever it is off the field that you have to deal with, whether it comes from the owner or the dry cleaner . . . your job is to pay attention and get ready to play between the lines."

He tells newcomers every season that if there's any significant news affecting them, they'll hear it from the manager first. And he'll always be the bearer of bad news, never delegating that part of the job to his coaches.

After playing parts of eighteen seasons in the majors, Torre is very sensitive to players' needs. He's also sensitive to perceptions, ever since someone came up to him in St. Louis a few years after he was traded there and said, "You're not a troublemaker." That was the label someone had tagged him with around the time he was a union representative. Back then, that was a highly unpopular stance to take, even though at the time the Players Association was fighting for pensions, not against drug testing.

He feels it's somewhat unbelievable that he's lasted eleven years, and those who witnessed the Steinbrenner–Billy Martin histrionics would certainly agree. But it also was very natural and very comfortable to Torre, who could still deliver a message with great success.

"The most satisfying for me is that when I do talk to players and stuff, they're attentive and listening," he said. "Because when you manage and the players all of a sudden are straying a little bit, you know your welcome is being worn out."

It took Torre a long time to get comfortable giving speeches as a manager, due to his shyness. Before he delivers a speech, he'll jot down notes for himself. He's able to improvise on the subject matter, and one thing usually reminds him of something else. In managing, as in rapping, keeping it real is of the utmost importance. No wonder Torre has the type of bling bling (four World Series rings) that would make most hip-hoppers weep.

"I'm not trying to sell anybody anything," he explained. "And that's the one thing I never try to do with the players.

"Because it's not like you're playing 12 games a year, you know? You're playing 162 games, so in my opinion, I have to make sense to these guys . . . It's gotta be *something they can hold on to.*

"When I have a meeting, I base it off what I see or what I don't see. And I pretty much—what's the word I'm looking for?—deal with facts."

Dealing with the personalities of the players is an ongoing thing, and handling egos can get tricky. Torre still laughs over the recollection of a young Lee Mazzilli telling rookie skipper Torre that he couldn't hit lead-off for the Mets in 1977. The beauty of the current Yankees is that, for instance, there's a number of hitters who could hit third or fourth. At least there was at the beginning of 2006. The manager didn't feel that any particular player was putting himself on a pedestal.

"It's a challenge because there's always more pressure with being expected to win," he said. "But I'll take that pressure, as opposed to trying to win when you're not as good. When you haven't got the ability, let's put it that way."

If there's been a criticism of Torre over the years, it's been his handling of the bullpen. After the Yankees blew a two-games-to-one lead in the 2003 World Series because the manager went with starter Jeff Weaver instead of reliever Mariano Rivera in extra innings of Game 4, people have honed in on Torre's moves with his relievers.

In his defense, he was spoiled in his early years in the Bronx, when Jeff Nelson and Mike Stanton formed a potent left-right combination leading up to Rivera. But that doesn't pardon his overuse of Paul Quantrill and Tom Gordon in 2004 and Tanyon Sturtze in 2005, which his detractors found criminal. Looking at the first- and second-half ERAs from Quantrill, Gordon, and Sturtze, it was clear that they were less effective in the second half of seasons. In '04, Quantrill recorded a 3.05 ERA in the first half and a 7.09 ERA in the second half, his arm shot. Gordon's second-half ERA in 2004, 2.77, was 0.99 higher than his first-half ERA. In 2005, Sturtze posted a 3.91 ERA before the break and a 6.07 ERA after the All-Star Game.

When Torre was asked for his take on that criticism, he said, "I can't deny that, other than the fact [that] Quantrill, his past history, has always been a workhorse.

"I don't think anybody was better than Mel at keeping track of and never overdoing and being protective of all these pitchers," he said. "Sturtzie's case, he was a workhorse for a while and there were situations that made us use him. But the fact someone all of a sudden shows they can't handle the load, then you back off and change the decision. You don't push the envelope.

"I don't proclaim that I know everything. The one thing I know, I'm smart enough to make adjustments as you need to."

As Sturtze became increasingly ineffective early in 2006 and finally went down with a shoulder injury by mid-May, Torre desperately needed to make an adjustment and find someone who could chew up innings in setup. He turned to Scott Proctor, a hard-throwing righty reliever whose fastball was straight and, therefore, whose tenure in the Bronx was usually short-lived. In 2004 and 2005, he had five separate stints with the Yanks. The club was actually developing him as a starter in spring training 2006, but he earned a spot on the team out of camp and was pitching effectively in long relief. Right before Sturtze was put on the DL with tendinitis in his right shoulder on May 14, Proctor had taken over his seventh-inning role.

As Torre remembered it, Cashman first addressed the issue with his manager in the middle of May.

"My feeling was, a lot of those innings came early, when he really wasn't part of our back end," Torre said. "He ate up some innings in games we were ahead or behind, because he was a starter in spring training.

"Since then, you try to be aware of taking better care."

By June 13, Proctor was still leading the major leagues in innings and pitches, the intrepid Peter Abraham of the Westchester *Journal News* reported, appearing in 31 of the team's first 61 games. Kyle Farnsworth had toiled in 30 of them, and he had a bad May and early June. On May 15, he allowed three hits and chucked a wild pitch in the eighth inning of a 4-2 loss. On May 26, working for the third straight game and third time in four days, he surrendered three hits and three runs in an inning. Paul Bako had the game-tying hit against Proctor that night, and Angel Berroa hammered a three-run homer on a hanging slider.

On May 30, a hit and two walks led to a run and a blown save in an 11-6 extra-innings victory. Farnsworth felt he was fortunate to get out of the eighth inning by only allowing a run.

Two days later, with the Yankees having a chance to sweep a four-game series in Detroit, Farnsworth was called on in a rare save opportunity, since Rivera had hurt himself bending over to tie his shoes. Farnsworth blew the save, for the third time in four chances. He allowed two runs on three hits and a walk, recording only one out. On June 11, he lost a 6-5 game on a homer by Oakland's Dan Johnson that Farnsworth said wasn't a bad pitch or a good one.

By the middle of the month, despite Torre's proclamations of "taking better care" and "making adjustments," Cashman said the issue was "definitely a concern" at Yankee Stadium. He said he'd try to come up with some alternatives if he could, but Octavio Dotel—whom the GM had optimistically signed hot off Dotel's Tommy John surgery—had had a setback and wasn't going to be available until later in the summer. Cashman said he'd "continue to have dialogue with the manager that he's got to rely on some other guys at the same time. No different than everybody else in the game."

Cashman summarized, "You can't have Farnsworth and Proctor pitching every other day as much as they were pitching. You just can't, to have them be at their best for the stretch drive.

"You've got to use the bullpen one through six, or seven. I think we've had a twelve-man staff most of the year. And he's got to spread the wealth. There's quality guys, three lefties out there. Ronnie Villone, there's other guys who can step up and hold the flag. We've got a number of major-league guys that can get the job done out there, but Joe's so used to going for the jugular to secure a win that he's going to try to gravitate to the guys who can do that for you."

To Cashman, there was no question that Proctor's struggles in June and later were because of his usage. He appreciated that Torre has a very difficult job in balancing the team's short- and long-term interests, and that sometimes tough choices had to be made. But Proctor was one of those young players who Cashman felt could help the Yankees in the present and future, if Torre would use him correctly.

"He's come a long way for us," Cashman said. "He's developed and cleared some hurdles, but at the same time, it's tough to be at your best if you don't get some consistent rest."

CHAPTER EIGHT

COACHES

Working for the Yankees "was the furthest thing from my mind," thought Joe Kerrigan when general manager Brian Cashman called him on July 1, 2005.

Kerrigan was signed on as a special advisor to Cashman, which meant he was a wild card in the GM's deck. Although it was a steep step down for someone who'd managed his own club a few seasons earlier, albeit briefly, Kerrigan jumped into the challenge. One of his main roles was breaking down opposing teams' hitters on video, something he'd pioneered with the Montreal Expos in the early 1990s, when the team was too poor or too cheap to hire advance scouts and Kerrigan gained an edge through a satellite dish and a TV. The Yankees spared no expense, so the tools at his disposal were significant.

"I always thought that was an integral part of pitching and playing defense," Kerrigan said. "A pitching coach almost had to be a defensive coordinator nowadays.

"Probably half of it is knowing your own staff and your own staff's mechanics. But the other half of the battle is how to use that stuff to attack hitters, and have a good game plan of attacking hitters and breaking down hitters.

"And their system here—their computer system and their data bases and their availability of resources—is second to none. They have the most modern, up-to-date video system in the world as far as tracking hitters. As far as statistical analysis, we have more information available with regard to breaking down the hitter than anyplace I have been."

Fifteen years after he was at the forefront of the movement, Kerrigan reported that nearly all of the upper-echelon teams and a lot of the middle-market teams were using video. Teams that didn't, Kerrigan said bluntly, were at a disadvantage.

"Let's face it: when somebody else is using it and tracking your hitters and your pitchers, they have an advantage over you because they have more information," he said.

Larry Bowa, who managed the Phillies when Kerrigan was the pitching coach, said, "Joe's as prepared as any pitching coach. He knows how to break down hitters as good as anybody I've ever seen by looking at film."

Although Kerrigan's expertise was in analysis, Cashman would've been stupid to discount one other line on his new hire's résumé. Kerrigan could counsel the most important pitching investment that the Yankees owned: Randy Johnson.

A few years after Kerrigan's middling four-year major-league career as a right-handed reliever ended in 1980 after one appearance for Baltimore (the last of 131 games in the bigs), he became the Montreal bullpen coach. That stint ended in 1987, when he accepted a job as the Expos' Double A pitching coach in Jacksonville, Florida, where he was introduced to a towering 6-foot-10 lefty. After Kerrigan worked with Johnson to produce an 11-8 record and 3.73 ERA, both men moved to Triple A Indianapolis the next year. Johnson—then a prospect who had problems harnessing his wildness—was traded to Seattle for Mark Langston in 1989. The rest was history.

"I think through these eyes, through someone who saw him as a young, raw, developing kid to now, I've kind of enjoyed him from afar— watching him in the opposing dugout, being on other teams, seeing how far he's come," Kerrigan said somewhat wistfully.

Kerrigan didn't need to take a bullpen coaching job with the Yankees. The job resides on the fringes of the majors, and the last person who'd held it with the Yankees was Gary Tuck, a man anonymous to 99 percent of Yankee fans. But Kerrigan had enjoyed working with Johnson nineteen years earlier, and he appreciated the efforts the Big Unit was making to stay on the mound in the present. Johnson was making adjustments on a daily basis due to his age and health, at a time when repeating his mechanics was becoming more and more difficult.

"I mean, I don't think people appreciate how hard it is for him to go out there with the number of pitches, the number of games he's thrown in his lifetime—the punishment that his body's gone through—to still be able to compete," Kerrigan said. "And I think he needs someone who understands that, who appreciates it. And I make sure. We have conversations.

"Say what you want about him, he's having a subpar Randy Johnson year. But people don't understand that he's forty-three years of age. And yet he still goes to the mound every fifth day—or was during the season. There's something to be said for that, for the type of warrior he is."

Johnson went 17-11 with a 5.00 ERA, and most Yankee fans never embraced him. Much of that had to do with the Madison Avenue meltdown before his first season in pinstripes, when Johnson confronted a TV cameraman and revealed himself, in essence, as a surly jerk.

"It didn't surprise me," Kerrigan said. "That's Randy: he likes his privacy. That's part of him.

"I could see him being a little upset by that, because he enjoys his space, his free space. He's probably a little less patient than the next guy about personal space. It was made a big deal of and showed over and over on the clips, but it didn't faze me one way or the other, except it was part of his personality."

Fans most identify with players who are (a) successful on a transcendent level and/or (b) share at least part of their personality with the general public. You can have one or the other, as with Barry Bonds or Johnny Damon. But when you have neither, as in Johnson's case, it's a tough case with the fans. While Johnson worked in the Bronx, he never reached out to fans with an olive branch. In fact, it was just the opposite—he once dared the Yankee Stadium crowd to boo him for Game 3 of the 2005 Division Series against the Angels if they wished, and they complied after he was bucked out of the saddle that night.

Although nearly all starting pitchers have only cursory relationships with their teammates because of the solitude of their training habits, the rest of the Yankees left him alone. And even those with the longest relationships with him, such as Kerrigan, often couldn't get inside his head. Sometimes Johnson would talk to his former minor-league coach about baseball or other issues, and Kerrigan would get to enjoy his sense of humor, which he called dry or sarcastic. But other times Johnson wouldn't talk to him for a week at a time. That's particularly strange, given that Kerrigan handled most of Johnson's work on the side between starts. But he respected the five-time Cy Young Award winner's privacy, and Johnson always knew where Kerrigan could be found.

"He's protective," Kerrigan said. "He keeps his friends at a distance. He does. He doesn't let too many people in. He doesn't let too many people know what he's actually really thinking or feeling. And he's always had that trait, even when he was twenty-one, twenty-two years old when I was around him and he was a little bit of a quiet, introverted kid then. But if you could see him then and see him now . . . and he's got some quirks now, but he was even quirkier then, believe me."

Even in Jacksonville, Florida, when Kerrigan would go to lunch with him in 1986, people would gawk at Johnson. No one knew who he was, but every head in the room would turn because of his height. Jacksonville is no small time, no Mayberry. But just by Johnson's sheer presence, people noticed him.

"So he's always had to battle that . . . even in the days when nobody knew who he was. And now that he's Randy Johnson, a lot of people notice him," Kerrigan said with a laugh.

Johnson was really fortunate he was in the Expo organization with the right teammates at the right time, according to Kerrigan. Otherwise, who knows how he would've ended up. Maybe his intense shyness and need for privacy would've sidetracked him from a Hall of Fame career. But instead of ostracizing him for his peculiarities and antisocial behavior, some future major-league teammates including Brian Holman, John Trautwein, and Gary Wayne took him under their wing, made him feel wanted, made him feel like part of the team, part of the group.

"They took him out and made him socialize a little bit," Kerrigan said. "And I think those guys helped his development as much as any coach or teacher along the way."

In some ways, Kerrigan helped the development of first-year pitching coach Ron Guidry. He took the daily grunt work off Guidry's hands, keeping a diary of every Yankee pitch thrown, chronicling how many times a pitcher had been up in the bullpen in a given week, compiling that data on a computer. Additionally, he did the videotape scouting and broke down the other teams' hitters. That left Guidry with the task of getting to know the pitching staff's mechanics and personalities, essentially managing the game responsibilities.

Guidry enjoyed a tremendous Yankee career from 1975 to 1988, and it's a sports cliché that sometimes the best players make the worst coaches. Even early in Guidry's tenure, that wasn't the case. Kerrigan felt Guidry did a "great job" of bonding with the staff.

"He's got a real, real good bedside manner," Kerrigan said. "He's a lot like Joe and Mel in that they never panic, they never seem to get upset with a pitcher. They're always supportive of their pitcher. And they have a good personality. Gator's got a great personality for a pitcher. And the pitchers know they got support from him.

"But that comes more from the man inside than necessarily the coach. That's more of the person who you are."

Guidry had had a couple of chances elsewhere since he retired as a player, but he couldn't do it. He was approached more than once over the years to become the pitching coach for a major-league team, but he always said the same thing: "If I ever wanted to do it, the only team I would do it for would be the Yankees." He couldn't envision himself in any uniform other than pinstripes. Even for his era, Guidry was a rare breed. Not only was he one of the finest left-handers in a generation, going 25-3 with a 1.74 ERA in 1978, but he was one of the rare players who remained with one team his entire career, never answering the siren song of free agency in an era when it was as seductive as the Playboy Mansion.

In the spring of 2000, former Yankee pitching coach Mel Stottlemyre was diagnosed with multiple myeloma, a cancer of the bone marrow. He went public with the news in April 2000, when it became clear he would need to miss a few games for treatment. One day in spring training, Joe Torre asked Guidry if he'd entertain the thought of being pitching coach if Mel ever left. Guidry told him it'd be something to think about, but until Mel made the decision to retire, there was no use dwelling on it. For the next couple of springs, though, Guidry was groomed for the role. He was already attending spring training on a regular basis as a special guest instructor. Many major-league teams invite the best players in their history to come down to Florida or out to Arizona and talk with the current players, sharing stories and giving a few tips. The thing that makes the Yankees unique is they have such a large roster of greatness to choose from. From Yogi Berra to Reggie Jackson, there was seemingly someone from every era who could play that role. When Guidry began making the annual trip to Tampa from his home outside Lafayette, Louisiana, in the new millennium, his stays lasted longer and his duties increased. Stottlemyre did a lot of work with him, explaining the exact duties of a pitching coach. Guidry called it a tutelage, and he learned plenty.

In the spring of 2005, when he was preparing to head back to Louisiana, the day before the team broke camp, Stottlemyre told him a secret he'd kept from nearly everyone else: he was retiring.

"This is going to be my last year," he told Guidry. "Do you still think that you might want to take the job?"

"Well, if Joe asks again, I can make a decision whether I want to do it or not," Gator replied. "But you have all this year, so at the end of the year if I'm the guy he's thinking about, all he has to do is call."

Stottlemyre had been a virtual stranger to Torre back in 1996, when the manager and the pitching coach both began with the Yankees. They became best friends, so Torre knew Stottlemyre was hanging up his spikes after 2005. He too made a recruiting pitch to Guidry that spring.

"Skip, whenever it happens, if I'm still on your mind, call," Guidry told him. "I'll make a decision. I'll talk to my family about it when I get home. We'll see. I'll have a good idea of what I need to tell you whenever it happens. Mel might change his mind at the end of the year. Who knows?"

As he promised, when he arrived home that spring, he discussed the idea with his wife and three children. The kids were elated and said he should take it, while his spouse said it was something to think about. By that time, Guidry's children were adults. Like fellow coach Don Mattingly, Guidry spent the years after his playing career ended at home being a full-time father, watching his kids—who were twenty-nine, twenty-six, and twenty by 2006—grow up. Major leaguers miss so many moments in their children's development, so many birthdays and holidays, over the years due to the constant rigors of travel. Guidry, like Mattingly, held off the call to be a coach for many years because of that.

The 2005 season ended for the Yankees with a Division Series loss to the Angels, and Stottlemyre indeed retired—but not before blasting his way out the door, firing verbal bullets at George Steinbrenner, who seemed to get pleasure in blaming the team's woes on the pitching coach.

In the past, Steinbrenner would boot coaches to get back at managers, much like firing a warning shot across the bow of the ship. Although Stottlemyre technically left of his own accord, he knew the writing was on the wall. He said the notion that Torre's job should be in jeopardy after 2005 was "absolutely ridiculous" and told reporters he'd laughed at a Steinbrenner press release that congratulated Angels manager Mike Scioscia on the job he did.

A few weeks after Torre and Brian Cashman decided to return for 2006, Gator received his phone call. It wasn't from either one of them.

"Gator!" the man on the other end of the phone bellowed.

"Yes, sir."

"It's Mr. Steinbrenner."

"How you doing today, sir?"

"I'd be doing a whole lot better if you tell me you'd take the pitching coach job."

"Well, have you spoken to the skipper yet?"

"No, I haven't."

"Well, you need to talk to the skipper to make sure it comes from the skipper. I'm not going to do nothing unless the skipper says."

About ten minutes later, Guidry's phone rang again. It was Torre.

"Gator, how you doing?"

"I'm doing fine. How you doing?"

"I'd be doing a whole lot better if you take the pitching coach job."

"You must've talked to Mr. Steinbrenner."

"Yeah, we just got off the phone. You're the guy that I want."

"Skip, if I'm the guy that you want, I'll take the job."

On Friday, November 4, the move was announced. Guidry and Stottlemyre talked frequently over the winter about how to structure the staff. But Louisiana Lightning was an apt pupil, and he kept all of Stottlemyre's old worksheets and charts on how to line up an entire organization's worth of pitchers in the spring. It's a balancing act akin to juggling, only with million-dollar arms (and egos). The projected starters need 25-30 innings to get into shape. Top-line relievers get anywhere from 10 to 20 innings, and second-tier relievers get 10-15. Some of the youngsters or non-roster invitees who won't make the parent club still need their work, and it's important for the coaches to look at them, too.

"The hardest part of my job so far has been the spring training," he said late in 2006. "Because you have thirty pitchers to worry about instead of eleven, trying to make sure that all of them get some throwing in.

"The regular starters have to get a certain pattern. The next group of guys have to fill in, and then you keep on going to where everybody's throwing every two or three or four days. A couple days off, relievers every other day, every couple days."

Whereas Kerrigan was the professor behind the Yankees' numbers, Guidry was the doctor who attended to the pitchers' mechanics and psyches. The former Cy Young Award winner never tried to make any of the pitchers throw the way he threw, never attempted to mold them in his image—not even Johnson, who like Guidry possessed a great fastball and tremendous slider. Instead, he tried to polish what each individual had, and get them all to pitch as well as possible with the stuff they had. He was on top of their mechanics, but he was able to relate to them off the field, too. Guidry came to the Bronx toting the well-worn cliché of any great leader: people won't care how much you know until they know how much you care.

"The strongest thing that I have is the ability to communicate with them," Guidry said. "Because you have to give some respect to them in order to get it back from them.

"And I think I have that from them. I'm not here to change anybody; I'm just here to make them better in any way that I can make them better. . . .

"I'm not going to try to do anything other than be myself with the guys I have. I think that's how it's probably going to work out the best. Because I don't know how long this job is going to last for me."

His rapport with Chien-Ming Wang was particularly special, and Gator was credited with drawing the twenty-six-year-old righty from Taiwan out of his shell. Guidry joked during the season that he was taking away two wins from Wang's season total because he didn't go more than five innings in those wins. In the midst of a two-hit shutout on July 28 versus Tampa Bay, he jokingly told Wang after the eighth inning, "I'm going to give you one more chance. No more."

Wang didn't understand much English, although he was a proud kid who refused another interpreter after his first one was fired. By 2006, he understood most jokes.

An international signing in the spring of 2000, Wang didn't exactly skyrocket to the top of the rotation, a spot he owned by Game 1 of the 2006

Division Series. He was no can't-miss kid. Although he owned a hulking frame for a Far East prospect, threw in the low nineties, and had seemed preternaturally composed on the mound in Taiwan, the Yankees offered him only $1.9 million, reportedly less than the Braves did. But Wang liked Roger Clemens, and came to New York.

Wang encountered shoulder problems in 2001 and 2003, however, and he didn't possess the one weapon that would have immediately propelled him into the stratosphere of AL pitchers: the two-seam sinker. Organizational pitching coach Billy Connors took credit for teaching Wang the sinker after his first full season, but Connors was a Steinbrenner lackey who was often given credit—warranted or not—after working with Yankee pitchers. The right-hander developed blisters and never developed a comfort level with the sinker until 2004, when he worked with pitching coach Neil Allen and catcher Sal Fasano, whom Wang credited with developing the pitch. That was a breakthrough year for him, as he was the ace of the Taiwanese team at the Athens Olympics and became the top starter for Triple A Columbus at the end of the season. It was also a serendipitous year, because the Yankees were desperately trying to acquire Johnson that season, but a Diamondback advance scout admitted to the *New York Times* that he wasn't impressed with what he saw from Wang, although he noted that the pitcher wasn't yet throwing 93 mph with jackhammer sink on his pitches.

By 2005, he was. Wang made his major-league debut on April 30, throwing seven innings and allowing only two earned runs. He went 8-5 with a 4.02 ERA, but the Yankees were frightened when he awoke the day after an All-Star break workout with major shoulder pain. He worked hard to return that September, but they babied him a bit throughout 2006, never letting him zoom much past 100 pitches. Although he became more comfortable with his slider, his sinker remained his out pitch, one that had such late, heavy movement that it caused hitters to beat it into the ground.

"It's like trying to hit a bowling ball," Guidry said memorably.

Wang lived a simple life in the United States. He lived in New Jersey with his wife, who cooked Taiwanese food, although they did venture to Flushing, Queens, for the Chinese food there. He said even down the road, he would resist the lure of Manhattan and stay in New Jersey. Two times a week, he called his family in Taiwan.

That's not to say he wasn't an interesting character, or a sought-after one. He told Peter Abraham of the Westchester *Journal News* that he listened to Snoop Dogg, and he copped to a smoking habit that he'd brought to the dugout with him in Class A Staten Island after he signed. He reportedly did commercials for potato chips and computers in his home country, modeled for the Taiwan version of GQ, and even filmed a TV commercial sponsored by the Taiwanese government touting tourism.

Guidry saw someone who was blossoming into the Yankees' ace, much the way he had nearly thirty years earlier. Like Wang, Guidry had been a shy kid from a remote place (southwest Louisiana) who spoke with an accent. But he didn't want to take total credit for the emergence of his pupil's personality, because Derek Jeter had teased him from day one with the mispronunciation of his name (Jeter called him "Wang"; his last name is correctly pronounced "Wong"), and third-base coach Larry Bowa also tweaked him frequently. Guidry didn't want to say he was responsible, but he acknowledged the truth.

"I probably had a big part in it, but getting him to loosen up a little means he's going to loosen up a little to everybody else," he allowed. "So then he's going to get comfortable with everybody.

"And it starts with one guy, and it starts to domino to the next guy, the next guy, the next guy. Now he's different to everybody. Now whether you say I'm the one who had more responsibility, I wouldn't say I was the one who totally had done it.

"I might have started it, but it steamrolled because I picked at him a lot. But I've been in that position where he's at with this team. I know what it takes to be able to get that guy to come out."

Guidry saw this as an important key to the Yankees' future, because he perceived the duties of the number-one starter differently than did many of the other people who had lived inside the Yankee Fishbowl. In the former ace's eyes, Wang needed to learn how to eventually take care of the rest of his staff. In other words, he needed to communicate effectively with the other pitchers, share his knowledge with them, teach them or counsel them when things weren't going right. Roger Clemens was the last team ace to fulfill such a role, taking Andy Pettitte under his wing in 1999. David Cone was also an alpha ace who was willing and able to talk pitching to nearly everyone. Since then, though, the ornery Randy Johnson and the standoffish Mike Mussina kept mainly to themselves. Mussina, to his credit, had warmed up to people such as Jaret Wright and Scott Proctor by 2006, but even he didn't feel able to approach the Big Unit with some advice during his struggles in '05 and '06. It's all about camaraderie, something the Yanks lacked in the eyes of so many people in the drought years since the twenty-sixth world championship.

"That staff's going to be built around him, OK?" Guidry said of Wang. "So he's going to have to learn how to accept that and work with that and deal with that.

"Well, I had to do the same thing. I was kind of quiet, but then within a couple years of starting, I was the number-one guy. So I had to be able to learn how to speak, because the staff is built around me.

"And I had to make sure that I have a good rapport with the guys behind me. Because if I'm trying to do the best job that I can do and lead a team to go somewhere, those other guys have to follow. So I have to be a good example. But I have to show them that I'm not just worried about me, I've got to worry about you, too."

For those who missed his tenure in Philly, Larry Bowa was a man who was fiery. This was a man who was intense.

"No, Bowa's psychotic," Lee Mazzilli put in with a laugh. "There's a difference."

Although Joe Torre was more low-key than Bowa, the former Phillie was impressed from the time of the first spring training meeting, when the Yankee manager told his players, "Everybody knows what our goal is. You have to be playing in October. That's the bottom line." Bowa remembered saying to himself, "All right. That's the way it's supposed to be here."

"You very seldom hear that in other clubhouses," he said. "And if you do make that kind of speech in a clubhouse, you have a lot of people say, 'Oh, you're putting too much pressure on guys.'

"That's a joke, as far as I'm concerned. That should be your goal."

The turning point of the 2006 season, many people in the Yankee organization agreed, came when both Hideki Matsui and Gary Sheffield were lost for months and the team had to get along without them. It was something Bowa had seen happen before in other organizations, and those clubs reacted differently. Bowa remembered Torre telling the players, "Nothing's changed, guys. We have two guys out of the lineup, but we're plugging in two guys. We've got to have the same mind-set, same determination, and same goals as if they were in there."

"Other organizations will say, 'Well, you know what, if we can just play .500 . . .' It's not acceptable here," Bowa said.

Torre delegated many of his responsibilities and often asked the opinions of all of his coaches. Most managers, Bowa observed from being one and watching countless others, asked only one coach—the one who was their best friend. That wasn't Torre's way. All the coaches knew he made the decisive call after sifting through their input.

There was a natural tendency to speculate how a coaching staff would work with four former managers on it, in addition to two of the most iconic former Yankee players in a generation. Yet Bowa echoed the other coaches' comments that it wasn't about them or their egos or who was in line to succeed Torre as the next Yankee manager. It was about making players better. As Bowa noted, virtually every manager in the history of the game was a coach before he helmed a team, and the 2006 coaching staff was no different. At least publicly, he betrayed no thirst to manage his own team again.

"It's not even an issue with me right now," he said. "If someone came up and said, 'You're going to spend the rest of your coaching career as a coach for the Yankees under Joe Torre and Cashman. Would you do it?' I'd say yes."

Bowa's enjoyment came in working with the players, from perennial All-Stars such as Derek Jeter and Alex Rodriguez to up-and-comers such as Robinson Cano. Those players made it very easy for him and his coaching brethren because they checked their egos at the door and never slacked off, never shortchanged themselves like some other superstars on other teams. They wanted to get better, they wanted to improve, and it's a mark of their character that they still yearned for that after winning as long as some of them have done.

Maybe the most impressive growth in 2006, and maybe the most impressive display of maturity before the season, came from the youngest infielder on the Yankees. Right after Bowa received Torre's assurances that he could be himself during that first conversation, he got another meaningful call. Cano phoned him in the dead of winter, at a time when most major leaguers were at vacation homes you could only get a glimpse of in the *Robb Report*. Cano called Bowa despite no prior relationship and a thirty-seven-year age gulf (yes, Bowa was old enough, in technical terms, to be Cano's grandfather).

"I want to improve my defense," Cano told him.

Bowa later told the *New York Times* that he was stunned by the phone call, that scouts had told him Cano was lazy. That couldn't have been fur-

ther from the truth. Every other morning in Tampa during spring training, Cano would show up on a back field between 8:30 and 8:45 A.M. ready
to field grounders, make throws, and learn the nuances of the position.
Similarly, in the middle of the summer, when it was scorching hot, Cano
would be at the stadium at 3 P.M. following an off day to do extra work.

"If the player isn't willing to work, then it doesn't matter how good
you are as a teacher," Bowa said. "It's not going to work.

"But all this credit, the way he's playing, goes to him."

Cano could walk with an air of arrogance through the clubhouse, but
he was a good kid who was nominated for the Roberto Clemente Award
in his second season for the charitable works he did. All you need to know
about him was that he actually volunteered to move to center field after
his rookie year, a declaration that undoubtedly made his agent gulp hard:
great-hitting, good-fielding second basemen are rare commodities, while
offensive outfielders aren't.

Cano is the son of a major leaguer—Jose Cano, who was originally
signed by the Yankees in 1980 and pitched six games for Houston in 1989.
After working with Luis Sojo in his first year, Cano hit it off with Bowa
immediately.

"I didn't know him as a manager before," Cano said. "But as a person,
for me, I like him a lot. He's the kind of guy, if he's going to tell you something, he tells you right in your face. He doesn't go in your back and say,
'Robbie's not doing . . .'

"It's 'You've gotta do this,' 'You're wrong,' or 'You're right.' That's
something that I like from people. I don't care if I play [good] every
day, but tell me the truth. Tell me what you feel like. Don't be like, 'Oh,
you're doing good,' and when I turn my back, 'Oh, you're fucking doing
horseshit.'

"That's something that I love from him. He tells you things right to
your face."

Once Bowa got to know Cano better, he began to understand that
what scouts saw as laziness was in fact a lapse of focus on the defensive
end. Cano made 17 errors at second base his first season. Only Milwaukee's Rickie Weeks and Texas' Alfonso Soriano (a predecessor at the position with the Yankees from 2001 to 2003) committed more at that position.

As much as Bowa worked with his pupil on ground balls, he also
instructed him on preparation, on how to mentally stay in a game. If he

popped out with the bases loaded to end an inning, it needed to be put behind him. It was time for defense.

"And he's done a pretty good job," Bowa said, before correcting himself. "Not pretty good. He's done a very good job. This kid has got a chance—in my opinion, if he continues to progress—to win a Gold Glove there."

In 2006, Cano shaved his error total to 9 and raised his fielding percentage from .975 to .984. Bowa remembered a game during the season when Cano did nothing offensively but made a couple of outstanding defensive plays. After the game Bowa told the twenty-three-year-old that he might not have come up with the winning hit, but he had won the game all the same. Cano, with his trademark megawatt smile, said, "You're right." It was a turning point for teacher and pupil alike.

"To get that point across to him . . . ," Bowa began, then stopped to collect his thoughts. "When you're young and coming up, all that matters is at-bats, hits, runs, RBIs. They don't care about . . . and it's not just Robbie, it's all young kids. As a coach, when you're able to tell them, 'Put the offense aside when you're in the field. And when we're in the dugout, think about offense. And when we're in the field, think about defense.'

"And we're almost there. He still gets a little [distracted] now and then. But let's face it: he has less than two years in the big leagues. People don't realize that. You look at all his skills, and you go, 'Well, this guy's polished. He's a big-time player.' Which I think he is. But nothing helps you more than experience, and he has less than two years. So he's going to get better."

As much as Cano improved defensively, though, 2006 was a breakout year for him offensively. After batting .297 as a rookie, he ranked third in the AL with a .342 average and finished tied for ninth in the league with 41 doubles despite missing 35 games over six weeks with a strained left hamstring. Most impressively, in his final 53 games after returning from the injury, he led the majors with 51 RBIs. Try projecting that over a full season.

"He's a great offensive player," Bowa said. "He can do whatever he wants. He can hit anywhere in the lineup. That's going to be something that Joe's going to have to decide later on down the road.

"If you want to hit him third, you could hit him third. If you want to hit him fourth, you could hit him fourth. Second. Seventh. It doesn't matter. This kid can hit."

Cano nearly wound up with the Yankees' sworn rival, the Red Sox. When asked who else was interested in the San Pedro de Macoris native, Cano smiled widely and said with a laugh, "Boston . . . almost." In the fall of 2000, two months before he signed with the Yankees, Cano participated in a Friday tryout in front of a highly impressed local scout who represented the Red Sox.

"They've got a guy down there in the Dominican, but you've got to wait for the American to come see you so they can give you the money," he said.

The Red Sox sent their scout down from the States the following Monday, according to Cano, but he had some tests at school that day. He never went to the tryout.

"I didn't want to go try out and miss school," he said.

The rest is Yankee history. Or, at least, it will be.

"For me, it was one of the best things that happened in my life, signing with the Yankees," he said. "I would like to end my career here."

The influence of a great coach or manager is priceless, and when Cano spoke of being a Yankee, he thanked Torre for the opportunity immediately after he thanked God. Cano will never forget how Torre spoke to him in early May 2005, when he couldn't buy a hit. His batting average after seven career games in the majors was .087. He was struggling and he knew it, but after one of his fruitless at-bats in a game against Oakland, Torre counseled him.

"Keep swinging the way you're swinging," Torre told him. "They're going to come."

After bottoming out at .087, Cano produced five straight multihit games and was up to .326 by midmonth. It was Torre's words that gave him so much confidence. Of the many managers he's had over the years, he ranks Torre at the top of the list. He was the kind of manager who never meddled when he didn't need to, the second baseman said. If he's going to give you constructive criticism, he'll often wait until after the game. Cano knew that Torre was a former player who understood that nobody wants to make a mistake, that every major leaguer wants to be perfect.

"He's the kind of guy who gives you the energy to play the game," Cano said. "And it's cool when you have the kind of manager that you can play the game you want to play."

While Torre always knew the right thing to say, Cano also had what amounted to two older brothers in the dugout. Derek Jeter and Alex

Rodriguez were carefully watching their young teammate that first year and weren't afraid to comment if they thought Cano was being lackadaisical or wasn't respecting the game. There were lessons to be learned.

"They don't go out there and play around," he said. "They want to win. And they do their job every single day. That's something I would like to do."

His sophomore season was not without growing pains. Cano was named to start his first All-Star Game in Pittsburgh, but on June 25 he pulled up lame after doubling in a game against Florida. Although he attended the Midsummer Classic and waved to the crowd, he was crushed that he couldn't participate. More frustrating was the slowness of his rehabilitation.

"They told me it was going to be ten days," he said. "When I went down and tried to run, twice I couldn't run," he said, referring to twin setbacks. "Straight was good. But turning, no chance."

Although hamstring injuries are serious, Cano hoped to be ready by the start of the second half. He wasn't, and he lingered in Florida for weeks and weeks while the strain worked itself out of his thick hamstring. Mired in Tampa, he admitted that frustration took over—yet he turned his emotions to good use and put himself to work. Once again, his work ethic shone through. Even when he couldn't run the bases, Cano hit every day in the cage and on the field. He wasn't sure how fast he'd get his stroke back when he returned to the majors, which fueled him even more. His only chance to watch the Yankees was when they were on ESPN.

"I was like, 'How's it going to be when I get back to the team?'" he said upon his return. "I was working every day, Monday through Sunday."

Whereas you might suspect Cano would be soaking up the New York nightlife, he actually lived in New Jersey across from a movie theater.

"First thing, I don't hang out in the city," he said. "If I go out in the city, it's got to be an off day. Not a night game. Day off. I hang out a little bit, not too late.

"I don't want to be in trouble or be in the paper, 'Cano's here' or 'Cano's there.' Right now I'm just focused on playing baseball."

Cano chalked up the spike in batting average to his experience and the fact he was facing pitchers he had faced before. Although winning a batting title was a real possibility once Cano qualified with the proper number of plate appearances in late September, he wasn't fixated on personal goals.

"I want to win a championship," he said. "That's what I've got on my mind right now. I know you can [compile] your numbers, but your friends got to decide where you're going.

"I don't [say], 'I want to be an All-Star.' Just 'I want to win.' I want to do good on a team that wins a championship. Because if you're an All-Star and you don't go to the World Series, it don't mean anything.

"If you do good and win a championship, that counts. You help your team."

One of the major ways Bowa helped the team had nothing to do with any work with Cano or anybody else. It came off the field, when Cashman was debating whether to acquire Bobby Abreu from the Phillies in late July. The GM was concerned about how Abreu would affect the chemistry of the club, which was as good as it had been in the Bronx for a few seasons. Bowa had managed Abreu for four seasons and knew him as well as any scout could. As Bowa noted, Abreu could play. Sure, his power numbers were down, but he still drove in runs at a respectable clip and still cranked out mesmerizing at-bat after mesmerizing at-bat. The big issue to Cashman was if he could fit into the clubhouse of established All-Stars under the white-hot spotlight, if he was comfortable enough to assimilate into the lineup.

"By all means," Bowa told Cashman.

Abreu was an extremely quiet star, one who could speak perfect English but would do so in a near-whisper. He wasn't shy, as he'd often look you in the eye, but he was a bit subdued. Still, he was the type of man who could get along with everybody, Bowa said, from the youngest rookie to the most veteran. Not only was Bowa flattered to be part of the process, but he respected Cashman and the Yankees for looking beyond Abreu's ability and asking the tough questions.

"And I'm honest about him," Bowa said. "If I didn't think Bobby could've fit in here, I'd have said, 'No.'

"Bobby's very easy to get along with. He's fit in very nice. He's sort of taken Cano and Melky under his wing. I know that's helped them out a lot."

Bowa gave the shirt off his back to Abreu in August, as the third-base coach had started out wearing 53, the uniform number Abreu made popular in the City of Brotherly Love. Although he liked the left-handed slugger, he'd often criticized him in Philly.

"Oh, yeah," Bowa admitted. "If I see Bobby not hustling or if I thought he went after a ball not as aggressive as I thought [he should], I'd say something to him. But one thing about Bobby is, most of the time when Bobby messes up—I don't mean physically, I mean mentally—he will come to you.

"That's what makes him special, I think. Because he's not afraid to say, 'You know what, you're right, I messed up.'"

Nobody messed up more in 2006, in a more scrutinized setting, than Alex Rodriguez. After committing 13 errors in his inaugural year at third base and 12 in 2005, he committed 24 over the entire 2006 season. By early June, he had already collected 10, but he was working at the problem, taking as much as thirty minutes of extra infield practice before games. Bowa had worked with A-Rod before on the 2000 Mariners, when A-Rod played short and Bowa coached third, so the window into A-Rod's soul was open a bit wider to him.

"Nothing's changed except the size of the checks," Bowa said. "He still works just as hard now as he did back in Seattle."

For someone who knew all about criticism from his Philadelphia days, knew all about being booed, knew all about angry fans and unmet expectations and out-and-out fanaticism, Bowa was nevertheless stunned by how A-Rod was treated in New York.

"Here's a guy who's at the top of his profession," Bowa said in June. "He could easily say, 'You know what? I'm going to play through it.' He's not like that. People don't understand: this guy wants to do good.

"I just don't understand sometimes the receptions that he gets. Because if they come out here and watch what he does, you can only do so much. He prepares, he does his extra work. Sometimes it doesn't work. Sometimes you're 0-for-12, sometimes you make some errors—but it's not from lack of work.

"This game's hard to play. People don't understand that it's very hard to play. And when you put up the numbers that he's put up over his career, I think you better reevaluate how you perceive this guy. Because there's a reason that he's one of the top players in baseball."

When A-Rod was going through a fielding lapse in the middle of the summer, Bowa went to him and immediately looked at his glove, which he deemed too small.

"This is a terrible glove to be playing third base with. It's terrible," Bowa told him.

"All right, I'll try a bigger glove," A-Rod said.

Immediately, Bowa noticed a difference, saying that A-Rod began making plays reminiscent of when he played short. Rodriguez admitted that he felt more comfortable, even felt more aggressive going after balls. There was more margin for error (no pun intended) with the bigger leather. In his old glove, if the ball didn't hit right in his pocket, it wasn't sticking.

"Things like that, when you talk to a guy that's an established superstar, and is willing to do that, that tells you all about his makeup," Bowa said.

The third baseman's makeup was constantly in question, and he found he had few supporters in New York in 2006 other than Bowa. Rodriguez knew the expectations were high, and he knew it was going to be very difficult to please Yankee fans. But he was besieged by doubters and haters in 2006. In Bowa's eyes, it was just like Mike Schmidt's ordeal. Schmidt was a Hall of Famer in Philadelphia, but he was never a fan favorite. Bowa and Pete Rose were teammates who enjoyed the love of the fans, while Schmidt endured their wrath despite being a prolific slugger and a very good third baseman. Schmidt was buried in Philly, as Bowa remembered it, but after he retired, people appreciated him.

"And that's probably going to be the case here," Bowa said of A-Rod. "And it's a shame because the numbers this guy puts up are off the charts. I mean, he's a first-ballot Hall of Famer.

"But it's a shame right now, it's like a quarterback. He's being judged by the ring. He hasn't gotten a ring. I was very fortunate to get a ring on the winning side. I think he's going to get a ring.

"Will it be this year? I don't know. And once the ring is on his finger, it's amazing. You go from 'You can't win a big game' to 'This guy's a great player.' That's just the way the game is. It's the way people perceive it, it's the way people write about it. And that's just the way it is."

While fans and media members were ready to tear down A-Rod for a subpar year, Bowa thought that Rodriguez pulled himself together by the final month. A-Rod himself famously said he was having a horseshit year, but his third-base coach respectfully disagreed.

"You take a look at Alex's numbers, there'll be a whole lot of guys saying, 'I'd like to have a horseshit year like that,'" Bowa asserted. "I don't think it's a horseshit year."

Nearly every major leaguer has a bad stretch, both offensively and defensively, over the course of a 162-game season, remarked Bowa. It was unavoidable, even for All-Stars. Usually only one aspect of a player's game goes off at any given time—an offensive slump happens in May and a fielding slump occurs in September, say, or a hitless skid takes place in June while a spate of errors occurs in August. For A-Rod, both happened in June, which made it more difficult. Nothing was good enough for the man who wanted to please everyone, the man who wanted to be universally loved. Bowa believed that by September, Rodriguez had come to the realization that it was physically impossible to silence all his doubters, and he finally stopped beating his head against a wall trying to please talk-show hosts and fans. He started realizing baseball was a game and that he was supposed to have fun. Others didn't buy it, believing that A-Rod's neuroses would rear up at the worst time.

"He constantly heard me say . . . , 'Hey, Alex, it doesn't matter, man. You could get three hits tonight and win the game and you strike out the first time up tomorrow, and they're going to be on you,'" Bowa said. "I constantly say it. Maybe after a while, not only me but I heard a lot of guys tell him. Joe told him, 'Don't try to please everybody, Alex. Go out and play your game.'"

While Bowa might have known A-Rod the longest, nobody had worked more closely with him since 2004 than Don Mattingly. There was more than a bit of irony to that fact. While A-Rod could do nothing right in the minds of some Yankee fans, Mattingly was lauded as the Golden Boy in the Bronx. While people were always trying to run Rodriguez out of town on a rail, Mattingly was being portrayed and set up as the next Yankee manager. Mattingly, who retired in 1995, is the most popular Yankee who never won a World Series. It's not even close.

Mattingly's contemporary, Hall of Fame third baseman George Brett, told a *Kansas City Star* reporter in 2006 that there were two jobs he'd never like to have in baseball. One was the title of general manager. The other was hitting coach. Brett, one of the greatest clutch hitters of his generation, reasoned that every hitter panics every time he fails to get a hit. Baseball may be a game of failure, but hitters are the Chicken Littles of the game. Hitters aren't above wondering if their careers are in jeopardy during every slump. And it's up to the hitting coach to help fix it—immediately—for each and every one of the thirteen or fourteen hitters on a given roster.

"There is an aspect of dealing with everybody," Mattingly said in July. "But I don't think it's quite the extreme that George is talking about.

"I look at it as teaching and learning and kind of growing in knowledge of the game and the whole thing. I feel like I try to learn from them, learn from the players. Hopefully they can learn from me.

"And sometimes I'm just helping to do maintenance. Guys who are more established, Jeet [Derek Jeter], I'm not really helping Jeet. I might catch something now and then when you're going bad."

Different hitters have different routines, and it's Mattingly's job to tailor a program for every one of them. Most hitters work every day in the cage, but some do less than others. Jason Giambi, for example, hates taking BP outdoors. He'll hit there only if it's a new stadium he doesn't know or a new background in center field that he needs to get accustomed to, and then only before the first game of a series. Giambi prefers to hit in the cage, but he doesn't do a ton of work there, either. Neither does Johnny Damon. Neither does Jeter, believe it or not.

"He'll hit on the field as much as you'll let him, but he's not a big cage guy," Mattingly said. "He doesn't like to hit in the cage."

Jeter will do the necessary drill work throughout the spring and season for maintenance, but he's not a player who needs to do "ten different things every day," as Mattingly put it. His workload is lighter than a lot of guys', but that's how he gets prepared.

Something the captain does without fail, however, is early hitting on the field after every off day. He'll show up at 2:30 or 3:00 P.M. and hone his swing after not playing the day before.

Some hitters, such as Jeter, don't make changes to their swing when they struggle. Others want to start tinkering with their mechanics. Mattingly was one of those guys, so he understands them. Although his paycheck is based on how well he can help All-Stars such as Jeter, Giambi, and A-Rod maximize their potential, bench players also need to stay sharp. Andy Phillips, for one, was a backup who constantly sought out extra hitting with Mattingly in the indoor cages, and seeing him overcome different barriers and hurdles was something the forty-five-year-old enjoyed.

"I don't really look at myself as being a guy who was overly talented," the 1985 AL MVP said. "If you look at me as a scout or an evaluator, you're going to look at a guy who, coming through the system, didn't throw well, didn't hit for power, didn't run well.

"I wasn't a five-tool guy. It was, 'Couldn't do this, couldn't do that.'"

The genius of Mattingly, though, was that the nineteenth-round draft pick worked his way through the system and made adjustments all the way through, even after he proved he could hit in the bigs. Although he once hit homers in eight straight games, tying a major-league record, he saw that there were many parts of the game that had nothing to do with sheer ability, nothing to do with raw power or speed. He realized that if he could understand the nuances of pitchers, get a handle on how to run the bases, and figure out how to play certain hitters while he was in the field, it would increase his major-league shelf life.

"And when I was able to get to a different level, a pretty good level, I was able to understand what a guy like Alex is feeling," Mattingly said. "Not to his degree, but at times at that level.

"I also struggled, too. I don't forget the times I struggled and scuffled."

When the 2005 season ended with a Division Series loss to the Angels and the coaching staff turned over, Mattingly had a gnawing concern that he wanted to address with Torre in the winter. Although the Bombers finished second in the AL in runs scored with 886, the hitting coach thought the club was too homer-happy. The lineup had socked 229 homers in '05, which was also second in the league, and Mattingly felt that the offense wasn't able to generate runs on nights when the long ball wasn't going to be an option.

So when Torre called to tell his hitting coach about the new coaching staff, Mattingly was able to express how he felt about the offensive philosophy: they needed to be able to move a runner without hitting the baseball beyond a fence. To some big boppers, the hit-and-run was sometimes treated like a capital offense.

"Not so much that we needed to go small ball, necessarily, but we needed to scratch for runs and get one here and get one there and not always rely on the three-run homer," Mattingly said.

Torre was in agreement, and they essentially told the players in the springtime, "Hey, we're going to ask you to do this. Not a lot—we're not going to ask Jason to bunt 999 times out of 1,000. But there may be that one time where we need that run, it's a big game in the playoffs and he might have to do something. And Alex might have to do something. Or Sheff."

Mattingly had seen it in the past, and he feared it in the future: when you get to the playoffs, you don't just bang out nine or ten runs every game. You never face a fifth (or even sixth) starter.

"You've gotta win 5-4 or 4-3," he said. "You just don't beat people up.

"You're facing the Schillings, Bartolo Colóns, [John] Lackeys, and then you get them back to Bartolo again. You're not going to get their fourth or fifth guy very often. He's in the bullpen now, so you don't get that middle guy, either. You don't get that long guy.

"You've got to be able to scratch for runs."

Mattingly wanted the philosophy shifted from the beginning of spring training, knowing that you can't just begin to bunt and to hit and run once the playoffs start. Throughout the year, there are times when the bats collectively cool off and an opposing team's ace is on the hill that night. You hope the Yankee starter is matching him zero for zero, and you hope you can fight for a run here and there. The difference, Mattingly felt, could be the fifteen or twenty games that define a season.

Even after Hideki Matsui and Gary Sheffield went down, the offense produced a better season in 2006 than they had the year before. Bolstered by Bobby Abreu's August arrival, they led the AL in runs, with 930, and homers, with 210. And to Mattingly's delight, their ratio of runs to homers was way up, from 3.87:1 in 2005 to 4.43:1.

Unfortunately, his greatest fears came to pass in the playoffs, and he was helpless to stop it. Even after he and Torre had emphasized that the team had to get away from the homer, the players couldn't do it when it counted most. One of the worst offenders was Rodriguez.

Mattingly came back to the Bronx the same year that A-Rod arrived, for the 2004 season. The hitting coach helped Rodriguez hit his way to the MVP in 2005, but by the following season things had gone south. Mattingly tried to get through to Rodriguez, both mechanically and mentally, but it wasn't working. On June 17, Mattingly actually called a hitting session an "intervention" when Rodriguez was in the throes of a horrible 4-for-25 slump, and according to *Sports Illustrated,* he told A-Rod in no uncertain terms to fix his mechanics.

On June 28, Rodriguez hit a game-winning homer against Atlanta and then called Lou Piniella "an angel coming out of the sky" because he had consulted and worked with his former manager the night before. It couldn't have been seen as anything other than a shot at Mattingly.

The Yankee hitting coach felt his duties were to prepare Rodriguez through his work, help him if he had a hitch in his swing, allow him to figure out how to be mechanically right. But Mattingly's own tenure in pinstripes as a player hadn't always been rosy; in fact, he'd clashed with owner George Steinbrenner over the years, and he knew about the pressure of playing in New York. The soft-spoken but tough-as-nails native of Evansville, Indiana, understood the Big Apple in a way only a few other people did. He didn't talk to A-Rod about the pressure of pinstripes every day, but he tried to share his own experiences.

"It goes back to that relationship thing, where you share how you felt, how you kind of dealt with things here, how you felt when people were getting on you or you had a down time," Mattingly said in July. "He'll sort it out. He keeps sorting it out. He's going to be fine. He's been fine, and I really don't have any fear for him in that direction."

But Mattingly then added a caveat: "Again, just help him prepare, and hopefully the relationship is enough where we can trust." Hopefully? If after two and a half years he and A-Rod weren't in a place of mutual trust, what did that say about them? What did it say about the Yankees? All Mattingly could do for Rodriguez—all he could do for any player—was pass on how he'd felt in the Yankee Fishbowl. But the player has to be receptive.

"When you share something with somebody, it's not necessarily something that you're telling them how to handle it," he noted.

In mid-September, after he had endured not one but two huge slumps, Rodriguez said all the right things about Mattingly.

"He's one of the most positive people I've ever been around," A-Rod said. "That, to me, is one of his greatest attributes if not his greatest.

"He has an amazing work ethic and [is] always ready to work and help you out. Always has a kind word to help you turn a corner."

During the 2006 season, Mattingly had many kind words for Damon. He told ESPN's Peter Gammons that the new leadoff hitter and center fielder had changed the dynamic of the clubhouse for the better. Damon was the opposite of many of the current Yankees: a loose, fun-loving, relaxed player.

"I think it's been great," Mattingly said. "I think it's good for us.

"He doesn't seem to worry about anything. It keeps guys relaxed. I definitely think Johnny's good for our club. There's no question he's loose, he's having fun. That's not to say he's not playing hard.

"You can have fun—and you should be having fun—when you're playing. If you're not having fun when you're playing . . ."

A-Rod often looked like he was having as much fun as a waterboard victim of the CIA, but Mattingly defended the more buttoned-down Yankees. They might look serious, but they were having fun, he said. That was their way of getting prepared, and that's fun for them. Damon, meanwhile, would have trouble trying to be serious all the time.

"Jason's like that," Mattingly said. "He's more relaxed, kick back. Al [Rodriguez] is not a guy who's joking all the time, but that's his own style. You have to have your own personality, and you have to be yourself number one."

From his first year as a coach, Joe Torre began touting Mattingly as a future managerial candidate, even though the new hitting coach walked back into the Bronx with zero coaching experience.

"Donnie to me is a manager if he wants to be," is how Torre put it during the 2006 season.

After he hung up his spikes following the 1995 season—due mainly to a bad back that curtailed his sterling career—Mattingly returned to Evansville to raise his three sons. He had earned enough money never to work again if he wished, but he served seven seasons as a special spring-training instructor in Tampa, the way many former Yankee greats do. There was something inside that still burned, still yearned to earn his keep.

While Torre's predictions of a managerial future made him feel good, it took Mattingly a while to get comfortable with the idea.

"First time I heard that, I probably didn't feel that way," Mattingly said. "I just started coaching, and all the focus was just in that little square, that little box. As time went on, I felt more and more confident I could manage. And feel like I had a chance to be good at it."

The learning curve was steep in Mattingly's first year, and he learned something about the value of patience and the length of the season. Players don't look at it in those terms, he said, especially in New York. In the Big Apple, if the team goes on a four-game skid, the tabloids scream about how they're done, the manager has lost control. A week later, the same team wins five out of six, everything's fine, they're the best team in baseball. Meanwhile, there are still ninety games remaining on the schedule. It's a dizzying ride, one that creates a certain type of understanding.

"So you really have to look [at the] length of the season," he said. "You know you're going to have lulls.

"You have to understand you're going to go through that and you can't panic during that period and say we've got to make changes, we've got to do this or that."

By 2006, Mattingly had begun visualizing his managerial future, whether it meant taking over for Torre in the Bronx or going somewhere else. He credited former coaches Roy White and Luis Sojo with helping him learn the ropes, also noting that special assignment instructor Rob Thomson's wealth of knowledge and understanding about the game had helped him along the way. Lee Mazzilli, the bench coach in 2006, and first-base coach Tony Peña were people he could lean on as well.

Torre, though, thought that one of the most important relationships for Mattingly was with Joe Girardi. Girardi, who played four seasons for the Yankees in the late 1990s and was the bench coach in 2005, was hired to manage the Marlins in 2006 and became a manager-of-the-year candidate before getting shoved out of Florida because of a disagreement with the owner. Torre watched Girardi, a highly detail-oriented individual, explain the organization of information and the nuances of preparation to Mattingly over the 2005 season.

Mattingly earned plaudits for his work ethic and success with the hitters, although the fact remained he had no managerial experience. He knows it will be a negative in some people's eyes when his time comes.

"But Willie [Randolph] didn't either, and Joe Girardi didn't either," he noted. "And somebody had to get the job the first time somewhere. It's a matter of having somebody who believes in you and has confidence in you. It's definitely something I think I want to do, I'm pretty sure I want to do. I don't know where that road takes you. It's not necessarily here all the time.

"Because maybe these guys, the front office, or Cash, doesn't feel the same way. They feel they need somebody experienced here. This is different from other places. So I don't know where that road takes me."

Mattingly took mental notes as he watched the Yankee manager, and he was impressed by Torre's preternatural calmness, impressed by how level-headed he was in the worst of times. Although many people thought Torre did a terrific job in 2005, Mattingly saw the 2006 season as the perfect example. Even when the team lost Sheffield and Matsui, Torre made sure none of the players got down on themselves.

Mattingly cited the Cleveland series in early July, when the bottom looked like it was going to fall out from under the Yankees' feet. On July 3 and 4, they lost 5-2 and 19-1 against the Indians, the latter falling on owner George Steinbrenner's birthday. Thing was, Boston lost on both days, too, and the Yanks never fell further than four games back.

The next day, with the season exactly halfway over with eighty-one games in the books, Torre gave a brief speech to his team. He didn't read them the riot act, but rather mentioned the positive things the short-handed club had accomplished in the first half. Players, Mattingly said, tend to get caught up in the short term: *it's seven days, we haven't been scoring, we need this game.* Torre's approach is the opposite: *it's OK, let's go forward and forget about the last few days.* He was always under control, always a steady hand, Mattingly observed.

The Yankees won the day of Torre's speech, picked up a game, and eventually won four of their last five heading into the All-Star break, trailing the Red Sox by only three games.

"He just keeps the ship going in the right direction," Mattingly said. "That's what I mean: things change so quickly, you can't panic about a little stretch. And Joe doesn't."

Mattingly played in only one playoff series in his career, and it didn't end well. The Yankees owned a two-games-to-none lead in the 1995 ALDS over upstart Seattle, a club that needed a furious finish simply to make the playoffs that year. Although he batted a terrific .417 (10 for 24) with four doubles, a homer, and six RBIs, it wasn't enough to get the Bombers into the ALCS: they lost an exciting Game 5 in the Kingdome. Mattingly retired that winter, and the team won the first of four World Series in five years beginning in 1996.

As said before, Mattingly is the most beloved Yankee without a World Series ring, and he said he hadn't given much thought to what the moment of a world championship would be like as a coach.

"It's definitely going to be different than if you were a player," he said. "You feel like you have hands-on contact with it if you were a player, I would think.

"And as a coach, it's more preparation and helping guys prepare. I look at what I do now, and even Joe, you have an effect on it, but it's a players' game.

"And your horses gotta run for you, they've gotta play, they've gotta perform."

The horses didn't perform in the 2006 playoffs, and some of them came up really lame.

CHAPTER NINE

THE BOSS

O n the same day Cashman was at the home opener talking about the voyage to the twenty-seventh world championship, George Steinbrenner completely lost his bearings. Steinbrenner, the imperious Boss who has lorded over the Yankees since buying the team for under $9 million in 1973, came to town for the home opener. Seventy-five years old when the season began, Steinbrenner lived in the Tampa, Florida, area year-round and usually didn't come to New York until the weather was permanently warm. When in New York, Steinbrenner stayed at the Regency Hotel on Park Avenue and 61st Street, and a Yankee-blue Lincoln Town Car would pick him up and drive him to Yankee Stadium.

On the day of the home opener, as Steinbrenner arrived at the place where he had been hundreds of times over more than thirty years, he stepped out of the backseat of his car and began heading in the wrong direction, according to an eyewitness. Instead of walking toward The House That Ruth Built, Steinbrenner began slowly, aimlessly walking the opposite way, toward the other end of the parking lot. An employee had to stop him and guide him toward the proper entrance. It would've been shocking if it wasn't so much in line with what people were seeing and saying behind the scenes.

There were other signs in 2006 that something was amiss. An eyewitness who rode the elevator with Steinbrenner and YES Network color man Ken Singleton during the first half of the season said Steinbrenner looked as if he didn't know who Singleton was. There was even a rumor floating around from reporters that one day The Boss forgot who Reggie Jackson was.

In spring training, Steinbrenner, while briefing reporters, wore the same blue Yankee windbreaker and aviator sunglasses that Yankee fans had come to love. He threw in a new twist, though: the elderly Steinbrenner, a grandfather, had dyed his silver hair black, as if he could turn back time at that stage. If Ponce de León had ever found the Fountain of Youth, Steinbrenner would've figured out a way to go partners.

Steinbrenner's son-in-law, Steve Swindal, had become more involved in the most delicate operations of the franchise, such as the re-signing of Brian Cashman, which led some to believe The Boss no longer had the energy or the desire for it. The Boss' right-hand man, president Randy Levine, told me on May 3 that wasn't the case.

"I speak with him many, many times a day," Levine said. "We talk about many issues, from very complex business issues—very complex, because this is a big company—to baseball, to life. And I find him engaged. I find him very agile.

"And I believe a lot of these rumors out there are nonsense. Obviously I get a much different perspective because I talk to him all the time and see him all the time, than maybe some folks in the media or other people do. Clearly, he's still the chairman of this company. The Boss. The managing general partner.

"We have discussions on the baseball side. We talk to Cash every single day. On the business side, me, Steve, George, Lonn, every single day, we have a lot of different issues going on between all these interests that I told you. He's on top of everything. I don't find him slowing down at all."

Another team employee, though, gave a different analysis. Steinbrenner is no longer the fearsome emperor who wields an iron fist, but rather an old man expected to play the same old role. People want the same old Steinbrenner, which is why every major New York paper stationed reporters outside the executive office doors every time he was at Yankee

Stadium in 2006. But he's like the aging TV anchor who needs larger and larger cue cards, or the geriatric movie star who still receives top billing but delivers increasingly muddled performances. Steinbrenner is becoming what Johnny Cash was at the end of his life: still lucid enough to draw upon his former glory, but not vibrant enough to do it the way he used to, the employee reasoned.

It was in December 2003 that concern began in earnest over Steinbrenner's health, when Steinbrenner passed out during the funeral of his longtime friend Otto Graham. Then, during a YES Network interview that was aired in May 2005, the owner often gave short, stock answers that led some to believe he was no longer completely coherent. New York *Daily News* media critic Bob Raissman was at the forefront of such speculation. Publicly, Steinbrenner's employees take great pains to assert that isn't the case.

"He looks in good shape," Levine reported in early May 2006. "He was just here in New York, I spent five days with him, many hours. He was very robust. We started the day with meetings in the late morning and went all the way through the end of games, which was late. And he was robust the whole time."

Only two months later, though, Steinbrenner barely avoided a catastrophic injury in what was a frightening scene. He tripped down three stairs outside the team's executive office entrance following an 8-3 loss to the Mets and nearly cracked his head open. The bodyguards and team employees who hover near Steinbrenner on a nearly 24/7 basis weren't close enough to prevent the tumble or catch his fall, and he nearly banged into metal barricades that were designed to protect him, ironically, from media and fans. Had he missed the barricades, he still could've split his melon open on the concrete plaza outside the stadium. Talk about a real-life Humpty-Dumpty—nobody in the Yankee kingdom would've been able to put The Boss back together again.

"Oh, whoa!" a shaky Steinbrenner yelped as he rolled down the steps. He regained his equilibrium and righted himself just before the metal barricade, but it was frightening to observers. A handful of reporters, including me, witnessed the event from about two feet away.

Afterward he answered a question in support of struggling ace Randy Johnson, who'd been blitzed for eight runs over six innings. He then appeared to have trouble articulating an answer about whether he felt his club would make the playoffs. Just as he opened his mouth, though, an employee shut the back door of Steinbrenner's Town Car and nobody could hear if he said anything or what it was.

It wasn't a good series for the Yankees' principal owner, who'd looked very frail on the first day of the matchup between the two New York teams. He held on to an employee's shoulder as he walked from the players' parking lot and through the press gate on Friday afternoon, the day before his fall.

One day after his near trip to the emergency room, Steinbrenner told me his health was "good" but declined to comment further on his team. He actually left during a rain delay in the third game.

Even if Steinbrenner's health had taken a turn for the worse, his expectations remained the same: win the whole thing.

"You talk about pressure," Levine said. "There is pressure here. Because there's pressure for us to be the best, there's pressure for us to win. It's self-imposed pressure, as well as everywhere else. So yes, there's great anticipation before the season, at the beginning of the season, and there will be all season.

"And his wishes are all our wishes, but we all hear what he wants. There's very small patience level for failure.

"The outcome is we've got to go back, reinvent the wheel, and fix it—not wait for it to just fail at the end of the year," Levine said, his voice rising. "Both on the business and baseball side, there's a daily evaluation going on."

Steinbrenner once said, "First breathing, then winning." He should have amended the statement thusly: "First breathing, then winning, then making money."

During the 2006 season, Steinbrenner's Yankees were valued at $1 billion by *Forbes* magazine. It was a staggering sum, one that made the $8.7 million that Steinbrenner paid CBS for the club in 1973 a mere pittance. One that made people who hate the Yankees despise them even more.

"One could argue that it's the greatest business deal ever done, maybe second only to buying Manhattan island," Levine allowed.

Not only were the Yankees the most valuable franchise, but the next nearest competitor wasn't even close: the rival Boston Red Sox were valued at $617 million.

You can't separate the Yankees from the issue of revenue sharing and the payroll tax, which is a socialistic system Major League Baseball put into place to prevent the Pittsburghs and Clevelands of the world from being squashed like bugs by big-market clubs. In 2005 alone, the Bombers paid a combined $80 million in payroll tax and revenue sharing. Privately, people inside the Yankees and other clubs fume that some small-market teams pocket the money and never reinvest it in their club. Kansas City, for instance, has been horseshit for years, and Cincinnati similarly was the dregs of baseball before a 2006 mini-renaissance. Keep in mind that the richest owner in baseball is Minnesota's Carl Pohlad, who treated nickels like manhole covers when it came to paying his players. The Royals are owned by David Glass, a former CEO of the Wal-Mart empire.

"We believe in revenue sharing, we believe in payroll tax," Levine said. "The question is always a question of, is it fair?

"Now, in the last labor negotiation, we voted no because we didn't think it was fair. When people complain about how much money we spend on payroll, the fact is that's our choice and we're following all the rules and that's what the Basic Agreement allows.

"As to revenue sharing, we didn't think that the amount that is under the present formula was fair. So our position is we don't have any problem philosophically with revenue sharing or luxury tax. The question is, when you look at each of them and you put them together, what's fair?"

The Yankees are a cash cow for Major League Baseball, and not only for the reasons stated above. Levine said he wasn't miffed by the current Basic Agreement, which was due to expire in 2007, but declined to comment on the Yankees' efforts to change the situation.

In his best legalese, Levine laid down the facts in short order: Fox and ESPN always televise the maximum allowable number of Yankee games to a national audience on Saturday afternoons and Sunday nights. The largest amount of team apparel sold by Major League Baseball Properties carries the Yankees logo.

(Indeed, former New York mayor Rudy Giuliani, a huge Yankees fan, once conceded that the symbol of New York might not be the Statue of Liberty anymore, but an interlocking white NY on a blue baseball cap. Proof? During the All-Star break, you could even find someone with a Yankees cap in the city of Argostoli on the Greek island of Kefalonia.)

Levine wasn't certain, but he said the Yankees.com Web site was either the first or second most popular Web site affiliated with Major League Baseball Advanced Media. XM satellite radio is another area where Yankees games are at the top of the pack, not to mention that the Yankees were a close second in road attendance in 2005. So they're making a lot of people beyond themselves very rich.

"That's in addition to the very significant revenue-sharing payments we make," Levine said. "I don't have a problem with revenue sharing, we don't have a problem with the labor agreement as is, except for the appropriation of the numbers. It's not fair.

"But I think it's very fair to say that in addition to everything, we provide because we're in New York, because we're the Yankees, because of everything that George has done—anybody, including the commissioner, will tell you that we provide a lot to everybody in this industry."

The thing of it was, the Yanks had truly just begun maximizing the value of their own franchise.

In 2002, the club started the home-owned YES Network, designed around live and taped Yankees-themed programming. Among the offerings, besides the games and pre- and postgame analysis, were an interview show called *Centerstage*, a documentary series called *Yankeeography*, and even a reality show titled *Road Trip*, which followed four fans around to all 162 games. The ironic part of the whole thing is this: The Boss bought the moribund franchise from a media conglomerate that had no idea how to run the team, and he eventually turned his team into not only a winner but a media empire.

"He deserves all the credit," Levine said. "Because when he bought it, they were having a hard time drawing over a million people, and they paid for their radio, to put it on.

"His leadership and the people who worked for the Yankees, it's quite a tribute. I don't know valuation, but I think a billion dollars—or higher—is probably right."

By 2006, the Yankees had shrewdly expanded the brand all over the world. The organization entered into a joint venture with media conglomerate Yomiuri Shimbun in Japan, which owns the Yomiuri Giants. It's a partnership spurred in part by the signing of former Giants outfielder Hideki Matsui, and Levine said it's not only a baseball relationship but a business one. Yankee Stadium had Shimbun signage on its left-field wall during the 2006 season, and the Yanks were widely believed to be the most popular team in the Far East.

The year before, the club also formed a new company with Steiner Sports, a memorabilia company that specializes in autographed, authentic sporting goods. It's called Yankees/Steiner, and fans can buy their Derek Jeter game-used, autographed jerseys right from the team, as it were. People love the Yankee history and tradition, and team officials wanted to capitalize on that, yet protect the franchise from the unsavory elements in the memorabilia business (forgeries are rampant, and the FBI considers it a serious, ongoing problem).

"We're always looking for new ventures, new opportunities to increase the brand," he said. "But each time, we understand the importance of the Yankee brand of tradition, of respect. It has to be done in a way that is not cheap and will only advance the stature and the prestige of the Yankees."

Levine, who works mostly out of a thirty-eighth-floor law office at 590 Madison Avenue in Manhattan, is senior counsel at the law firm of Akin, Gump, Strauss, Hauer, and Feld. His corner office has soaring north and west views of the city. The issue that consumes his every conscious and subconscious moment, however, is how to improve the Yankee brand.

He joined the Yankees in 2000 after forays into baseball, politics, and law. The 1977 George Washington grad earned a law degree at Hofstra and once worked at the Department of Justice as principal deputy attorney general. He was director of Major League Baseball's Player Relations Committee before he became the first Yankee team president since 1986.

Yet Levine was probably best known as one of Rudolph Giuliani's deputy mayors, and he actually ran one of Giuliani's campaigns. Levine saw strength and intelligence in both The Boss and Rudy, but both men were secure enough to heed Levine's counsel when warranted, he said. Each was single-minded about the thing he loved the most.

"They're both twenty-four-hour, seven-day-a-week guys who basically put everything they do into running their organizations," Levine said. "They are both not afraid to get off the corporate perch and to really get down below to understand what the problems are. They pride themselves on that."

Levine said he never gave much thought to how the two men differed, although it's hard to believe anyone ever rode his subordinates harder than The Boss did in his prime. You can never rest, Levine said, and you always need to be on the lookout for creative, innovative solutions, whether you're improving the team or improving the brand.

"That's the measuring stick that George Steinbrenner requires of all of us, and what we require of ourselves," he said. "On the field, unless we win a world championship, it's a failure of a season.

"In business, unless we're maximizing everything we can do and cross-ing new ventures and new opportunities and breaking barriers into things, it's a failure. That's the standard we all hold ourselves to."

Levine was the point man for getting a new Yankee Stadium pushed through, having previously specialized in economic development, plan-ning, and administration with the city as deputy mayor. For years and years, the team's efforts to build a new park were stuck in the mud. Years ago, Steinbrenner threatened to move to New Jersey. There were also some discussions of a ballpark on Manhattan's West Side. After Levine joined the team in 2000, studies and surveys were commissioned that con-cluded that the best location for a new site was right next to the old site in the Bronx.

In 2001, Giuliani signed an agreement that allowed both the Mets and Yankees to go forth with plans for new ballparks. When Michael Bloomberg became mayor, he put the projects on hold because of the pri-ority of recovering from the September 11 terrorist attack. However, the planning money remained, and the club spent about four years sketching out the new ballpark.

The Yankees felt the only way they could maintain their tradition of excellence was to build a baseball-only stadium, one without a roof. Also, they felt that the renovation that began after the 1973 season erased so many of the park's best-loved characteristics. They decided to honor the team's past by re-creating, as much as possible, the stadium as built in 1923. That meant four specific things, according to the team president.

"One, restore the great grandeur of it, and tradition," he said. "The great façade, the great cathedral windows. The great markings along the lines of the stadium.

"Two, replicating the great frieze on top of the stadium, which is now in the outfield. Three, preserving the great traditions: Monument Park, the short porch in right field . . . And then fourth, with all of that great stuff, make it as state-of-the-art, modern, fan-friendly as possible."

Most current stadiums have over a hundred luxury box seats. The Yan-kees will have only sixty in their new park, which Levine said is because they want all the seats to be closer to the field.

The dimensions and direction of the park are exactly the same as those of the original park, down to the limestone arches and the bullpens in right (home) and left (visiting). You can see the field from any spot in the ballpark, Levine said, even while getting a hot dog at a concession stand. Whereas the old park had only about 20,000 seats in the lower bowl and over 30,000 in the upper part, the dimensions will be reversed in the new park.

"So it's the tradition of the old stadium with the phenomenal state of the art, spare no expense of the new stadium," he said. "And it will be the most expensive baseball stadium ever built. Maybe the most expensive stadium, one of them, of all sports, ever built."

The cost, as announced in the team's 2006 media guide, was a staggering $800 million. Just as staggering, though, was one reported estimate that the team would need to rake in an additional $50–60 million per year in revenues to pay for it.

Construction of the park was slated for the location of Macombs Dam and John Mullaly Parks, across the street from The House That Ruth Built. The architects, Hellmuth, Obata + Kassabaum, also did Baltimore's Oriole Park at Camden Yards and Cleveland's Jacobs Field, two wonderful architectural triumphs. Since the team was taking public parkland, it had to replace it with an equal amount of acreage elsewhere. Technically, the city owned Yankee Stadium and leased it to the club. But Steinbrenner was building the new park with his own money, seeking only infrastructure help from the city. New York City promised to spend $160 million to build 27 acres of new parks and sports facilities, according to Bloomberg. A $45 million Yankee Stadium Metro-North station was also promised.

A press conference unveiled the plans on June 15, 2005, and the club hoped to break ground by the spring of 2006, but that was delayed due to an IRS ruling. The process was not without its hiccups. Unlike the Jets, Nets, or Mets, Levine noted, the Yankees wanted to go through something called the city uniform land use review process. According to Levine, the team had about eight public hearings, during which they talked to advocacy groups and community leaders. There were disagreements and hard feelings.

"This is New York: everybody has an opinion, everybody is entitled to their opinion," he said. "There are going to be critics.

"Some people are always against the building of anything."

On August 16, 2006, under a cloudless sky on an unseasonably warm morning, the Yankees began breaking ground on a new Yankee Stadium.

Exactly fifty-eight years after Babe Ruth died, they had finally put in place all the political and financial capital needed for a successor to The House That Ruth Built. Multiple white tents stood side by side for the ostentatious ceremony, making it appear as showy as a Hamptons fund-raiser. Up until a few days before, the land adjacent to Yankee Stadium was being used as public parks, which included a track and ballfields. Politicians (Mayor Michael Bloomberg, Governor George Pataki), dignitaries (baseball commissioner Bud Selig), and luminaries (comedian and actor Billy Crystal) showed up. The dais alone was three rows long and held up to sixty people, and there were aluminum bleachers on each side that held others who were deemed slightly less important. The backdrop behind the dais was an architectural rendering of the new Yankee Stadium. Green artificial turf covered the ground, and a white NY logo was right next to the spot of the groundbreaking. The silver shovels used for the event were fashioned with baseball bats for handles. The program featured an announcement by the timeless Yankees announcer Bob Sheppard, whom Reggie Jackson has dubbed the "Voice of God"; a West Point color guard; a recording of the national anthem by the late Robert Merrill; three masters of ceremonies; a procession of children from six different community organizations, from the Bronx YMCA to the Robotics Team at Morris High School; and fourteen scheduled speakers.

The ceremony took place hard by the subway tracks for the number 4 train, and occasionally a loud rumble pierced the oratory. If you listened real closely, you could hear the protesters who'd been barred from the proceedings. A group called Save Our Parks had tried but failed to stop construction through a court injunction. Their gripe was that the community wouldn't have the needed parkland between the time the Yanks took over the current parks and when they built the new ones, presumably in 2009. This was truly a David versus Goliath venture, though, and David missed his mark in this instance.

"How many places do you have a chance to get $800 million of private money to build something that we can all use?" Bloomberg asked after the ceremony. "It happens very seldom. This is a win-win-win for everybody, unless you just don't like anything.

"Unfortunately, there are some people like that. And I'm sympathetic to that, but they can't be those who stop everything that we have to do so our children and our grandchildren will really have a future."

On the dais, the speakers tried to outdo each other with florid rhetoric.

"A great day for baseball, for the Bronx, and for New Yorkers" is what Bloomberg called it.

"This is truly a historic occasion," Commissioner Selig said. "I look forward to the day of walking into new Yankee Stadium with my granddaughters."

"Greatness is truly getting a new home," COO Lonn Trost said.

"No one will ever forget The House That Ruth Built," Deputy Mayor Daniel Doctoroff said. "But this will be the stadium that built the Bronx."

Of the fourteen scheduled speakers, Steinbrenner was the penultimate one. As he rose from his seat on the dais, he looked frail. One report stated that he needed to lean all his weight on MC John Sterling to keep from falling. Steinbrenner has a bad knee, and he limped to the podium before delivering one of the most underwhelming speeches in Yankee history for such a momentous occasion. He was front and center for barely thirty-five seconds, which included the cheering he received before and after the speech.

Wearing a black suit and his signature white turtleneck, Steinbrenner seemed reluctant to speak.

"I'm very happy for everybody that's . . . we're all here today to celebrate the new Yankee Stadium," he said. "It's a pleasure to give it to you people. That's what we're doing. This is for you people.

"And we think very highly of all of you, and I just want you to know that. It's very hot sitting up there, but you can get a good feeling for how we all feel. We're just happy to be able to do this for the Yankees. We're happy to do it for you people. Enjoy the new stadium. I hope it's wonderful."

The key phrase, recited three times, was "you people." The speech struck an odd chord. When you look at the subtext, it was almost as if Steinbrenner didn't think he'd be around for the new Yankee Stadium's opening day in 2009. The mention of giving it to people, like something you'd pass on through a will. The notion of telling others to "enjoy the new stadium." Wouldn't he also be enjoying it? The remark where he hopes it's wonderful. Won't he have a say in its construction? Won't he be able to see for himself?

Sure, Steinbrenner was seventy-six and the opening was nearly three years away, but for someone whose PR flack had repeatedly described him as fit and in good health, it sounded a little like a man who could see Father Time gaining fast down the homestretch. Steinbrenner sat back down, Lonn Trost came up and called the new stadium "The House That The Boss Built," and the official groundbreaking commenced in front of the dais. Steinbrenner didn't wear one of the hard hats, which had Yankee logos on them.

Less than a week later, though, a picture of a different Steinbrenner emerged. During a phone conversation with *USA Today*'s Hal Bodley, The Boss sounded giddy while describing his team's utter demolition of the Boston Red Sox in a five-game series at Fenway Park.

"Can you imagine that, five games?" he asked. "It's hard to believe. I'm sitting at my desk celebrating by eating a hamburger."

In late August, Cashman said in no uncertain terms that Steinbrenner is "still The Boss.

"He's very engaged and keeps me jumping," Cashman said. "He's got more energy than I do, I can tell you that."

At seventy-six?

"If you can bottle it up, you'll make a lot of money selling that."

But when Cashman was then informed that there were widespread reports and speculation that Steinbrenner was in failing health, the conversation about The Boss' energy quickly ended.

"That stuff, I'm not going to speak to," the GM said.

On September 20, Steinbrenner could celebrate a ninth straight division title. The Yankees were only the second franchise in baseball history to accomplish the feat. The week before the Yankees clinched the AL East crown in Toronto, Steinbrenner did a lengthy phone interview with the Associated Press from his office in Tampa.

"No, I did not have a stroke," he barked. "I am not ill. I work out daily. I'd like to see people who are saying that to come down here and do the workout that I do.

"I have relinquished pretty much all control of the Yankees," Steinbrenner continued. "I had to make room for the young people. You can't hold them back. I miss the day-to-day, but I still talk to Cashman every day. I talk to Torre a lot. I still offer my opinion. They still listen quite a bit.

"My sons and son-in-law are running the team. They learned hard under me about how to succeed. . . . I want the Yankees to keep on winning. To keep in contention. I hate to lose. To lose is a failure in my book."

Steinbrenner also pointed out that the Yankees were the first billion-dollar team and that when he bought the team for $8.7 million, he never dreamed the value would soar so high.

"I'd say that was a pretty good investment," he crowed.

The Boss may have been more hands-off in 2006, and he may have worried observers and those close to him with his declining hearing, eyesight, and mobility. But when it came to the thing that counted, George Michael Steinbrenner III was as militaristic, imperious, and emphatic as ever: this year would be the end of the World Series drought.

"We're going to win it," he told the AP, repeating himself from the springtime. "We're going all the way."

CHAPTER TEN

MATSUI

Even for someone preternaturally calm, someone always unruffled and prepared for anything, 2006 was the most disconcerting year of Hideki Matsui's life. Godzilla—a man who had become a legend in the Far East—suffered the most painful injury in his career, and an entire country waited for his return with concern and bated breath.

The year began with a decision that promised to define Matsui's season, until a twist of fate on May 11 changed everything inside the Yankee Fishbowl. In the off-season, Matsui had been faced with one of the most harrowing decisions of his professional career: would he abandon the Yankees, contrary to the wishes of owner George Steinbrenner, and represent his country in the nascent World Baseball Classic? Or would he honor his contract and say no to his heritage?

This wasn't a decision to be made lightly, and Matsui knew the consequences would be great either way. If he went to the WBC, he wouldn't be able to prepare for the season with the same comfort level as in the past. He would need to develop a new routine in a variety of different locales, instead of training in the familiar environment that Tampa had become since he arrived before the 2003 season.

On the other hand, he'd once again be playing with his countrymen for a prize that was coveted all over the planet: bragging rights in a true "World Series." Playing for Japan in the WBC was a matter of pride, which is paramount in Japanese culture. Losing face is considered shameful and is usually avoided at all costs. Sadaharu Oh, the all-time home-run king in Japan, was managing the club. Ichiro Suzuki, the Mariners outfielder whose journey to the United States preceded Matsui's, was on board to play.

But Matsui could get hurt playing in such an exhibition, and if he did, Steinbrenner would never view him the same way again. After all, the left fielder had signed a four-year, $52 million contract just a few months earlier—getting that accomplished had been GM Brian Cashman's first priority for the off-season. He'd departed from Japan years ago after having fulfilled every goal, winning every award, and earning every trophy imaginable. The final step in his journey was winning the World Series for the Yankees, a team more revered than his former employer, the Yomiuri Giants.

But in many ways, this decision was as gut-wrenching as his initial choice to come to the United States. About three years earlier, the unemotional Matsui nearly cried as he addressed his countrymen inside Tokyo's Imperial Hotel and bid them farewell during a forty-minute press conference. There, he made a remark that might ultimately come back to haunt him.

"I hope people don't think I'm a traitor," he said.

Since his days as an adolescent, Matsui seemed predestined for greatness. He grew up in Neagari Town (now called Nomi City) in Ishikawa Prefecture, where the biggest, unglamorous industries were textiles and construction machinery. Its closest U.S. equivalent is Milwaukee, one native helpfully suggested. The official bird of the prefecture is the golden eagle, and Matsui certainly soared like one. After flirting with sumo and judo as a youngster, he found his life's work on the baseball diamond. He was so much bigger and stronger than his adolescent classmates, the legend goes, he batted left-handed instead of his more natural right-handed stroke in order to give them a fair chance. Eventually, it stuck.

In Japan, high-school baseball is followed much like college basketball in the United States, and Matsui attended one of the most successful schools in the prefecture's capital city, Kanazawa. He reached the National High School Baseball Championship all four years at Seiryo High School, and he made his first trip to the United States as a sophomore. His initial taste of Western culture came during a national tournament with Korea and the United States in Los Angeles.

"I don't quite remember if I really hit much," he said, "but I remember [Nomar] Garciaparra hit a home run off one of our pitchers. And I remember that Chan Ho Park, his velocity on his pitches was up there."

As a senior in 1992, Matsui smashed 60 homers, and the nickname Godzilla stuck—in part for his raging acne as well as for his raging bat. In his final high-school game, he was intentionally walked by Meitoko High five times, a feat even Barry Bonds would be impressed by. Matsui, a center fielder then, was snapped up by Yomiuri in the first round of the draft and played ten seasons there, becoming an All-Star nine times, winning three Gold Gloves, three MVPs, and three Japan Series titles. Those accomplishments—plus his three home-run titles and batting title—were only part of a bigger picture, though.

The Japanese worshiped him for his yeoman effort, and he left there with a string of 1,250 consecutive games, which was the second-longest streak. He was every bit as rugged as Lou Gehrig or Cal Ripken Jr., often playing through serious injuries and nagging aches and pains that would sideline teammates.

"I love baseball," he said in 2006, "and if there's a game, I'm going to play. It's really that simple."

Many U.S.-bound stars such as Tsuyoshi Shinjo, Ichiro, and Kazuo Matsui flaunted their individuality, but Matsui provided a stark, boring contrast. He was anything but controversial, giving fans substance in lieu of style. In junior high, the story goes, he once flung a bat at a pitcher who wouldn't pitch to him, and was slapped by his coach. He would never again lose control of his emotions that badly in a game. The baseball field was a place to perform, not to act out.

"When I was fourteen, I promised my father I would always be nice to people and I have done my best to keep that promise," he told author Robert Whiting, a renowned expert on Japanese baseball. "Sure, sometimes, I get upset. I get mad like anybody else. But I try to hold it in."

In the winter of 2002–03, Matsui tried to hold in his wanderlust. He tried to do it for the good of the country, for the good of the sport, for the good of his team, even though he had other desires. He had accomplished everything in the Japanese game, yet he was worried about the slew of defections to Major League Baseball.

So was his owner, Yomiuri Giants head Tsuneo Watanabe, who incidentally was like a cross between George Steinbrenner and Rupert Murdoch. He ran the Giants, the premier franchise in his country, as well as the Yomiuri Shimbun media group, which included the largest newspaper in the world. Watanabe was a kingmaker, someone who could steer the news instead of reporting it, someone who could influence politicians and the voters who elected them. Years earlier, Watanabe had criticized Ichiro for heading to foreign shores, but his own jewel did the same after much soul-searching.

There was nothing left for Matsui to accomplish as a Giant, and he eventually realized as much after praying and discussing the issue with friends and family. The Yankees, who'd foolishly failed to bid for Ichiro's services a few years earlier, were the obvious choice. It was really the only place Matsui wanted to play. They signed him to a three-year, $21 million contract with yearly salaries of $6 million, $7 million, and $8 million.

To the Bombers, it was a bargain. Whiting speculated that Matsui would mean $500 million to the New York economy. The Yanks inked a business agreement with Yomiuri Shimbun soon after.

Still, there was risk involved. Although he was the seventeenth Japanese player in the majors, Matsui was still a trailblazer: someone who came from the Land of the Rising Sun as the game's first Japanese slugger. His success or failure would affect how major-league executives viewed those who came after him, especially purported power hitters.

Matsui was welcomed by New York's mayor, Michael Bloomberg, in an unprecedented Yankees press conference at the Marriott Marquis in New York, where there were at least four hundred people in attendance. Normally when the Yanks sign someone, they hold the press conference at the Stadium Club Suite in Yankee Stadium.

When Matsui first arrived in New York, he visited Ground Zero. He called the city beautiful and the Yankees beloved, and manager Joe Torre—who had only seen sparse video of him at that time—was impressed by his remarks.

"Today has been one of the happiest days of my life," Matsui said at the time.

Three years later, in the midst of a season wracked with disappointment, he could still wax poetic about the meaning of the pinstripes and the interlocking NY, the symbol that had come to represent the Big Apple.

"Everybody has their opinion for what the NY means for them," he said. "But from my standpoint, as a baseball person, there's nothing more satisfying than having that symbol and wearing that uniform and playing baseball with it."

When Matsui played in Japan, 50 percent of the baseball fans were reportedly Giants fans. All of his team's games were broadcast regularly on national TV. (Of course, it was said his media mogul boss influenced that, too.) He was always willing to sign autographs or conduct interviews with the media, so New York wasn't that much different from Tokyo. The main difference was that in Japan, scribes aren't allowed into the clubhouse.

If Matsui had willingly dived into life in the Yankee Fishbowl, he had just completed a starring role in another drama that had played out in a parallel universe: the Matsui Fishbowl.

"When you compare the Yankees and the Giants in the sense of pressure to win the championship, it's actually very similar," he said in 2006 through his personal interpreter, Rogelio Kahlon. "The owner is very similar, and that transcended down to the clubhouse and to the field.

"When I was there, the pressure that's here to win a championship, it's the same kind of pressure that I played with when I was in Japan as well—the responsibility that comes with it."

There was much hand-wringing in both countries as to whether he'd hit homers at the same clip. In 2003, his first season as a Yankee, he hit 16. In 2004, he managed 31. In 2005, his total dipped to 23. He adapted to the American League well, though, driving in at least 106 runs per season and averaging .297.

Matsui was welcomed as a Yankee by the rank and file ever since his grand slam against Minnesota in the home opener in 2003. His teammates found him to be a likable guy who owned a bigger porn stash than a houseful of college frat brothers. Indeed, Matsui's pornography collection would make an editor at *Maxim* magazine blush. When he suggested that he passed his time on the DL "watching movies," you got an idea of what he was probably talking about.

Godzilla wasn't expected to carry the franchise the way he had with

Yomiuri, although the media demands were the same or greater. In his first season in New York, about a hundred media representatives followed his every move.

"When I first joined the Yankees, I didn't know what to expect," he said. "So it was hard for me to say.

"Looking back, everything has been just refreshing, and everything has been really just a great experience. It's disappointing that we haven't won a World Series yet, but perhaps that's the only thing that's missing in the whole experience."

So there he was in the spring of 2006, wrestling with the same decision he'd grappled with three years earlier: to which team did he owe his loyalty? To which country did he now belong? Ultimately, Matsui sided with the man who signed his paychecks, and explained the decision in a letter written to Oh.

"The priority was that time period was very important for me to get ready for the season," he said. "I found that that was really my prime responsibility.

"As far as writing the letter, it was a way to show respect. I don't know if it's a cultural thing, but it's a way to show respect. I think you can really express yourself well through a letter, all your feelings and the decisions that led to that. And that's a way of kind of showing respect."

Reportedly, Matsui's camp was approached by organizers and union people who pushed hard for him to play in the WBC. Yankee officials were said to be equally persuasive about getting their opinion across. Before Matsui's decision, Ichiro was thought of as the more self-involved player, the one who would look after his batting average in lieu of the team's needs (as he did with Seattle in 2004). Watanabe, the Giants' boss who'd once groomed Matsui for bigger and better things and criticized Ichiro, met with Ichiro in the off-season and told him a managerial job in Yomiuri was waiting for him if he wanted it.

Then, in a tournament filled with strong Latin American teams as well as one from the host country, the United States, the Japanese won it all. Ichiro, Matsui's only real rival in popularity in Japan, played well there while assuming a strong leadership role.

"We really wanted to win this championship today, and I didn't even think about the upcoming regular season of 2006," Ichiro said, according to MLB.com. "It's not an ideal thing for a player to think, but I didn't really care if I would get injured in this game; that's how much I really wanted to win this one.

"That's how we were driven to this championship."

Reportedly, Matsui was received coldly in Japan for his choice, even more so when the results were in. Once he'd been the most popular player in that country's most beloved sport, but he was on the sidelines while Ichiro was doused with champagne in San Diego on March 20. It was something no record book, or Japanese fan, would ever forget.

Months later, he was asked whether he regretted the decision or worried whether his star had fallen.

"I'm not sure as far as the reputation being tarnished. In my position, that's really hard for me to say," he said. "As far as Japan winning the Classic, I as a Japanese citizen was very happy we won."

For the furor to die down, Godzilla needed a monster year. He needed to finally claim his own championship on American shores. Japan was watching, to see if he could make his decision pay off in October. And then the unthinkable happened in the finale of a three-game series with Boston on May 11.

With nobody out in the first and Kevin Youkilis on base after a Derek Jeter error, Mark Loretta took a called strike from Yankee starter Shawn Chacon. The next pitch, which Loretta blooped into shallow left, redefined the season for the Yankees.

Matsui, whose outfield play had been steadily declining during his time in New York, sprinted toward the ball and slid onto the turf, landing with weight on his left arm. His glove hand buckled back, and it was calamitous. Matsui grimaced in pain immediately, but he did something that many ballplayers—veterans even—wouldn't have had the presence of mind to do. He retrieved the ball, which had fallen in for a single and trickled behind him, and threw in to his cutoff man before completely succumbing to the pain. It was another little detail that defined who Matsui was: even with his broken wrist dangling like a rusty door hinge you'd find at some flea market, the play was the thing.

Time was called; trainer Gene Monahan came out and immediately grasped the severity of the injury. Monahan felt around the wrist and brought Matsui back to the dugout, holding the Japanese superstar's wrist with his right hand and his Mizuno glove with his left. Even for Matsui, this was obvious pain: his cheeks were bulging as he tried to deal with jangling nerves that were setting his entire body on fire. That was as much as he would reveal; Torre said after the game that Matsui didn't moan or complain in any way.

The Yankees wasted no time spiriting Matsui off for X-rays: he exited Yankee Stadium in full uniform with his arm in a sling and headed to New York-Presbyterian Medical Center. Team doctor Stuart Hershon and the team's hand specialist, Melvin Rosenwasser, examined him, and tests showed a broken wrist. The next morning, May 12, he underwent surgery at 7:30 A.M.

In an odd twist of fate, Matsui didn't officially play in the game that ended his remarkable consecutive game streak. According to baseball rule 10.24(c), "A consecutive game playing streak shall be extended if the player plays one half inning on defense, or if he completes a time at bat by reaching base or being put out." Matsui didn't finish the half inning, so his streak of 1,768 straight games ended. He played in 518 with the Yankees and 1,250 with Yomiuri. The next day, he released a statement following surgery.

"Due to this injury, I feel very sorry and, at the same time, very disappointed to have let my teammates down," he said. "I will do my best to fully recover and return to the field to help my team once again.

"I would like to thank Joe Torre from the bottom of my heart for having been considerate of my consecutive games played streak these past several years and for placing me in the lineup every day."

In spring training, the Yankees had boasted a threatening lineup that was expected by some to score nearly 1,000 runs. Torre was constantly asked questions about who would bat third and fourth. Now, that had gone out the window with the second catastrophic injury of the early going.

"I feel terrible for him," Jason Giambi said. "He's a big part of this team and a big part of this lineup."

"You can't replace what he does," Jeter added.

In late April, Gary Sheffield had gone down in a collision with Toronto's Shea Hillenbrand at first base. Sheffield was on the DL at the time of Matsui's injury, although the Yankees initially expected him to be fully recovered by late May. He wasn't, and instead also needed surgery.

With two heavy hitters out of the lineup, this was equivalent to an eighteen-wheeler that had blown out four wheels. The Yankees lost that night, 5-3, to fall into second place, where they would spend nearly all of the next two and a half months.

But the Yankees weren't going to throw any pity party for themselves with Matsui potentially lost for the year, because Torre and GM Brian Cashman wouldn't let that happen.

"Everybody is going to have to do a little something extra, play the game the way we know how," Torre said at the time. "We're not going to be sitting around saying 'what if,' because that's not what we do. We're going to rely on finding other ways to win games."

CHAPTER ELEVEN

GIAMBI

Virtually every working day over the last couple of years has begun the same way for Jason Giambi. The lefty slugger enters the Yankee clubhouse from the side door, often wearing blue jeans and a T-shirt with a "Simms" logo on it (one of his best friends is a Bay Area–based custom motorcycle builder named Ron Simms). Giambi, with backpack slung over his shoulder, heads immediately to the personal computer off the Yanks' players' lounge and fills out his ticket requests for that night's game. Sometimes he stops into the lounge for a quick drink, snack, or joke, but he's never in there long. He doubles back to his locker halfway between the lounge and the trainer's room, and the race against time begins.

Giambi quickly steps into his locker and grabs his baseball clothes (compression shorts, socks, jock, T-shirt, uniform pants) off hangers before making a beeline for the trainer's room a few feet away. Unlike the rest of his teammates, Giambi won't dress at his locker.

It's not that Giambi needs constant medical attention or treatment, although he has been banged up over the years. Rather, the face of

BALCO can avoid a flurry of media inquiries this way. If he times it just right and the media folks don't converge on him quickly, he can escape for another day without answering too many questions. But it wasn't always that way, and that's the part that seems so sad.

When Giambi emerged as one of the best young hitters in baseball in the late 1990s, he was under contract with a small-market Oakland franchise that reveled in its outlaw image. The A's of the 1970s, winners of three straight World Series, were known for their facial hair and attitude; the pennant-winning Oakland teams from 1988 to 1990 were either loved or hated for the caveman clout of Mark McGwire and Jose Canseco. By the late 1990s, around the time Canseco had begun to reveal himself as a circus act and McGwire was emerging as the Baseball Bunyan, Giambi was leading the charge of a talented young group as Oakland became good again. After suffering through a 97-loss season in 1997, Giambi was soon joined by peers who helped turn the club around. Barry Zito, Tim Hudson, and Mark Mulder were Cy Young Award candidates known as the Big Three, and Miguel Tejada and Eric Chavez were a shortstop and third baseman who showed nearly unlimited potential.

In that clubhouse, Giambi was the alpha dog. He was touted as the frat-house king in national magazines and newspapers, the go-to guy on and off the field. The cover shot in *Sports Illustrated* in July 2000 of a long-haired, tattooed, hulking slugger was an image he reveled in and, ultimately, set him up for his fall.

"I love being The Guy," Giambi told the *Baltimore Sun* in 2001. "That's the exciting part—[teammates] expecting me to get the big hit or take the big walk or put ourselves in a situation to win a game.

"But at the same time, I've always been man enough when I didn't get it done to tell you I didn't get it done. The biggest thing for me is the respect I get from my teammates."

Giambi was the rare superstar who not only enjoyed mashing the game-winning homer but could provide the pithy sound bite to the TV cameras or joke about it with the beat writers afterward. And the Oakland clubhouse was his Eden; he told the *Baltimore Sun* in 2001 that he didn't have as much fun when he was playing Pony League ball. One of his T-shirts from that era said it all: "Party like a rock star. Hammer like a porn star. Rake like an all-star." He still looks back fondly on that time.

"I would never change those days with the A's, because those were the greatest times of my life," he said. "I had my brother [Jeremy] on the team, we all grew up together. And that's what we needed to become great players. We needed that fun."

In New York, though, he's mostly a ghost. To be fair, he will accede to many requests, but not always on the same day. And he doesn't have a bristling disdain for the media, like some of his teammates (Randy Johnson comes immediately to mind). Although he talks less to the press and makes himself scarce, there's still an unmistakable humanity about him; on two separate occasions in early August, Giambi approached reporters who had scheduled interviews with him, asking them if they were ready to begin. Many times in a baseball clubhouse, players will need to be reminded of a previous agreement to talk, either forgetful or begrudgingly willing in the first place. Having access granted can be like pulling teeth, and many athletes feel they need to assert their star power on workaday journalists. Giambi isn't like that.

There are even still a few glimpses here and there of a carefree, fun-loving California lug, one who's politically incorrect. When the Paul McCartney–Heather Mills McCartney breakup made the cover of the *New York Post* and speculation abounded that the former Beatle could be on the hook for hundreds of millions of dollars, Giambi couldn't resist. Speaking with his teammates that afternoon, Giambi made a crass joke as he came out of the players' lounge that the money would buy Mills McCartney—who lost a leg in a 1993 traffic accident—an enormous amount of wooden legs.

"Triple-dipped," Giambi joked, providing the punch line. That's a process used to make Louisville Sluggers harder and resistant to chipping. Derek Jeter shook his head and told Giambi that the joke was just wrong, but the boys in the players' lounge laughed and lapped it up.

The anecdote reveals more about Giambi's simplicity than it does a mean streak. He lunged for the easy, if totally inappropriate, joke like a BP fastball. Actually, it's not hard to like Giambi, and he clearly has empathy for others. In April, a young cancer patient walked into the clubhouse and Giambi was drawn to him like iron filings to a magnet.

"How are you doing?" Giambi asked.

"I've lost a little bit of hair," the young boy glumly replied.

"You're still sexy. That's all. That's all," Giambi said reassuringly, rubbing his head.

The slugger then asked if anyone gave them baseballs, and he immediately went to get baseballs for the child. In the Yankee clubhouse, you'll often see players sign for a kid, but you'll rarely see them go out of their way as Giambi did.

Giambi sees his lack of media availability more as a function of the team he's now on than the circumstances he's now in, as the biggest alleged confessor to the steroids scandal that rocked the national pastime. The thirty-five-year-old sees himself as one of twenty-five superstars, someone who must carefully guard his privacy in the tabloid sensibility of the Big Apple, where everything the buttoned-down Yankees do is news.

"See, I don't think you can compare apples to oranges, either," Giambi said. "It was like Little League when I played for the A's, but we also grew up together, too. Other than Robbie [Robinson Cano], we don't have twenty-two-year-olds in this clubhouse. Everybody's got fucking ten years in the big leagues.

"So I also think you start to change with age. You get families, guys get married. And also, I don't know if you can have that same fun here in New York. There's no way."

There are no remote-controlled cars in the Yankee clubhouse, as there were in Oakland when Giambi played there. The only cars Yankee players are interested in are the real ones with names like Ferrari and Mercedes-Benz. And Giambi has a point when he said that if the Yankees had ever lost 97 games, as Oakland did during the growing pains of 1997, fans and media "would've been going fucking apeshit. They would've burned down the stadium, the fans."

In 2001, Oakland lost to the Yankees for the second straight time in the ALDS, in a deciding fifth game, and Giambi decided to be a Yankee since he couldn't beat them. His father, John, had rooted for Mickey Mantle, and Jason was indoctrinated at an early age. The A's whiffed on their chance at keeping him when they wouldn't give him a no-trade clause, and the Yanks gave him almost $30 million more than the A's offered during his last season there. Still, Giambi didn't say it was about the money.

"I think a lot of people want to come and have a chance to play in New York because Mr. Steinbrenner every year is going to put a team on the field with a chance to win the World Series," Giambi said. "You come here to win. You get an opportunity to play for the Yankees, you've played probably six years in the big leagues, you're a free agent, and you've already made money and now it's about winning."

Since Giambi has been a Yankee, though, his team hasn't won, at least not the big prize. In spring training, he told a reporter that he and the other post-2000 newcomers are well aware of the void on Steinbrenner's mantle.

"What those teams did, the Yankees from '96, it's not that easy," Giambi said. "Everybody wants it to be that easy, and it's just not. That's the part that people just don't get. They made it look easy, I know they won a ton of games. They had all the breaks.

"I know with the A's, [the Yankees] could've lost two of those World Series [appearances] if we had just played a good Game 5. They would've not even got out of the first round of the playoffs!

"There was a lot of luck that went into that [2001] series, they came back from 2-0. They could've booted a ball . . . it's over. So I think luck plays into it."

When Giambi signed his seven-year, $120 million pact, he quickly came to realize that he couldn't act the same way in the Big Apple as he had in the Bay Area.

"A lot of things change, basically," Giambi said. "You learn real fast it's great to have [attention], but you also have to be careful with the media. Because for every five guys that you have a great relationship with, there's always one that wants to turn the story into something that's negative— 'Oh, they're not focusing. They're having too much fun!'"

Giambi doesn't seem to miss the give-and-take with reporters at all, although there are one or two he'll whisper to occasionally. He sees it as a necessary sacrifice to superstardom.

"That's what it is. You look at this room now, the media outweighs the players," he said, scanning a clubhouse filled with fifty reporters on Bobby Abreu's first day as a Yankee. "That's just something that comes with the job.

"Derek, from what the media sees of him, is a lot different person off the field than he is here [in the clubhouse]."

Giambi explained that you have to learn to be "that guy," presumably the way Jeter has. Although he left his meaning purposely vague, apparently he was referring to the type of bland, cliché-spewing ballplayer who's as dull as Alan Greenspan. It's an issue Giambi seems to have put a lot of thought into. As he explained it, in the Bay Area the newspapers enjoy their own readership areas, such as San Francisco, San Jose, and Oakland. The people who live in those cities are their main readers, and so the same story can be written by every paper without affecting the circulation on a given day. In New York, a handful of newspapers fight for the coveted area in and around Manhattan.

"You're competing for such a small area," he said. "You've got to have something different. Which is great.

"This is why this is the media capital of the world, there's no doubt about it. And you just have to be more careful, because a lot of things sometimes get taken a bit further than what they're meant to be. You know what I'm saying?"

As a bit of an explanation, take Giambi's outsize reputation as a party machine. He can go out anywhere in Manhattan on any night, unlike in Oakland, where certain hot spots were hopping on fewer nights. The trade-off is that a Yankee superstar like him is watched like a hawk by everyone, and there's nowhere to hide. If he gets into a late-night altercation, it will be on the front of the *New York Post*. Everyone of a certain age knows who he is, so as he put it, he has to watch his "Ps and Qs."

As a member of the A's, Giambi and a teammate were pulled over one evening reportedly driving at "outrageous speed" across the Bay Bridge, according to a story in *GQ*. A police officer escorted them home without issuing a ticket. The incident never saw the light of day until it turned up in a *GQ* profile of Giambi in 2005, long after he had become a Yankee. In New York, that cop might be a Met fan. And that story might get into the hands of an intrepid reporter.

"I saw it firsthand with David Wells," Giambi said. "As much as they loved that he was like a party animal, they couldn't wait to fuckin' get on him when he didn't play well. You kind of just guard yourself a little bit and you don't take anything personal here."

Nobody would blame Giambi if he took everything said about his fall from grace personally, if he took every sling and arrow fired in his direction to heart. His honeymoon with the Yankees didn't last long. In 2002, the Bombers were summarily dismissed from the playoffs in the first round by the Angels, something that hadn't happened that early since 1995. Giambi hit .357 in that ALDS, with one homer and three RBIs.

In 2003, Giambi's close work with a personal trainer, Bob Alejo, caused much ink to be spilled in New York, as it was an issue that apparently rankled team officials and teammates. Giambi wanted Alejo to have unfettered access all over the stadium, which the team was reluctant to allow. Non-Yankee employees usually have restricted access, even if hired by a player. At the end of 2003, Giambi experienced left knee pain that ultimately made him beg out of a World Series game with Florida, for which he was ripped up and down.

On December 11, 2003, he testified to a grand jury in the BALCO steroids case, reportedly admitting to using steroids and human growth hormone. The testimony was leaked and reported by the *San Francisco Chronicle* on December 2, 2004, which was a fitting way to end the worst year of his life. In 2004, he was having all sorts of physical issues, from knee problems and back spasms to an intestinal parasite and respiratory infection. Ultimately, he was found to have a pituitary tumor, and the season was nearly a total loss.

For the rest of his life, Giambi will be known as an admitted steroid user. Was the fallout from the BALCO trial more painful than the terrifying physical ailments that plagued him?

"Well, I think [criticism about] BALCO would've been a lot less if I had been healthy," he said. "Does that make sense?

"And if I had hit, it would've fuckin' taken that away. There still would've been a lot of talk about it, but I think the situation of me being sick made that even bigger. I mean, as I look back now, if I had just been healthy, gone out there and played . . . because once I started playing great, then it went away. Because it was, 'Oh, he's fine. He's great.' I think that kind of went hand in hand.

"To me, maybe at the time it occupied my mind, trying to get myself physically [fine] other than dealing with that. It could've been a blessing. I don't know, because I wasn't healthy and didn't have to go through that. Because it was more constantly like, God, [I just want to] one day wake up and feel good."

In 2004, Giambi hit .208 with 12 homers and 40 RBIs in 80 games, and he was sick from the beginning of June through the rest of the season. Doctors could find different symptoms but couldn't seem to get to the cause of the problem, while Giambi lost almost 15 pounds and was constantly nauseated and dizzy. There were days when he couldn't even get out of bed, and a few times when he was too sick to drive himself to the ballpark. His wife, Kristian, chauffeured him.

"When people say, 'I feel terrible, like death,' I had never felt like that," he said. "All of a sudden, you go, 'Wow, when people say that, I know what it means now.' I just couldn't even function."

Added to some serious ailments was the mental drain of the incomplete diagnosis. Doctors could see different problems at hand but for a long time couldn't figure out the real issue, which was a pituitary tumor.

"It's like, God, what is it?" he said. "Every time you go to the doctor's, it's like, 'All right, take these pills. OK, you're not better?' Fuck. It's like, 'All right, well, let's knock this out.' Well, we knocked that out, and I still don't feel any better. That was probably more frustrating than anything, was just trying to get the bottom line."

When the pituitary tumor was found and treated (ironically, with steroids), Giambi tried a futile comeback in September. He was 4 for 33 with 13 strikeouts and wasn't on the ALDS or ALCS roster. The Yankees flushed a three-games-to-none lead to Boston in the ALCS, which people called the biggest choke job in history. The first baseman watched it all, helplessly.

When the BALCO testimony was leaked that winter, the Yankees briefly pursued the idea of voiding his contract, and it was a messy off-season story. In February 2005, right before spring training, Giambi held a strange press conference in which he appeared contrite and repeatedly apologized about the subject—but he never mentioned the word *steroids*. He couldn't say the word and give the Yankees an opportunity to fire him.

He also looked embarrassed, and rightly so. It was the second most bizarre press gathering in New York baseball history, slightly trailing the impromptu, on-field press conference Mike Piazza had held in 2002 to proclaim he wasn't gay (contrary to a blind item in the *New York Post*).

Although Giambi looked healthy at the start of 2005, he was a shell of his former self in the early going. He took two cortisone shots in his left elbow even before his average plummeted to .195 on May 9, leading to an infamous meeting with the Yankee brass. Manager Joe Torre and general manager Brian Cashman called Giambi into Torre's office on Tuesday, May 10. For thirty minutes they discussed different ways to get Giambi back to his old self.

The Yankees wanted Giambi to go to the minors, but both he and hitting coach Don Mattingly resisted. Ultimately, they had their way.

"Hey, we're close," Mattingly told Cashman and Torre. "I know the hits are kind of sparse, but we're not that far away."

"Then all of a sudden, I took off," said Giambi, who said he holds no grudge over the issue. "We got our work in, and then the singles and doubles started turning into home runs. Before you know it, I had a great year."

Indeed, Giambi won the American League's Comeback Player of the

Year award, batting .271 with 32 RBIs and 87 games. In his final 112 games, he drove in 81 runs and smashed 29 homers. He also led the AL in on-base percentage with a .440 mark.

"I don't know if I ever slipped into like, 'It's over,'" he said. "I always had that drive like, 'If I can just feel better, I know it's there.' I just kept holding on to that."

Giambi didn't make the All-Star team in 2006, but he could've. He was batting .260 with 27 homers and 72 RBIs at the break, and Torre—who about fourteen months earlier was doubting Giambi's ability to regroup—called him one of the most valuable players on the team just before the All-Star Game. On the day that Abreu and pitcher Cory Lidle, a high school teammate of Giambi's, arrived in the Yankee clubhouse for the first time, Giambi was highly optimistic about his team's chances. By August 9, the Yankees owned a three-game lead on Boston.

"I think we're a lot better," he said. "Trust me, we've really, really stepped it up. We're hopefully right on track in being the team we want to be."

At the end of 2006 the West Covina, California, native looked swollen again, the way he had when he was the AL MVP in 2000. Naturally, there's speculation that he's on to the next thing, be it human growth hormone or another performance enhancer. He told the *New York Times* in 2005 there was "no way" he'd take a chance on doing anything. He hasn't heard the whispers that maybe—even after all he's endured—he's as all-natural as a Twinkie.

"I'm sure people talk about it, but I don't [listen]," he said to me. "Because I can only do what I can do. I can't control [it].

"It's almost a waste of time to stand up there and get up on a soapbox. I'm glad they have implemented the testing, because there's not that gray area to be in. I just go about it like everybody else. I think the thing people forget is I was a great player before, and now I'm a great player again. So it wasn't by accident."

Giambi is quick to say that the BALCO confession, combined with the overcoming of his physical ailments, "definitely made me more of a man." What it really did was make him less of a pariah than the other supersized sluggers of the steroids era.

"He did something that our former president didn't even have the balls to do, which was to come clean and admit to his mistakes," Barry Zito told *GQ* in 2005.

"Giambi was treated worse than a serial killer," one highly placed Yankee executive tried to claim.

Of course, many serial killers don't confess.

In the same trial as Giambi, Barry Bonds reportedly claimed he never knowingly did steroids, and a grand jury reportedly looked into perjury charges in April 2006. McGwire stood up in front of a congressional committee in March 2005 and said he wasn't there to talk about the past, ruining his image enough that Hall of Fame voters, if one 2006 straw poll was any indication, weren't going to elect him to Cooperstown in his first year of eligibility. Rafael Palmeiro was indignant in telling Congress he'd never taken steroids, and then failed a drug test. He'll be known as one of the greatest villains of the steroids era. Somehow, it seems like Giambi won't. By the end of 2006, it seemed as though the storm had passed.

"Back then, it wasn't maybe the greatest decision, you know? But now, hindsight is 20/20," Giambi said with a smile.

Giambi said he never does much soul-searching on the issue and doesn't wonder what his fate would've been if he had taken the route Bonds did that day in San Francisco. In the past, he always played the what-if game after a tough day at the ballpark, telling his wife, "If this ball had gone through the infield . . ."

"I've never really gone backwards about it," he said. "Because I don't think you can grow if you keep going what if, what if. In the past, I would probably be the worst. . . .

"You just go on and . . . stand up and be a man about it and go forward and go from there."

In addition to the hostility Giambi faced from baseball fans and pundits, he also lost his Nike shoe endorsement in the last year of his deal. Giambi admitted to being a bit disappointed that Nike wouldn't stand behind him (he now wears Reebok cleats), "but then you just learn that the world's about money. You grow up fast."

Although Yankee fans were fed up with Giambi at the nadir of his career in 2004 and 2005, he had nothing but praise for them, calling them "incredible" and saying he was grateful beyond belief. The BALCO issue vilified him and humanized him at the same time, although Giambi focuses on the latter part of the equation.

"It's made me more popular," he claimed. "And I don't know how many more people come up to you and say, 'You know what? I really wasn't a fan of baseball. But I think you're a man for what you did. I enjoy watching you, and I enjoy that you're playing well.'

"I don't know how many people I've heard that from. Even Yankee fans.

"You sit there and kind of sometimes ponder it," he said, scratching his head, "and saying, 'Wow!'

"Because it would be an easy shot to take at the time. But they just don't do it. It's incredible."

CHAPTER TWELVE

SHEFFIELD

G ary Sheffield once actually boasted that the Tampa neighborhood of Belmont Heights that he grew up in was so bad, it was bull-dozed to the ground, a casualty of urban renewal. In recounting that tale about his neighborhood and some longtime friends there, he only half-jokingly told me, "I could have you taken out for [the cost of] a ham sand-wich." I believed him, and not only because Sheffield once took a bullet off his left shoulder.

When Sheffield talks, he looks at you eye to eye, his stare frozen, seemingly defiant. It often feels as if he's sizing you up and then dismis-sing you as disgustedly as if you were a weak breaking ball he'd hammer foul into the third-base seats or over the left-field fence.

To him, performing in the Bronx was no big thing. Players such as Kenny Rogers, Ed Whitson, Jeff Weaver, Jose Contreras, and Chuck Knoblauch had failed under the microscope, but Sheffield was a tough superstar who adapted to New York right off the bat. To him, the pressure didn't exist.

"What's pressure?" he asked in early August.

For the Yankees, it means that if the team doesn't live up to its only real goal—a World Series title—George Steinbrenner is pissed off, it's hell on the front office and coaching staff, and at least some major changes usually occur before the next season, with nonperformers dumped into other cities.

"Is it life or death?" Sheffield asked. "Well, then, it ain't pressure.

"That's how you look at it. If you start looking at 'I can't fail,' that's when you're gonna fail. Because you can only go one of two ways, so if it ain't gonna kill me, why worry about it? So then you play better by not thinking about it."

Some players—some great players—can't help thinking about it. Knoblauch, a cornerstone of the previous three championship squads, developed an ugly throwing problem, one that was unrelated to physical issues. Knoblauch eventually couldn't make an easy throw from second base anymore, and he was moved to left field before retiring prematurely after 2002. Sure, Knoblauch was an extreme example, but players psych themselves out of success every day in the batter's box, on the mound, or in the infield. The curious case of Alex Rodriguez in 2006 is the prime example.

"Guys think about all the scenarios you thought up," Sheffield said. "The failure. You can't be afraid to fail, because you are gonna fail. Kirby Puckett told me, 'You play this game long enough, you're gonna fail, and you're gonna struggle, and you're gonna struggle bad. And you ain't gonna be able to explain it. You're gonna feel great. Everything is going to be intact, and you're gonna fail.' So you're not immune to it."

The Yankees have always said they value players who can handle the white-hot spotlight, can handle life in the Yankee Fishbowl. That's what made the question of whether they'd re-sign Sheffield so intriguing. But the serious left wrist injury he sustained in late April, which torpedoed most of his third season in the Bronx, essentially torpedoed his chances of returning in 2007 also.

Although the intimidating right fielder had won a World Series before coming to the Bronx, he was searching for closure to his career. On one of his first days as a Yankee in the spring of 2004, Joe Torre called him into the manager's office in Tampa to break the ice. Sheffield was immediately drawn to one of Torre's World Series rings the way a young woman might be drawn to a friend's gigantic Tiffany engagement ring.

"I want one of those," Sheffield said.

"You have one," Torre answered, alluding to the world championship Sheffield won in 1997 with the Florida Marlins.

"No, I want one of *those*," Sheffield said, meaning a ring with an NY on it. "That's exactly what I'm playing for. I'm not coming here for a contract, I'm not coming here for the glamour of it. If I wanted to do that, I'd go to a team where I'd have been the only star on the team. But I'm not interested in being a star. I'm interested in being an individual as well as a teammate, as well as a piece of the puzzle. And that's what I look for."

Torre told him, "You're in the right place, you're in the right situation. You're in the right opportunity."

By that time, Sheffield was on his sixth team—with more baggage than the Acela Express. He was a first-round draft pick in Milwaukee in 1986, the sixth overall selection, and he reached the majors only two years later. He quickly decided that Milwaukee wasn't for him and even boasted years later that he would make throwing errors on purpose so that the Brewers would trade him (sportswriters and historians could never verify Sheffield's claim). He was traded to San Diego before the 1992 season but lasted only a year and a half there before being sent to Florida, where Sheffield felt he established himself. He earned a ring in '97, but the entire team was ripped apart in a fire sale in '98 and he was shipped to Los Angeles for Mike Piazza. After tearing into management and the contracts of his teammates while asking for a contract extension with the Dodgers, Sheffield was dealt to Atlanta before the 2003 season.

His reputation as an angry, seething player had been cemented, but Sheffield was treated warmly by Braves fans. He didn't really understand until getting there that the reach of the team's superstation, TBS, was national, and for the first time in the cable era baseball fans could see him on a regular basis.

"Oh, man, I'll tell ya, the love that I got from the fans . . . my fan base has grown out of control," he said. "That kind of made me look at things a little different.

"When people try to bad-mouth you and say what you can't do and put you in a negative light, there's people out here, millions of fans out here, letting me know you can't do that. There's millions of fans out there rooting for me. And that's one thing I keep on my brain and remember. Because the one article that anybody writes, millions of people don't want to hear it. And that's all I need."

When he was granted free agency, though, Sheffield set his sights on New York. His uncle, Dwight Gooden, had always told him he'd be the type of player who could thrive in the Big Apple, and he negotiated his own three-year, $39 million contract.

But the thirty-seven-year-old didn't win a ring in either 2004 or 2005, and there were indications that Sheffield wasn't a good long-term fit with the Yankees. By spring training of 2005, he had already worked himself into a lather about his contract situation. That spring, he initially refused to do promos and other work for the team-owned YES Network unless or until his contract was renegotiated. He reached an agreement with Steinbrenner regarding the interest he felt he was owed on the deferred money in his contract, but not before the issue became public.

For Sheffield, money equaled respect. And when Hideki Matsui and Johnny Damon signed contracts for $13 million per season in the winter before 2006 began, it didn't escape Sheffield that two statistically inferior outfielders were now matching his average annual salary. The nine-time All-Star was in the last year of his contract in 2006, and the Yanks held a $13 million option for 2007. In spring training '05, Sheffield said he didn't want a contract extension.

"When this is over, that's it," he reportedly said.

Almost exactly a year later, he groused about having his option year picked up and seemed to insinuate that he wanted an extension.

"They can't just use me like that, waiting to see what I've got," he reportedly said. "They should be glad they got me at the [price] they did. There are a lot of players with better contracts."

On Tuesday, February 21, 2006, the day he reported for his physical, general manager Brian Cashman sought out Sheffield in regard to his option year. In the winter of 2003–04 Cashman and Sheffield hadn't gotten off on the right foot, as the player felt he was lowballed.

He eventually went over Cashman's head to George Steinbrenner to get the deal done, because Sheffield was Dwight Gooden's nephew and a Tampa native, and The Boss had had Doc on the payroll for years and always craved Sheffield.

Sheffield had buyer's remorse, both immediately and again in the spring of 2005. The whole incident was a cautionary tale for anyone trying to negotiate on his own (Sheffield had fired superagent Scott Boras and was trying to make do with a "business advisor," Rufus Williams) and reminded one of the adage that the person who represents himself has a fool for a client. Additionally, Cashman couldn't have been pleased that a player had gone upstairs to his boss to get the deal done. When Sheffield was part of trade talks during the 2005 season, that didn't help matters.

By early 2006, though, even Sheffield said the relationship was better, and Cashman was trying to meet a potential problem head-on and stamp out the controversy. He didn't guarantee that the Yankees would honor the option, but he indicated that the Yankees were happy with Sheffield's performance and would likely exercise the option if Sheffield had a season like 2004 and 2005. However, Cashman stressed that the topic would be revisited at a later date. That day, Sheffield led some reporters to believe that the Yanks were definitely going to pick up the option, and confusion ensued.

"He didn't have to bring me in today to tell me that he would pick it up, so I appreciate that," the player told reporters.

"I'd be surprised at the end of this thing if we're not picking the option up because of who he is and what he's capable of doing now and going forward," the GM told the media. "There's nothing official."

Sheffield thought ESPN and other media outlets suggested that he had been duped, that he was portrayed as "a two-year-old" who couldn't make the distinction. On Friday, February 24, he ranted and raved.

"Tear up the whole contract," he fumed. "Send me somewhere else. It doesn't matter. I'm sick of it. . . . Just like all those other guys feel comfortable here, I want to feel comfortable, too. Why do I always have to have my back against the wall and prove something to everybody? . . . Do I still want to keep putting up with this every year, or go play someplace where it's simpler? Now I have to go make that choice. Since you can't appreciate what I do, maybe somebody else will."

Sheffield felt he was being "played" by the Yankees, which offended his sensibilities at the deepest level.

"On one side, I trust you, but don't play me," he said. "I don't care if it's The Boss. I don't care if it's him. Don't play me."

That day, Cashman pulled Sheffield aside for a second time, this time for thirty minutes, to reiterate the club's position on the matter. Basically, the Yankees were hedging their bets in case Sheffield's numbers declined or, more likely, he succumbed to injury. Cashman's words soothed him, and he calmed down when he spoke to reporters a second time that day.

"I'll be fine tomorrow. I'm just venting. . . . I'm cool with the Yankees."

Sheffield said he thought about going right to Steinbrenner, as he did a few winters earlier and in the spring of 2005, and asking that the option be exercised.

"But you know what? I said, let the chips fall where they may," he said in August. "Because when you try to block something, you try to force something, force to stay somewhere, you kind of block your blessings.

"And I'm not going to block my blessings, because when one door closes, another one opens."

The truth was, Cashman was handling all of the baseball operations in 2006, and Steinbrenner said as much when asked about Sheffield's contract that spring. In August, the veteran was asked what his relationship was with The Boss, and he answered, "I don't determine relationships until it's all said and done. . . . I'm not playing anymore, then I'll judge our relationship."

He then said that he and Steinbrenner had had "a great relationship" in the past.

"If I had any issue, I'll take it straight to him," he said. "I'm not going to go through a middleman to deal with my issues. But if something's out of my control, I'm not going to worry about it. I'll just move on. That's the way I look at it."

In 2006, however, the Yankees cooled on Sheffield like Viacom cooled on Tom Cruise: the great track record wasn't worth the predictable future aggravation. It looked like it was time to move on. And it all started with an injury that seemed pretty minor.

On April 29 at Yankee Stadium, Sheffield was hurt running out a two-run infield single during a 17-6 victory over Toronto. The ball was hit to the right side of the infield, and second baseman Aaron Hill made a throw that drew first baseman Shea Hillenbrand directly into Sheffield's path. The Yankee slugger collided with Hillenbrand, and both men tumbled to the ground. Sheffield hurt his left wrist getting entangled with Hillenbrand, and he appeared to be momentarily knocked out. He was helped off the field, as was Hillenbrand, but he told Jason Giambi he felt all right.

But Sheffield missed four games, and he wasn't himself when he returned. Initially, he was diagnosed with a left wrist contusion. Although he could still rip the ball in BP, he couldn't speed up and slow down his swing against real pitching or handle the various speeds of breaking pitches and change-ups. Moreover, he vowed that he wasn't going to go out and play injured anymore.

"Been there, done that, not doing it again," he told reporters. "It's just that simple. When it's right, I'll play. Until then, I'm not playing. . . . At this point in my career, I'm not going to tolerate a lot."

He initially refused to take a cortisone shot in early May, but he did receive an injection to relieve the pain. He went on the disabled list, played an exhibition game at Double A Trenton, and pronounced himself fit. That wasn't the case, though, as he went 6 for 25 without an extra-base hit. And on May 29, he felt pain in his wrist during a game against Detroit. His first injury was on the inside of the wrist, but he said this was on the outside. When he tried to swing a bat before a game on May 30, he told two reporters, "It felt like my wrist came off." He was scratched from that game and went on the DL on June 1 after an MRI revealed a torn ligament and a dislocated tendon. He said later that he probably wound up tearing the ligament during his aborted comeback.

The Yanks initially hoped rest could be the elixir, but he went under the knife on June 13, a procedure that was expected to keep him out around three months—possibly for the remainder of the 2006 season.

June was the worst month of the season for the Yanks, who went 14-12. At the beginning of the month, they were in a first-place tie and had ended May with three straight victories over the upstart Tigers. But Kyle Farnsworth's blown save on June 1 in Detroit was a foreboding moment, and the Yanks trailed by as much as four games before the calendar turned. Even Sheffield had his doubts that the Yankees could make the playoffs. On July 4, Steinbrenner's birthday, they were trounced 19-1 by a Cleveland team that had already revealed itself as a pretender.

"It was looking pretty bad when we were four or five games back," he said. "Because we didn't have any room for error right there. Because if you lose a couple games and go farther than that, it can be difficult.

"I think we won at the right time, especially at the All-Star break. These guys beat the White Sox, and I think that's probably the series that's going to turn the season around."

Since he arrived in New York, Sheffield wasn't afraid to criticize his teammates or his team, wasn't afraid to point out that something was lacking. He was in the minority as someone who had won a World Series (the others were Mike Myers, Johnny Damon, Carl Pavano, Randy Johnson, Jeter, Posada, Williams, and Rivera), and he sensed something in this 2006 team that his 1997 Marlins had had and that recent editions of the Yanks had lacked: chemistry.

"I can tell you exactly what it is," he said, putting his hand on Sidney

Ponson, the player at the locker next to his. "Just like me and this man just met, we can sit here and talk to each other like we've known each other for ten years. That's what that team was about."

Indeed, Ponson, who was designated for assignment in August after a few uninspiring starts, was one of the few players who dressed and stayed in the large clubhouse area, rather than retreating to the trainer's room or players' lounge to avoid the media. Jason Giambi wouldn't even dress in front of his locker, and Alex Rodriguez was another rare sighting in the clubhouse.

It was a drum that Sheffield had beaten before: that until or unless the Yankees stopped hiding from the press and started taking back ownership of their clubhouse, how could they own the diamond in October?

"You don't see guys in this locker room, you don't see nobody in their seat," Sheffield said. "And that's the thing. You deal in camaraderie and friendships, even if you don't like the person. But I know when he looks in my eyes and I look in his eyes, we're going out there to kick some butt. If we lose, they knew we was there.

"And I think that's the thing we had [in Florida] with Moises Alou, Devon White, [Liván] Hernández, [Alex] Fernandez, we had it all the way across the board—[Jeff] Conine. Some of it clicked, some didn't. Kevin Brown. But you know what? When we went out on that field, we fought as one."

As Giambi noted the day Bobby Abreu arrived, the media horde often outnumbers the players. But the Mets across town spent more time at their lockers or on the couches in the clubhouse, while the Yankees never used theirs. Only the clubhouse attendants sat there.

The Mets had two flat-screen TVs in the home clubhouse at Shea, and it wasn't unusual to see stars such as Jose Reyes, Billy Wagner, or Carlos Beltran sitting down and watching a hunting show or a B movie. No such televisions existed for the Yanks, except in the off-limits players' lounge.

Really, the Yankee clubhouse was one of the few that seemed to be "owned" by the media, as even in Boston players such as David Ortiz open mail or watch TV on the couch. There are exceptions, of course. But on twenty-nine other teams, players don't disappear into the back rooms as much or as often. Sheffield believes that has a tangible effect on the makeup of the club, that bonding is more difficult in New York.

"Absolutely," he said. "You people, it makes it tough to do. See, me, I don't see certain things, I'll walk through certain things, where it don't faze me.

"I'll get myself in front of the media, in front of anybody. Because I'm going to be myself. A lot around here, we let other people dictate how we act. And I'm not going to let you dictate how I act. I'll act how I want to act, and then I'm going to be respectful. But at the same time, this is my house. I'm here more than I am at home. A lot of guys are not bold enough to go the route I've gotta go. That's the thing. There's consequences to be like me."

As Sheffield finished his thought, he let out a laugh. Asked exactly what the consequences were, he implied that it was negative press, which he claimed just rolled off his back.

"C'mon, man, you know," he said. "Because I don't take myself too seriously. Y'all take me serious. I don't take myself too serious. Why am I going to get all flustered because you write something negative about me? It's just making people interested in me. . . .

"If you're image-driven people, always conscious of your image, you're not going to walk in the middle of the floor. You're going to try to stay on the edge. With me, I don't care about my image. My image is good inside. You can think what you think, but I ain't that way. I'm a family man. And the thing is, I'm going to walk in the middle of the aisle. I'm going to walk where I'm comfortable."

Sheffield said he loves the give-and-take with the press, because he doesn't take anything personally that's said about him.

"You can't hurt me," he said. "Because anything you say negative—and I'll do what you say I can't do—you're the one who will look bad, not me."

At first, Sheffield was teeming with optimism about his comeback, mentioning that he'd be fresh while every pitcher in the majors would be tired by September. Three days before the trade deadline of July 28, he said he was still pushing for a September 1 return.

"The way I feel now, I see no reason why not," he said.

Two days later, though, the Yankees pulled the trigger on a trade that would likely shove Sheffield out of town, acquiring right fielder Bobby Abreu from the Phillies. Sheffield dutifully played the role of good teammate, hugging Abreu and welcoming him aboard. He even said that if the lumbering Jason Giambi could play first base, he easily could. He began breaking in a new first-baseman's mitt soon after and took grounders at first. While people scoffed at the notion that Sheffield—a full-time outfielder since 1994—could transition to first, he took it as a challenge.

"It's funny how people think for you and tell you what you're going to do," he told reporters. "That's funny to me. Y'all think you know what I'm going to do. Y'all don't. Nobody knows. That's the mystique of me."

"The mystique of me" evoked an earlier proclamation from another self-absorbed Yankee star—Reggie Jackson, who'd spoken of "the magnitude of me" a generation earlier.

To Sheffield, his contradictions—hypocrisies, even—represented not failings on his part but an essential misunderstanding of who he was. Here was a man who said he'd quit alcohol and never touched drugs because of his uncle's well-publicized descent into addiction. But actually, one longtime observer noted that Sheffield used to pour Kahlúa in his chewing tobacco because he liked the taste. Sheffield may have tried to stay away from addictive drugs, but he allegedly injected testosterone and human growth hormone (most of which he denied) and admitted in a *Sports Illustrated* article to having taken performance enhancers "the cream" and "the clear" (albeit unwittingly).

Yet to him, even the perceived essence of him as a player—a power-hitting corner outfielder—was wrong.

"Everybody's got their perception of people, and they don't know what they're talking about," he said in early August. "I came up as a shortstop. I didn't have a choice of moving to third base, but I had a choice of moving to the outfield or not.

"I chose to look at the organization's best interests as opposed to my own. I could've said my legacy is at shortstop, and where would I be right now if I had stayed at shortstop, as far as the offensive numbers I've put up?

"So people don't look at that when you retire. They look at, 'Oh, you were an outfielder.' No, I wasn't. I was a shortstop. But I'm putting up outfield numbers."

When rumors of Abreu's arrival started to make the rounds, Sheffield said there weren't five better players in the game than him. He wouldn't back off.

"Name 'em. Name 'em," he dared. "I ain't smacking, I'm packing. I'll tell you, go get the bubble gum card."

Whether it was Abreu's arrival or a rehab that was going slower than expected, by August 17 Sheffield told a reporter, "I'm not sure if you'll even see me out there this year. I'm just not sure. I'm not in a hurry. My plan isn't short-term; it's long-term."

On August 23, GM Brian Cashman was told by Sheffield's hand specialist, Charles Melone, that the slugger wouldn't be cleared to hit off a tee for three more weeks, around September 15. Whispers in published reports were that Sheffield was protecting himself for free agency in the winter, and he felt screwed over and unwanted by the Yankees. Will Carroll, who writes the acclaimed medical column "Under the Knife" for the Baseball Prospectus Web site, noted on August 24 that Sheff's rehab was officially behind schedule.

Two weeks earlier, in a lengthy conversation with me, Sheffield had said, "I look at winning and losing. Did I fail as a teammate? Could I have given a little more to the team to get us where we need to go?"

In the darkest days of recovery, when his wrist wasn't improving as fast as he would've liked, he doubted whether he'd ever fulfill his "mission" of winning a championship in New York. Sheffield actually considered quitting a number of times. Plenty of people in his life convinced him otherwise.

"I made a dedication to myself that if I come back, I'm going to come back better than I was before," Sheffield said. "My trainers wouldn't let me quit, my doctor wouldn't let me quit, and my wife didn't want me to quit. I had to rededicate myself and put my priorities back in order."

A self-aware man (some would say extremely self-centered, too), Sheffield also went to Tampa and got away from his family during the rehab process, à la the title character in *Rocky IV*. There, he evaluated how much longer he wanted to put on a major-league uniform. He evaluated what he had to put into his profession.

"I'm playing three [more years]. No doubt," he said. "I just got my head clear and said, 'That's what I want to do.' When I set my mind to something, it'll get done."

"I want to go out a certain way—on top," he added. "I knew if I put in the work and got back to normal, I can go out on top. When you quit, there's no returning. I don't want to look back and say I should have kept playing."

When the Yankees returned from a road trip on September 12, Sheffield was cleared to take live BP for the first time. That it was the day Hideki Matsui returned was coincidental, but Sheffield—always with a chip on his shoulder—warned reporters not to forget about his pending return, either.

"Don't look at me as a handicap anymore," he said. "I don't have to worry about 'I've gotta see how I feel' and all that. Those days are over."

Sheffield had been working out in a cage for the week before, but he really believed he could've begun activities on September 1. He "waited patiently," mentioning that the Yankees and his doctor held him back, which he acknowledged was the right move. Indeed, he beat Melone's estimate by about a week. For all the talk that he was dogging it or protecting his wrist for free agency, it appeared he was ahead of schedule.

Sheffield turned introspective on the eve of his first live BP session.

"Imagine not being able to do it for twelve weeks, not knowing if you're ever going to come back from it, if it's career-ending," he said. "I was told when I went in the operating room that it's not career-ending and I'm going to be stronger than I was before. All of that sounds great until you go under the knife. Now I'm doing it and doing it pain-free, and I see it's true. . . .

"To know that you couldn't do something on a baseball field, that was a tragedy to me. To know that I can do it again, where you can say to yourself, 'Now I can hit another home run,' that's all you need to tell yourself. And that's what I'm pleased about."

There was plenty to be not so pleased about. Sheffield was irked that he'd have to play a new position (first base), although he reasoned to himself that it would help his value if he became a free agent. He also wasn't happy to be hitting lower in the batting order than the accustomed number-three hole. He was already planning life after the Yankees, too. Sources told the *New York Post* that the Red Sox would target Sheff in the off-season, and he reportedly would want to play in Boston if the Yanks didn't re-sign him. On a parallel note, when a son of Toronto GM J. P. Ricciardi came through the clubhouse late in the season, Sheffield not only said hello but told the youngster that his father was one of Sheffield's favorites and asked him to relay the message.

Sheffield considered himself a businessman, however, and there was still business left to accomplish in 2006. The only reason he'd come to New York was for that World Series ring, and his laser stare remained fixated on that goal, no matter how much pride he'd have to swallow in the final weeks and no matter what the future held for him.

"I don't have nothing else to prove," he said. "Anything else I do is a bonus. So you get my ring, and I'm complete."

CHAPTER THIRTEEN

BOSTON

As the sun rose over Boston on July 31, the Red Sox held a half-game lead over the Yankees. They had led the division for all but eleven days through the first four months of the season, had won twelve straight in late June and generally looked like a dangerous, playoff-caliber club. In reality, they were as phony as a $3 bill. All year, really, the Yanks had hung close to their archenemy despite serious injuries to three starting players—Hideki Matsui, Gary Sheffield, and Robinson Cano—and they became emboldened that Boston hadn't run away with the division while the Bombers were licking their wounds.

That night, a David Ortiz walk-off three-run homer gave Boston a 9-8 victory over Cleveland and boosted its AL East lead to one game. As thrilling as Ortiz's game-ending blast was, though, there was another moment in the game with larger implications: catcher Jason Varitek twisted his left knee overrunning second base in the second inning, and it was an injury that required the DL and surgery. Starting right fielder Trot

Nixon had just been placed on the DL with a biceps strain, and an injury avalanche was under way in Boston—even if the Sox didn't know it yet.

Moreover, the 4:00 P.M. EST trade deadline came and went in Boston without the Sox making a trade, while the Yanks had acquired right fielder Bobby Abreu and right-handed starter Cory Lidle from the Phillies the day before and first baseman Craig Wilson from Pittsburgh that day.

Earlier in the season, a notion became popular that the banged-up Yanks simply needed to hold the fort until the cavalry arrived. Cynics predicted a baseball Alamo. The July 4 massacre in Cleveland, which put them four games back, was the low point, although the club regrouped before departing for the All-Star break.

Still, even a week before the trade deadline, the Yankees looked like a team about to fall apart. They lost three of four in Toronto to a beefed-up Blue Jays squad that was expected to challenge for the wild card, and at one point trailed Boston by three and a half games while north of the border. Alex Rodriguez was making so many throwing errors, people compared him to Chuck Knoblauch, whose mental block had forced a move from second to the outfield and hastened his retirement. It was an uneven, inconsistent patch for the Bombers, but they again regrouped and pulled within half a game on the day they acquired Abreu.

At Fenway Park on July 31, Curt Schilling expressed his bad feelings about the implications. The Yanks had sent four prospects of various ages and abilities to Philadelphia—none of whom would help them in 2006— for Abreu and Lidle (who, it turns out, the Red Sox were interested in). Schilling and Boston manager Terry Francona knew Abreu well. Schilling had played alongside Abreu in Philly from 1998 to 2000, and Francona managed the Phillies those years.

"He could be the best player in baseball the last eight weeks of the season," Schilling told Francona that day. "He's that kind of player." Francona agreed with Schilling and conveyed the same thought to Boston GM Theo Epstein.

It wasn't a cut-and-dried decision for Brian Cashman, who agonized over the trade for a week. He spent his days canvassing everyone in the organization and his nights—restless nights—mulling over the scenarios in his head.

Abreu was a left-handed slugger who had mysteriously lost his power after winning the Home Run Derby in 2005 in Detroit. He had belted only

14 round-trippers after winning that crown (6 in 2005, and 8 with Philly in '06). Additionally, the knock against him was that he wouldn't dive for balls or crash into fences in right field. Sometimes, his critics even said, he preferred to take a walk instead of expanding his strike zone in an RBI situation.

Despite a 2006 power outage that rivaled Con Ed's neglect of Queens that summer, Abreu was still the best run producer on the trade market. At the time of the deal, he led the majors in pitches per at-bat with 4.47, ESPN's Buster Olney reported, when the major-league average was approximately 3.75. He was averaging 0.9 walks per game, another indicator of his incredible batting eye and patience.

He was an attractive get, but there were only a few teams that could afford his salary. He was due a remaining $6 million for 2006 and $15.5 million in 2007. Abreu also possessed a 2008 option of $16 million, or a $2 million buyout. Perhaps the pivotal part of the trade was that the Yankees wouldn't exercise the option, which Abreu had wanted. That's where Cashman had to draw the line.

When 2006 began, Cashman's grand strategy was to make it through the season without adding payroll and then integrate more homegrown talent into the big-league club. But he called the injuries to Sheffield and Matsui "catastrophic," and each week he watched the Yankees decline further in the major offensive indicators. It was like a car with an oil leak: it might not break down immediately, but you could predict the ugly ending.

He knew all the negatives about Abreu, but he also received positive recommendations from Yankees third-base coach Larry Bowa and bullpen coach Joe Kerrigan. Like Francona, Bowa had managed Abreu in Philly (and frequently criticized him there), and Kerrigan was also in that organization for a period. Scouts watched Abreu regularly, and the player development people had apprised Cashman of what the Yankees should be willing to give up and whom they shouldn't trade. Cashman said he engaged nearly every important voice in the organization, asking them, "What would you do if you were me?"

By the night of July 29, Cashman had already talked with team president Randy Levine, COO Lonn Trost, Steve Swindal, Steinbrenner's son-in-law, and The Boss himself. Levine gave Cashman the financial rubber stamp to make the trade, and Steinbrenner gave him the royal blessing. Still, the Yankee GM went to bed that night not sure whether he'd pull the trigger.

"I remember it was a tough call," Cashman said. "It was a very sleepless night for me. I wrestled on it—hard. It wasn't an easy call, because it was a lot of money.

"Bobby looked like he'd be the classic fix, the quick fix, and I was wrestling: do you deviate? I had a business plan, and with something catastrophic, how are you going to adjust to it?"

When Cashman finally dozed off, a reporter called his home in Connecticut. It was 12:42 A.M., and his wife was woken up by the ringing phone. The reporter had heard an Abreu deal was complete, which Cashman denied before hanging up, returning to bed, and tossing and turning nearly until dawn.

When he woke up on the thirtieth, Cashman already had a proposal from Philly GM Pat Gillick that he could've moved on. Gillick, the first-year executive who had won two world championships in Toronto and later built up the Mariners, had talked with Cashman for much of the season about parameters of an Abreu deal. However, the right fielder wasn't officially put on the trade market until late July, when he agreed to waive his no-trade clause for the Yanks, Red Sox, Angels, and Mets. Cashman, meanwhile, had irons in a number of different fires, but there was no guarantee anything would get done.

"We were working on all three ends, possibly doing no deal; I was trying to line up a few small deals, and they were difficult," he said. "Actually, I was unable to do that. But I was on the verge of doing four different deals total, but [one] didn't go down.

"And I had the big deal I was dealing with. So to be quite honest, I didn't have it measured against another alternative. It was more of doing this one, or none. I had a number of deals lined up where I had one more thing to finish off, and if that did, I would've done four different things, probably. That was not to be, so it was a decision to stay pat or do this bigger deal with Bobby and Cory Lidle."

As his car wound down the parkway from Connecticut to Yankee Stadium on a Sunday morning, Cashman had decided that he would swing for the fences.

"I'm going to tell Pat Gillick my bottom line, what I'd be willing to do," Cashman told himself, "and if he was acceptable, we'd probably get it done."

"I had to make a decision on the run, and we made the adjustment," he said. "It wasn't an easy one, but we made it."

One of the reasons Cashman made the move was the state of Gary Sheffield's recovery. In mid-July, Cashman had had a phone conversation with Sheffield's hand specialist, Charles Melone, who gave him a pessimistic outlook on the prospect of getting Sheffield back in 2006.

"Don't listen to Gary," Melone told Cashman. "He's not going to be hitting off a tee until mid-September."

"Really?" Cashman asked, disappointed and a bit surprised. "Doc, you know there's only like fifteen more games left after mid-September, and you're talking about tee work in mid-September?"

"September 15 right now," Melone confirmed. "Could it be earlier? Yeah. But you're talking September 15 to be cleared to be hit off a tee."

That changed Cashman's perspective, and he decided not to count on either Sheffield or Matsui, who was only a few weeks ahead of Sheffield in his own rehab. The way the Yankee GM looked at it, if either player returned, it'd be a plus, but even then nobody could be sure what kind of player they were getting.

"This team has fought too hard for me and did way too much," he said. "They deserved a chance to get the ring."

The proposal Gillick gave Cashman the day before wasn't the proposal the Yankee GM took. Instead, Cashman put together a mélange of four minor leaguers, including 2005 first-round pick C. J. Henry, a shortstop from an Oklahoma high school. When the Yankees took Henry as high as they did, they were ridiculed throughout the baseball community. Oklahoma isn't a hotbed of baseball talent, and some thought Henry was a more talented basketball player. Moreover, the Yanks had passed on a local kid, Craig Hansen of St. John's University, ostensibly because they didn't want to give the $4 million contract Hansen sought through agent Scott Boras. Instead, Hansen was drafted by the Red Sox and reached the majors by the end of the 2005 season. Henry got off to a rocky start in the minors and was still in low Class A in 2006, batting .240 with 86 strikeouts in 77 games and only two homers. There was no guarantee he'd ever be a major leaguer.

"It had no influence on the deal at all, actually," Cashman said. "You draft players to create value, and hopefully those players can translate into immediate value for your major-league club.

"And in C. J. Henry's case, it did. We got immediate value for our major-league club that will hopefully have a major, major impact. And hopefully C. J. Henry will have an impact there for them, too."

The Yankees were off the hook for Henry, and they were privately thrilled. After the trade, Steinbrenner told a reporter, "Cashman did a wonderful job negotiating down to get the deal with Philadelphia we wanted. Now I think we're in good shape with Boston."

Years before he was dealt, Abreu bought a luxury residence in New York at One Beacon Court on the Upper East Side, where teammate Johnny Damon and singer Beyoncé Knowles lived. It was convenient that his agents were based there, and Abreu loved the nearby restaurants such as Tao and the corresponding scene. It was a good city to do business in, he explained about his purchase.

But what else did it say about a player who had never tasted a championship in professional ball—not even in the minor leagues? Did it say his desire, deep down, was to live somewhere that really mattered on the baseball landscape? Or was it more about the trappings of fame and money?

When Abreu was initially asked about waiving his no-trade clause in July, he wanted a financial sweetener. The Yankees wouldn't budge, though, and exercising his 2008 option was out of the question. Abreu was left with a soul-searching dilemma. His condo might have been in Manhattan, but his home was in Philly. It was a tough choice.

"It's not that easy," he said quietly a month after the deal. "You've been there in the city [of Philadelphia] for ten years. You already pretty much know everything there.

"This is something that they came to me that, 'You have a chance now to be in the playoffs.' I think this is something that would be good. I took it."

Outside the Yankee Fishbowl, the perception is that the team is filled with buttoned-down automatons and cold-blooded mercenaries. That they don't have fun like other major-league teams, or that the camaraderie doesn't exist. Abreu quickly found out that it wasn't like that, that the Yankees had an esprit de corps but also played the game right, a criticism leveled at the Phillies for years.

The only current Yankee Abreu knew well was Miguel Cairo, whom he'd played with in winter ball in Venezuela. Yet when he arrived on August 1, Bowa gave him the number off his back (53), his teammates welcomed him warmly, and even Sheffield, whom he was replacing in right field, gave him a hug.

"You see the Yankees from outside, they're a contender team," he said. "They're a traditional team that always everybody wanted to beat. But you never realize until you get here how good they are, how they treat you, the friendships there are, especially in the clubhouse.

"The whole team of players is so close. I think it's made everything a little more easier because you always have somebody to pick you up. . . .

"It's nice to be a Yankee. Big things happen to them."

Abreu was asked if he thought the situation was weird given that he was replacing a more established player in Sheffield, who was still walking around the clubhouse and frantically rehabbing to return in late September.

"Not really," Abreu said. "Sheffield is a good guy. I came here, he told me, 'Welcome' and 'You're going to like it.'"

As far as one player replacing another, injured one, that was baseball, right?

"Yeah," Abreu answered with a thin smile, the smile communicating that it wasn't his cross to bear.

Abreu made a big impact right off the bat, batting third (where Jason Giambi batted much of the first half). In the sixteen games between the trade deadline and the season's defining series versus Boston, he was 22 for 61 with a homer, four doubles, nine walks, nine runs and six RBIs. He won his first four games as a Yankee, and the team climbed into a first-place tie after his first game on August 1. That was truly a notable night of firsts, as the Yanks spent the rest of the season atop the division. And the best was truly yet to come, as Schilling feared it would be.

Although they were in first place, the Yanks were still playing uneven baseball on the eve of the five-game, four-day series with the Red Sox, and Cashman feared that the bullpen was getting burned out. The team was in the midst of a twenty-one-game, twenty-day gauntlet that was physically and emotionally draining. Baltimore beat them two out of three at Yankee Stadium, and the last game, a 12-2 loss, was a pitching bloodbath. Jaret Wright bucked the saddle after three-plus innings, and Joe Torre called on Ron Villone—who had become one of his most trusted relievers—for the third day in a row and fourth time in five games. Villone allowed a three-run homer to Nick Markakis that clinched the loss. But Torre also called upon Octavio Dotel, who had just come off a grueling stop-and-start rehab after 2005 surgery, for a second straight day. He also called on Mike Myers, who was ostensibly a situational lefty more apt to throw to one batter than one inning, for 2⅓ innings.

"I was worried about our pitching big-time," Cashman said. "We went up there dragging."

Due to a May 2 rainout, the Yanks and Red Sox were scheduled to play a day-night doubleheader on Friday, August 18. Since 49 percent of all twin bills in the last twenty-five years have ended in splits—and because the Sox and Yanks were equally matched—it seemed unlikely one team would sweep the other. Similarly, it seemed unlikely either team would win more than three games of the five-game set. The teams were tied, 5-5, in the season series. And since 2003, the teams were practically tied, 41-40, in their previous 81 games—including matching 7-7 records in the postseason.

"Five wasn't what I was thinking. Three out of five, yeah," Cashman admitted a few weeks later. "Selfishly, you want to win all of them. But you have too much respect for your opponent and the way they play in that ballpark . . . it's become a house of horrors for teams to go in there.

"And they're so strong late in the game, it's unbelievable. Seventh, eighth, and ninth innings, they're a completely different team offensively. They're built for that park, it seems. They're a tough team to play in that park, so I never, ever would've expected it 5-0. If anybody was going to Vegas, I have no idea what the odds would be."

From the first at-bat through the end of the series, though, the Yankees dominated in a way never seen before. Johnny Damon, who was treated so harshly back in May, tripled and scored in the first inning of the doubleheader opener, a rousing 12-4 victory for the visitors. He smashed a two-run homer in the fifth and drove in four. While the Yankees were flexing their offensive muscle and rubbing their new acquisition in Boston's grill (Abreu stroked four of their seventeen hits), the Red Sox were proving inept. Boston went 0 for 16 with runners in scoring position. Joe Torre shrewdly pitched his young stud, Chien-Ming Wang, in the first game to get an advantage, and Wang improved to 14-5.

Torre's decision was partially based on the fact that Sidney Ponson, who was waived by St. Louis earlier in the season, started the nightcap. Ponson was a low-risk acquisition by Brian Cashman in July, before the Yanks acquired Lidle to help their staff. Predictably, he stank, losing the 5-1 advantage the Bombers had handed him in the middle of the second inning. Ponson lasted only three-plus innings, allowing nine hits and seven runs, and he was designated for assignment the next day. After Boston tied the game in the third, Damon smashed a two-run homer to put his team ahead again. Still, Ponson and Villone couldn't stem the tide, and the visitors trailed, 10-7, entering the seventh inning.

That's where the most difficult decision of the series rested with Torre. With three games in a twenty-eight-hour span between Friday and Saturday afternoon, Torre had planned to rest both Giambi and Jorge Posada. Neither started the nightcap.

Craig Hansen—the St. John's University fireballer whom the Yanks had passed on for C. J. Henry—started the seventh, and he retired Robinson Cano for the first out. That's when Torre pinch-hit Giambi for Wilson, and that's when the series, and maybe the pennant race, was irrevocably changed.

"The management part of it was tough, but it didn't take much coaching for me to do that," Torre explained a few weeks later, "because I just felt like we had an opportunity to take a game here. They were there ready.

"The whole ballclub was ready for whatever we needed to have done."

Giambi drew a walk. Bernie Williams—Mr. Old Reliable—followed with a single. Then Torre made another move: with weak-hitting backup catcher Sal Fasano scheduled to bat, Posada replaced him, and he stroked a single to left that loaded the bases.

"That made me feel good, because you knew they had to stay in the game, and they were gonna have to play tomorrow afternoon," Torre said.

Mike Timlin replaced Hansen, and he fared horribly. Melky Cabrera— who was six years old when Timlin made his major-league debut in 1991— mustered a single that brought the Yankees to within two, 10-8. Timlin got Damon to pop up, but Derek Jeter, who was being touted as an AL MVP candidate, was the next hitter. The numbers clearly didn't favor the captain, who toted a 3-for-20 mark against Timlin into the at-bat.

Somewhat predictably, Jeter fell behind 1 and 2. But then he fouled a pitch off, took two balls, and fouled off another pitch. He was wearing down the forty-year-old Timlin, who had already lost something by this point in the season, and on the eighth pitch of the at-bat he ripped a ball just inside the right-field line. Three runs came home and the Yanks led, 11-10. Captain Clutch, as some New York writers gleefully call him, had come through again.

A-Rod doubled home another run and Cano added a two-run single for good measure. It was the longest nine-inning game in major-league history, at four hours and forty-five minutes, but Mariano Rivera closed out a 14-11 victory that ensured the Yanks would leave Boston with an AL East lead. Having dropped two games in the standings and now trailing by three and a half games in the division, Boston's clubhouse was morose. And naturally so: a split would've kept the Yankees' lead at a game and a half.

"We're in trouble," David Ortiz told reporters after the loss. "Any time you score eleven runs and lose, you're in trouble. I feel like I just got my ass kicked. And I did."

Meanwhile, the Yanks were already looking forward to the Saturday matinee clash, even though they had played a combined eight hours and forty minutes and the finale ended at 12:52 A.M.

"The more they won, the more anxious they were to play the next game in spite of being tired," Torre marveled. "Because we knew the psychological part of it. We knew we were tired.

"We knew that they were tired, and being tired and winning and being tired and losing is a lot different, having been on both sides of that thing."

Saturday's game went the same way, and the Red Sox allowed twelve or more runs in a third straight game for the first time in franchise history. Josh Beckett, who was acquired during the winter along with third baseman Mike Lowell for touted prospects Hanley Ramirez (a shortstop) and Anibal Sánchez (a right-handed pitcher) and two other minor leaguers, walked nine men during 5⅔ innings of a 13-5 loss, and the Yanks drew thirteen walks overall. Eight of them scored.

While Randy Johnson wasn't super, he lasted seven innings, until Torre could turn the bullpen over to Jaret Wright and T. J. Beam, two pitchers who needed the work, and gave the rest of the bullpen the day off.

The teams didn't reconvene for about twenty-four hours, due to the scheduling quirk of the ESPN *Sunday Night Baseball* game. That gave the Yanks a chance to revel in their bulging lead and a chance for the city of Boston to be mired in mass depression. On Sunday, August 20, the Red Sox gathered for a team photo in late afternoon, where owner John Henry, CEO Larry Lucchino, and other front office members were on hand. After the players stood in the outfield against the Green Monster, they were summoned for an additional photo with team personnel in the red field box seats behind home plate. In what was certainly an unusual sight, Sox players were interspersed with regular workaday employees, from PR people to ushers. It was an odd scene, but maybe the most telling one of the weekend. Finally, this was a photograph that could sum up the series: the Red Sox were mere spectators at what was happening. They were seemingly as powerless as Lucchino, Henry, or the white-haired ticket takers from stopping the Yankee juggernaut.

As soon as the photos ended, GM Theo Epstein was converged upon by the media just off the first-base line. For the next twenty-five minutes he defended Boston's failure to make a deal at the trade deadline, the franchise's philosophy, and its uniqueness in contrast to the Yankees. In fact, he took some veiled shots at the Yankees, calling them an "überteam," even though he backpedaled after making the analogy.

It sounded like a politician's speech, coming from the mouth of a frustrated ideologue who was convinced his philosophy was right but conceded the numbers suggested otherwise. In other words, he was the John Kerry of the AL East (someone he had stumped for during a similarly failed campaign).

"Tough times are always just a character test," Epstein began. "Personally and as an organization, you've got to find a way to get through it and get better.

"It's in the results, near-term and long-term. You've gotta get stronger. If you're not getting better, you're probably getting worse. Adversity like this makes an organization stronger. No one's ever gotten anywhere with smooth sailing only. You don't have the good times without going through bad times. This is a tough week. We'll get through it and get better."

Varitek's absence essentially buried Boston. His game-calling ability, knowledge of opposing hitters, leadership, and offense in a lineup that was trying to keep up with the Yankees were critical. Epstein cautioned that the injury shouldn't be used as a crutch, but a few moments earlier Lucchino had called Varitek "the rock on which the church is built."

One of the biggest mistakes Epstein made during a miserable year of wheeling and dealing was trading backup catcher Josh Bard, whom the Sox had acquired in the winter from Cleveland in the Crisp trade, to San Diego for backup Doug Mirabelli. Bard had a terrible time catching knuckleballer Tim Wakefield in April, to the point where he was dealt along with young reliever Cla Meredith for Mirabelli, an otherwise undistinguished journeyman who had a reputation in the Boston clubhouse as a bad teammate. The night Johnny Damon returned to Fenway, so did Mirabelli. Boston fans gave Mirabelli a standing ovation, and the Boston police gave him a motorcade to the ballpark while he changed in the car. His lack of production was arresting, though, and the Red Sox were forced to acquire the graying Javy López from Baltimore. López was once known as one of the best-slugging catchers in the game, but he was never known for his defensive prowess. Greg Maddux famously preferred not to pitch to him in Atlanta. More to the point, López's game had declined in the steroid-detection era after he belted 43 homers, drove in 109 runs, and hit .328 in 2003, his last good season.

"Varitek was a huge loss for them," Brian Cashman said in late August. "He means so much to that franchise.

"He's one of the best you'll ever see. As a catcher who controls every pitch thrown on their side, you're gonna feel his loss."

Epstein, once a golden boy in Boston who was almost as popular as Patriots quarterback Tom Brady, was taking a beating in the papers, sports radio, and blogs. He gave away Bard (who batted .333 with 9 homers and 40 RBIs in 100 games) and Meredith (who went from July 17 to September 17 without allowing a run, a span of 34 innings) for an over-the-hill backup. And not only did Mirabelli stink in 2006, but he burned bridges on his way out of San Diego, asking San Diego GM Kevin Towers to send him back to Boston.

More troubling to the future of the franchise, Epstein also traded Bronson Arroyo—a key part of the 2004 world championship team—to Cincinnati for the perpetually tantalizing, disappointing slugger Wily Mo Peña. It was a questionable move to begin with, but it looked downright foolish when Arroyo restored respectability to Cincinnati by starting 8-2 with a 2.31 ERA into June, Peña struck out on a Dave Kingman–like pace, and starters David Wells and Matt Clement succumbed to injuries.

By mid-September, even Boston ace Curt Schilling admitted the obvious in panning the trade to reporters, saying, "We came out of spring training, everybody said, 'Well, you have extra starting pitching.' Nobody ever has extra starting pitching. If you have it on Monday, you don't have it on Sunday. It never fails.

"So many things happened to us so fast that it became a surplus to a lack of very quickly here. I think it's a lesson that people like Theo will have to learn only one time. I don't think it will ever be an issue again."

Fans and media also questioned Epstein's unwillingness to make a deal at the trade deadline. A common complaint was that he and other front office members were more emotionally invested in 2007, when key prospects would blossom. Epstein mostly ignored the squawking on the radio and only read the papers to the extent that he needed to be aware of what was being reported.

Boston was no stranger to deadline deals, as Epstein had made a name for himself trading Nomar Garciaparra two years earlier and bringing in Orlando Cabrera, Doug Mientkiewicz, and Dave Roberts, all of whom contributed to the first world championship team in eighty-six years. Frankly, it was a ballsy move. Garciaparra was once baseball royalty, his name spoken in the same sentence as A-Rod's and Derek Jeter's at the beginning of his career. Epstein worried soon after the deal that he'd be pilloried if it didn't work out.

Similarly, there were rumors that the Sox were involved in something big at the 2006 deadline. There were whispers that they would make a play for Atlanta's Andruw Jones, and reports that they were willing to deal Coco Crisp for Chicago's Mark Buehrle. One report stated that the Sox were asked about Hansen in a package for Abreu but wouldn't consider it.

Epstein stressed, again and again, that the Red Sox had one eye on 2006 and one eye on the future. The more he talked about it, the more it conjured up the image of a distracted driver talking on a cell phone and veering off the road on the way to a horrific crash. He was getting crushed by critics for making that distinction in word and in deed, although the former wonder-boy GM claimed the criticism was fair.

"Anytime you're not winning, you're not happy with the way things have gone," Epstein said. "You're always kind of looking at things you could've done differently.

"The process was good. We weren't going to be in a position to just bring in guys for the sake of bringing in guys. We wanted to find someone who was better than what we had. There's a lot of talented guys on this team who aren't pitching very well right now.

"We've got to find a way as an organization to turn that around. Certainly as an organization, we're probably more critical of ourselves than anyone else would be. At the same time, we're disappointed. We'd love to find a way to make something happen and bring in real quality arms to make a difference. . . .

"Anything you can say after you've probably played three of your worst games of the year can be unfortunately taken out of context. I prefer to take the broader look. We've used the same principles this year that we used to win 95-plus games the last three years in a row and make the playoffs three years in a row. We maybe had a little bit less room for error this year, and if a number of things went wrong, it was going to be more of a struggle for us. And it's proven to be more of a struggle for us. That doesn't mean we can't win. That doesn't mean we're giving up."

As bleak as things looked with a four-and-a-half-game deficit (and things would get much, much bleaker in Boston the next two weeks), Epstein spun the season in a positive light. Players such as Jonathan Papelbon and Kevin Youkilis had thrived in larger roles in 2006 (but pitchers Hansen, Manny Delcarmen, and Jon Lester hadn't). He cautioned that anytime farm-developed players were on the roster, there are bound to be ups and downs in performance. He noted that originally Keith Foulke was expected to close and Timlin, Rudy Seanez, and Julián Tavárez were expected to share setup duties with Papelbon, who emerged as one of the best closers in the game.

"I think we'll come out very well in the long run for having gone through this," Epstein said. "Obviously every loss hurts, and we don't want to miss the playoffs even one year. And we have to put ourselves in position to make sure that doesn't happen. But obviously it is a balancing act. . . .

"Sometimes you don't have an überteam. That's not our dynamic. We're not going to try to build an überteam every year."

When Epstein uttered the word *überteam,* it certainly sounded like another shot at the Yankees. Lucchino had so famously called George Steinbrenner's team the "Evil Empire" back when the Red Sox came up short in their bid to sign Jose Contreras in the winter following the 2002 season, and this seemed like another snipe at the most successful franchise in sports.

"We are not the Yankees," Epstein said a few minutes later. "We admire the Yankees. I admire the Yankees. I respect them. When they were beating us, I've said that, and when we were beating them, I've said that.

"We have to do things different. Our approach is a little bit different. Given our resources relative to the Yankees, we feel our best way to compete with them year in and year out is to keep one eye on now and one eye on the future . . . and to build something to sustain success.

"They're also very good at that. We just do it in a slightly different way. We've gone toe to toe with those guys taking that approach. I think we're what, one or two games under .500 against them since '03 and have won one more World Series than they have taking that approach. And have been in the playoffs every year, just like they have.

"We're not going to change our approach and all of a sudden try to build an überteam or try to all of a sudden win now at the expense of the future. That's not an excuse. I'm not trying to throw some sort of cloak over the clear holes on this team by sort of talking about the future. I'm not. Our goals are now, and our goals are to put ourselves in a position to win every single year. That's the reality.

"It's going to occasionally leave us short. It's going to leave us short every time there's a player who's available in a bidding war. Taking on a contract. Getting the best free agent. We're never going to sell ourselves out just to get that one guy. We have to take a long-term view. Given our resources relative to the Yankees, it's the only way to do it. I think we're good at it, and I think it's going to prove successful in the long run."

When asked to explain what, exactly, an überteam was, Epstein said it was code for a team with no weaknesses. An überteam, when you go around the diamond, has high-paid, impact players at every position and an extremely deep pitching staff. If three or four players go down, an überteam has a very good player waiting in the wings. An überteam, Epstein said, was "sort of a monolith of a team, a team that really has no weaknesses, perfectly constructed for the now with a redundancy at all spots."

Naturally, he was asked if *überteam* was a synonym for the Yankees.

"No," Epstein answered. "I think they achieve it sometimes. They do. If you look around the diamond, they have some of the best players in the game, some of the highest-paid players in the game. They've also done a good job of producing a couple good young players who are making no money. I don't think they're a one-trick pony by any stretch of the imagination. I don't think we do things exactly the same way. That's probably by design. They've got a great plan, and we have a plan.

"We're in a position competing directly with them with less resources than they do, we have to keep one eye on the future. We can't do certain things that on paper would look good without thinking what the ramifications are on future payroll, on future roster construction, et cetera. That's the reality. We've operated exactly the same way since day one of the off-season following the '02 season.

"Conceivably, that's an example of where we didn't have the resources to take on [Bobby Abreu's] salary, this year or next year. But we have tremendous resources, don't get me wrong. We have fantastic resources. An upgrade in right field is not worth that to us. We have to spread that money around to execute that plan and build the '07 team."

Publicly, Cashman refused to get drawn into a war of words regarding the überteam designation.

"The rivalry is already at its height," Cashman said at the end of August. "I don't need to take it higher. I think there's an obvious conclusion that anyone can conclude and come to. And I'll leave you to do that."

Although on one level Epstein was correct, examining the Abreu trade in its full context reveals the hypocrisy of the Boston front office. Perhaps in July an upgrade in right field wasn't worth the financial hit to Boston. But Epstein was incorrect to say that the Red Sox didn't have the money to take on Abreu's 2006 salary. Since March, Boston had hoped that Roger Clemens would come out of retirement and pitch at Fenway Park, and the team drew up plans on that contingency. Team officials from owner John Henry on down fantasized about the perfect closure to the career of The Rocket as he finished with the team that had drafted him. They even produced an off-season video (that one report described as "poignant") in an effort to recruit Clemens.

So when Clemens decided to return to Houston in 2006, what happened with that money? The Astros paid Clemens about $12.8 million for half a season. Abreu was slated to earn about $6 million as a Yankee. Did that contingency money just evaporate in the ether, disappear into thin air, or get swallowed up by a black hole? It's an interesting question, and one Yankee officials were privately asking with bemusement.

Hours after Epstein gave his State of the Sox address, Boston had their chance to reverse momentum and save face. Their ace, Curt Schilling, faced off against Mike Mussina, and if Boston could take the final two games of the five-game series (with big-game pitcher David Wells starting against Lidle on Monday), they would've trailed by only two and a half games with six weeks remaining. When Schilling outlasted Mussina, who left after four innings with a tight groin, things were looking Boston's way. The stubborn Schilling had outlasted a fifty-seven-minute rain delay, and his only mistake over seven innings was a three-run bomb he allowed to Jason Giambi. Boston led, 5-3, going into the eighth.

For the third straight game, though, Boston could not hold a lead. Timlin, horrible in the Friday night loss, faced two batters and allowed a single and hit a batsman. Javier Lopez, whom the Red Sox recalled before the game because they didn't have a situational lefty in their bullpen, walked Abreu. Giambi once again came up clutch with a sacrifice fly, just missing a grand slam to right, but the Red Sox escaped without further damage. However, this was the one loss in which Francona mismanaged the game.

Before the game, Francona said his closer, Papelbon, was available for six outs. Instead of starting the eighth with the dominating flamethrower, he went with Timlin, who was looking every bit his forty years, and Lopez, who wasn't even good enough to be in the majors hours earlier. Although Papelbon escaped by whiffing Cano and Posada in the eighth, the twenty-two pitches took a toll on him for the ninth. Melky Cabrera, the unflappable rookie, doubled to right center to lead off the inning, and Papelbon wild-pitched him to third. Papelbon recovered to strike out Bernie Williams and Damon, but Jeter blooped the second offering from Papelbon into shallow right to tie the game. On this night, it was the perfect result from his inside-out swing, and it was the hardest evidence yet that the Yankee captain was the league's Most Valuable Player.

And in the tenth, Giambi hit the go-ahead solo homer off the battered Hansen (there's that name again) and Jorge Posada added a two-run shot. The Red Sox were so worried about Hansen's rattled psyche, they optioned him to Triple A Pawtucket after the game. By that point, the former St. John's product was baseball's equivalent of a punch-drunk boxer.

Virtually everyone was stunned at the events, and David Ortiz said he was "almost 100 percent sure" that was the best he'd ever seen the Yankees play.

"It's not fair, man," Ortiz said from his chair in front of his locker. "Those guys are not playing around. They should let us win the game to make the series interesting.

"It's like they have a secret weapon every time for every situation. Their lineup is very deep. They're on top of their game. I'm telling you, this is my ninth year in the big leagues, I've been playing the Yankees a lot since I got here. I think this is the first time in a long time I have seen the Yankees all compact all the way around. It's hard to beat a team that is locked in like that."

Ortiz called Boston's predicament a "ride-or-die situation." "We've gotta fight with what we've got," he said.

Schilling was complimentary in defeat, praising the Yankees and saying that Jeter was to the Bombers what Ortiz was to the Sox: the one player you wanted at the plate (or didn't want, if you were an opponent) in that situation.

"Those guys over there have done a phenomenal job," Schilling said. "They've had every bit if not more of the injuries that we have going through the year.

"The guys they've lost and they have guys struggling they didn't expect to have struggling. And they found a way. . . .

"We keep playing like this, we won't be playing in October. . . . We're what, five and a half out? We haven't proven anything. We've proven we're not better than one team in our division. It's August, and we're five and a half out in a division we led most of the year. Again, we've had our bad breaks and injuries and whatever you want to say as an excuse for not playing well, but so have the Yankees."

Schilling saved his highest praise for the acquisition of Abreu.

"Bringing in a guy like Bobby Abreu I think was a much bigger thing than people realized," Schilling said. "He's come in full bore and made a difference."

The finale to the second Boston massacre on Monday afternoon had a certain symmetry to it: the Yankees started their trade deadline acquisition, Lidle, and the Sox started Wells, someone they'd soon trade in a white-flag move. Digging even deeper, Wells was a former Yankee who loved the drama of a must-win game and loved sticking it to his former employer even more. And Lidle was coveted by Boston in late July.

Back in July, the Phillies had been adamant about tying one of their salaried starters, either Lidle or, preferably, Jon Lieber, to any Abreu move. Lieber wasn't pitching well (he was 1-3 with a 6.75 ERA in July) and was due $7.5 million in 2007. Additionally, Cashman had heard the Red Sox were pursuing Lidle.

"I know that for a fact," Cashman said a month later. "Yeah, I could use the extra starter. We valued Lidle. He has a history of strong second halves every year, his ERA is a huge drop every year. He's a different pitcher in the second half than the first half. We needed him.

"We could use him, and knowing that they needed him too, if we could take him for ourselves to our benefit and at the same time keep him away from them, that was cooler."

The day after the trade, Cashman felt compelled to angrily defend the addition of Lidle during the most contentious exchange he had ever had with WFAN sports radio host Chris Russo. Cashman went nuclear on July

31 when he heard that Russo had called him a liar for saying that the Yanks wouldn't have done the deal without Lidle. Russo, much better known by his moniker "Mad Dog," was frothing at the mouth over the deal, calling Lidle "not a good pitcher." He also ripped Cashman, ostensibly a friend of his, for signing Jaret Wright before the 2005 season.

"I'm biting my tongue because you are irritating the heck out of me," Cashman reportedly said at one point.

The fifteen-minute conversation was great radio, at times comical and other times combative. In the days after the trade, Cashman had people come up to him saying, "Great job!"

"Thanks," Cashman would reply. "Yeah, we hope the trades work out."

"No," a few fans corrected him, "great job giving it to Mad Dog. You really told him off!"

Although Lidle was inconsistent down the stretch and couldn't even earn a starting spot at the beginning of the postseason, he pitched his finest game in pinstripes under tough circumstances. He missed the first three games of the series while attending the funeral in California of his ninety-seven-year-old grandmother, and took the red-eye to be in town on Sunday.

The afternoon matinee played out like the fifteenth round of a title fight in which both boxers had punched themselves out, but the Bombers took a 2-1 decision. Cabrera, who had seemed to play his best against the Yanks' biggest rival, led off the sixth against Wells with a single, stole second, and scored when Abreu once again proved worthy of Schilling's praise, knocking a double to left center. They added a run on a double by Nick Green, a sacrifice and a wild pitch in the eighth, and Kyle Farnsworth nailed it down in the ninth because Mariano Rivera was unavailable, having thrown two clutch innings in the Sunday night victory.

The Monday victory was icing on the cake, even Torre admitted. The Yanks had swept five games in Boston only two other times, during the championship years of 1927 and 1943. In the cramped visitors' clubhouse, the manager tried to stop and talk to each player and convey his appreciation before the Bombers packed and left for a six-game West Coast trip to Seattle and Anaheim. Players were gushing about the teamwork that secured the sweep, as everyone from one to twenty-five contributed something.

"It's unbelievable. If anybody would have said that either team would win five games in this series, I would have laughed," Scott Proctor told a reporter.

"Some of the greatest teamwork I've ever been involved with," Giambi told reporters.

"We always attacked," Bobby Abreu said later, after a few weeks of reflection.

Although it wasn't known at the time, the Red Sox were a team in real turmoil, with harrowing issues that extended beyond the playing field or win-loss column. It turned out Ortiz had heart palpitations and was admitted to a hospital for tests between the Saturday and Sunday games. In the ensuing days, he would again check into a hospital and be fitted with a heart monitor, although eventually he was cleared to return.

Lester, one of the most promising young pitchers Boston had seen, was diagnosed with anaplastic large-cell lymphoma, a rare cancer of the lymph nodes. He left the team and sought treatment immediately.

The injuries went from the supine to the ridiculous. Ramirez had tendinitis in his knee, but on the ensuing West Coast road trip, reporters questioned whether the mercurial, wacky Boston left fielder was sitting out. Reportedly, he had to be coaxed into playing the Sunday night game against the Yankees because he was enraged by a scorer's call on Saturday that took away a hit. Not exactly the type of team spirit you look for in the pennant race. Schilling strained his right lat and missed a start. Papelbon went down on September 1 and didn't pitch again. Peña sprained his wrist and shortstop Alex González strained his oblique. Crisp was bothered by an injured finger that he'd broken at the beginning of the season.

While the Yankees only went 2-4 on the West Coast trip and needed Jeter to bail them out with two homers in the finale against the Angels, they didn't lose ground. The Red Sox also went 2-4, and from the time the two teams left Fenway until the time they met back up for a four-game set on September 15, the Yankees lost ground in the division on only two days. They gained five games in that span.

In the end, there were a number of baseball lessons from the series, ones that, to paraphrase Schilling, Epstein and his bosses had best only learn once. On the field, the Yankees utilized an entire team over an entire weekend, as in-season pickups such as Green and Brian Bruney were just as critical in victories as Damon or A-Rod. Bullpen depth and confidence were obvious keys: the Red Sox blew leads in the middle three games, while the Yankee pen slammed the door when necessary.

The importance of taking walks was underscored: the Yankees drew 33 walks to Boston's 22.

One of the obvious lessons was that luck played a part over the course of a successful season. It was much easier to cope with serious injuries sustained early in the year, as the Yanks did with Sheffield, Matsui, and even Cano. Boston couldn't overcome Varitek's injury and the tsunami that followed.

Lastly, Epstein and his bosses remained adamant about standing pat at the trade deadline and not potentially jeopardizing the future. Instead, they mortgaged the season on an uncertain future while Cashman transitioned on the fly. The Yankee GM later explained that making the playoffs wasn't good enough in 2006, a goal that Epstein and company seemed content to reach before letting the playoff gods determine a World Series winner.

No, in the Yankee Fishbowl, there is only one goal, and Cashman made the one move, Abreu, at the one time he could in order to do his part. He described it as putting all his chips in the middle of the table, a poker cliché that fit perfectly. Heading into the final stretch of the season, Cashman held a great hand.

The Red Sox walked away, dazed and confused about how they could get their pockets cleaned. One consolation to their fans: Schilling, who had the ear of the ownership, reported that their club would be upping the ante for 2007.

"I think there will be less attention paid to the payroll number than there has been in the past," he said in mid-September. "I don't want to say the handcuffs are off, because they're never really on here.

"But this team has always operated with an eye toward the luxury tax and trying to play within the rules, so to speak. They'll go over the tax number to a degree, to get players in here, but they're not going to get absurd. That might not be the case [in 2007]."

For Red Sox fans, it confirmed what many believed all along: 2006 was collateral damage. Next season was when the team would be really going for a world championship.

For the Yankees, aiming for a World Series is simply business as usual every year. And they looked well on their way to that after humiliating the Red Sox.

CHAPTER FOURTEEN

PAVANO

One lazy day in mid-February 2006, Carl Pavano was perusing a newspaper inside the clubhouse at Legends Field in Tampa, reading the extensive coverage about Dick Cheney's hunting accident. During a weekend quail hunt, the vice president accidentally shot seventy-eight-year-old Texas lawyer Harry Whittington in the face with birdshot, a story that became national news for days and the subject of jokes for weeks.

Nobody around the Yankees pegged Pavano as an intellectual. He'd never attended college and spent his off-field life dating gorgeous women and/or driving fast cars (a combination that would end his 2006 season), so he wasn't exactly someone with high-minded pursuits. Politics didn't seem to be his bag, either. Thus it was something of a surprise for him to even be reading about current events. Of course, Pavano spoiled it by opening his mouth.

What's this country coming to, he announced, when there's such a furor over congressmen shooting citizens? Maybe it was a joke, maybe it wasn't. A couple of people who relayed the anecdote couldn't reach a consensus. It didn't matter, because either way Pavano revealed himself as a fool.

"You idiot," Tanyon Sturtze told him, breaking out in laughter. "He's the vice president."

"I knew that," Pavano said, trying to cover with his own laugh.

Already by the spring of his second season in pinstripes, Pavano was an unpopular teammate, evidenced by the preceding story. A veteran couldn't wait to call the beat writers over who hadn't witnessed the event firsthand and reveal the depths of Pavano's stupidity, couldn't wait to mock the buffoonish figure.

A's manager Ken Macha told a different story to *Sports Illustrated* about managing Pavano for Triple A Pawtucket of the Red Sox system in 1997, when the right-handed pitcher was coming back from arm problems and the organization wanted to protect him. Pavano couldn't grasp the concept of a pitch count, as Macha left him in during a rough outing when he was on a 75-pitch limit but yanked him a few days later when he reached 90 pitches in a stellar outing.

"Carl was not the sharpest knife in the box," Macha told *SI*.

Years later with the Yanks, Pavano's vapid mind wasn't what made him so unpopular. Well, not mostly. He was already injured again by the spring of his second season, once again beset by a vague malady that couldn't be corrected with surgery or disproven by skeptical teammates. He was already considered a malingerer for failing to pitch in the second half of 2005 with rotator cuff tendinitis, shutting it down for good after a June 27 start at Baltimore. Nobody liked the fact that Pavano (4-6, 4.77 in 17 starts in 2005) was waylaid by an injury that didn't require surgery during a season when fellow starters Jaret Wright and Chien-Ming Wang worked hard to return after shoulder problems they deemed more serious. He made one rehab start for Class A Tampa on August 3, 2005, and didn't appear again after that.

Now, in 2006, Pavano couldn't pitch again. A week before spring training, he informed the club he had back pain. Back specialist Robert Watkins told him to take two weeks off from pitching and do back exercises. During the first meeting of the year with beat writers on February 15, manager Joe Torre announced the news, and the Yankee manager cautioned that Pavano might not be ready for Opening Day. That day, the pitcher told GM Brian Cashman that he felt good, and Cashman responded by telling him he wanted Pavano feeling good in May and June.

By the end of February, Torre announced that he wasn't banking on Pavano for Opening Day, although the pitcher vowed he would be ready by then. He wasn't. He was expected to be ready by late April, but a one-inning appearance against the Phillies on March 28 was as far as he got. The first hitter he faced, Bobby Abreu, hit a nubber down the first-base line, and Pavano tripped while fielding it and stumbled to the base, diving to record the out. He then allowed a homer to Chase Utley but retired the next two men, and nobody thought the incident was much more than a punch line.

"You had to know something like that would happen," Pavano told reporters with a smile.

"We didn't plan on the swan dive," Torre said. "We were happy to see him get up. The first one is under his belt. At least we can start the clock on him."

During the interview session afterward, Pavano was described as excited about his performance and genuinely pleased, and he mentioned the fall was no big deal. A few days later, all that changed. Pavano was diagnosed with a butt bruise and he added that he also hurt his back, and he was shut down indefinitely. The punch line was that the Yankees still planned to employ him in the rotation.

"When he gets here, we'll fit him in," Torre said at the time. "We're not going to go through all we've gone through for him not to be a starter."

Pavano waited more than a month before getting on the hill in a competitive situation. He didn't pitch again until he threw five innings of shutout ball during an extended spring training start on May 2. He made a rehab start on May 7, which began an approximately four-week window in which he needed to be activated or shut down. In his next start, Pavano complained of triceps tightness after 63 pitches. He told reporters he didn't originally think the triceps tightness was a major issue, but he complained during the entire drive to his rehab start on May 17, having gone through a bullpen session on May 14 in which the tightness lingered. He exited after one inning that night for Double A Trenton, and he was scheduled for elbow surgery to remove a bone chip a few days later.

"The fact that he warmed up and felt OK is puzzling," Torre told reporters that night.

From the freshest-faced youngsters to his peers in the rotation, nearly everyone had turned against him by that point. One veteran pitcher mocked Pavano outright to reporters after the Yankees' 4-3 victory over

Texas on May 17, calling it "unarmed robbery" that the perpetually injured righty was still picking up paychecks.

After all, Yankee reliever Tanyon Sturtze had poured out his heart and soul on the Yankee Stadium mound and had continued pitching despite bursitis and a small rotator cuff tear. Sturtze wouldn't even tell anyone he was injured, which pissed off Torre. In the same week that Pavano came out of a rehab start after one inning, Sturtze was scheduled for surgery that he feared would end his career.

By late June, Pavano once again rejoined the club, but he was a pariah.

"The thing that's important for him is to be here, and whatever abuse he's going to take—when I say abuse, agitation—might as well get it out of the way," the manager said in mid-June. "The only way he's going to, first of all, feel good about himself—and not even concern himself with how others feel about it—is to get out there and pitch. He certainly doesn't feel good about what's going on.

"Once he gets out there and becomes a part of what we're doing, I think whatever whispering that goes on will be a thing of the past. That's gone on in baseball forever, whether it's been kidding guys about being hurt or whatever.

"That's part of the fabric of the game, that you basically have to get out there."

Perhaps naive, perhaps disingenuous, Torre said that he didn't think "there's anybody who thinks he's faking it."

"It's just one of those things that it's just a bad run of luck for him," Torre said with a shrug.

By then, Pavano was overdue. The 6-foot-5, 240-pound native of New Britain, Connecticut, was a major-league underachiever who was best known for being traded from Boston to Montreal for Pedro Martinez in 1997 and surrendering Mark McGwire's 70th home run in 1998. When the Yankees signed him to a four-year, $39.95 million contract, Pavano was a career 57-58 pitcher with a 4.21 ERA with Montreal and Florida. But he allowed one run over eight innings in Game 4 of the 2003 World Series for the Marlins against the Bombers, which opened some eyes in New York. He followed it up with an 18-8 record in 2004, compiling a 3.00 ERA in his walk year.

In the winter of 2004–05, small-time agent Scott Shapiro began a tour of cities with Pavano, calling it the Carlapalooza Tour in a play on the popular Lollapalooza music tour. He ate with Torre and visited Boston ace Curt Schilling at his house in Massachusetts, and he also went to a number of other cities.

Pavano was one of the trio of pitching mistakes in the winter of 2004–05, with Wright and Randy Johnson being the other two mistakes. The trio made only three combined playoff starts in '05 and '06, with two losses and a no decision. Those were decisions that came to haunt the Yankees still two years later, decisions that revealed the soft underbelly of the organization. Both Torre and Cashman were in agreement that the Yanks should make a competitive offer to sign Pavano, who had already developed a reputation as soft.

"He was high on both our lists," Torre said eighteen months later. "You can't feel bad about it. You make a decision at the time you have to make a decision, and if it works out that way, it works out that way. There's really nothing you can do about it. You can't read a crystal ball.

"It's not like you signed the wrong guy," Torre continued. "It's not like the guy is not handling being in New York, know what I mean? It's just a matter of he hasn't gotten a chance to get out there and show who he is."

In the middle of the year, the manager was still preaching tender loving care for Pavano. Although many managers usually use a hands-off approach to injured players and don't spend a lot of time thinking about or counting on them, Torre seemed particularly disengaged about what was truly going on. Pavano was revealing himself as a coward or a malingerer, and neither boded well for the franchise.

"On the management side, you have to take care of the people you make investments in," Torre said. "Otherwise, you're making a big mistake—especially when it's pitching. You're not going to get the guy you want."

But did the Yankees still want Pavano after 2006? He attracted trouble the way Paris Hilton did. In his first rehab start after the surgery to remove a bone chip, Pavano reportedly got into an altercation with a fan. It was August 10 in Tampa, and the fan heckled Pavano from his first pitch, according to reports. The pitcher snapped and called the fan a derogatory sexual slur, asking him what he was doing at the Florida State League game. The fan was said to be demanding compensation for the verbal abuse, although witnesses reportedly said he was setting Pavano up for an altercation.

As far as Pavano's bad judgment went, that was the tip of the iceberg. The *Titanic*-sized mistake came ten days later, and it sank his chances of pitching for the Yankees in 2006. Around 11:00 A.M. on August 15, Pavano drove his 2006 Porsche into a parked sanitation truck in West Palm Beach, sustaining $30,000 in damage to his car and $20,000 to the truck, according to a police report. He made his third rehab start for the Yankees that night and hid the injury from the Yankees for two weeks, until the pain from his two broken ribs worried him to the point where he needed to speak up. Pavano injured the driver of the truck, Ernest DeLaura, but he also erred after the accident by having his passenger, an attractive model named Gia Allemand, ushered away before the police arrived.

This was no minor fender-bender, either. "I was calling my boss and saying, 'They're dead, they're dead, they're dead,'" DeLaura told the New York *Daily News.*

What's crazy is this was the closest Pavano had gotten to a return to the majors. Cashman told him that there was a chance he would bring him aboard for a start in Seattle, but he decided against it. Around the fourth inning of an August 25 rehab start for Triple A Columbus, Pavano began complaining of pain. Finally, he copped to the car accident.

"Of course I'm angry," Cashman said. "I think it's obviously frustrating, disappointing. There's a lot of words which would come to mind."

Cashman was particularly galled that Pavano made such an error in judgment after the accident, which of course was unintentional. He forced the pitcher to do a conference call with reporters on Monday, August 28, at which time he was still scheduled to make his next rehab start and then join the team for a start against Detroit.

"It just seems like it's one thing after another," Pavano said at the time. "I'm not impervious to this because I make a lot of money and I play baseball.

"It just seems like there's a lot of distractions that are caused by me that go around with the team, and I figured that, at the time, it was something I could get through. I just didn't seem to get better, and that's the only reason why I really went to the team.

"I wanted to make a decision that was good for everyone and it wasn't good for anyone. It backfired on me."

Pavano was originally scheduled to remain on turn for his August 30 rehab start, but after being examined by the Yankee team physician on the twenty-ninth, he was shut down for a couple of weeks. That essentially ended all chances of his being a contributor to the 2006 team.

"Two years into this thing, it hasn't worked out thus far," Cashman said. "I've got two years left and he's got two years left to salvage it and make good. It just makes no sense to jeopardize anything going forward because of the emotions of the moment.

"There's no doubt that fans, front office, players, his teammates—everything is about earning respect on a daily basis. Hiding injuries and stuff like that loses credibility, loses respect, and clearly he's got a mountain to climb to get back into the fold, and that's on him. That's for another time, another place.

"Like any person, you're going to want to earn that back and fight for it. That's one of the challenges in front of him going forward, is to get back credibility and respect from the people that he has respect for."

The next day Cashman ordered Pavano to Tampa. Pavano implored the GM to let him come to Yankee Stadium to face the music with the press, but Cashman told him not to bother. Both Cashman and Torre were angry at Pavano, although they both insisted he wanted to pitch for the team. Cashman revealed that Pavano was on standby for a possible start in Seattle in the last week of August if the Yankee pitching staff was completely depleted, and the pitcher told him he would be available. That was before he complained of the pain from the broken ribs.

"The only people who would stop Carl from pitching would be us," Cashman said. "It won't be Carl. I believe he wants to pitch."

When Torre did a pregame press briefing just outside the Yankee clubhouse on August 29, he was in an angry, dismissive mood.

"I'm not going to sit here and wonder when he's going to pitch, because we've got work to do at this point," he said. "Every time we think we have something solved, something else pops up. You sort of shake your head."

The manager refused to believe that Pavano had some sort of performance anxiety or fear that prevented him from wanting to compete in New York, a charge that was now being leveled against him.

"I have to assume he wants to pitch," he said. "I would not believe that someone who's gotten that far in his career and really got to the point where he was our number-one choice a couple of years ago, all of a sudden he decides he doesn't want to pitch. I don't believe that."

That day, the players barely hid their utter disdain of Pavano, taping up a collection of back pages in his corner locker. The Daily News had "Crash Test Dummy," while the Post had "Crash Dummy" and Photoshopped the black-and-yellow circular crash-test dummy symbol onto

Pavano's body for good measure. Jorge Posada warned reporters not to ask him about Pavano, and Derek Jeter was described as annoyed by the topic—although he chuckled when recounting the back-page picture of Pavano he saw in the *Post*.

"I haven't been sitting around saying, when is Pavano coming back?" Jeter said. "Or waiting for Pavano to come back. I can't worry about guys who are not here. It's not a letdown if you're not counting on it. No, it's not hard to believe. That's what's been happening."

Torre, who had been sympathetic a few months earlier, seemed content to throw Pavano to the wolves in the clubhouse.

"Whatever the situation is, whether it's fragility or not, he's going to have to deal with it," Torre said. "He has to come and you have to walk into this clubhouse, dress next to these guys, and carry your share of the load, that's what it amounts to. And if it's a little tougher to do at first, so be it."

Not long after, Torre compared Pavano unfavorably to another brooding, unpopular former pitcher who formerly dressed in the same locker as Pavano: Kevin Brown. Late in the 2004 regular season, the cantankerous Brown broke his pitching hand by punching a wall in the Yankee clubhouse following a disappointing outing. He was unable to heal in time for the playoffs, and his start in Game 7 of the ALCS against Boston was a disaster that sealed the greatest playoff choke job of all time. Less than two years later, Torre seemed to absolve Brown more than Pavano.

"It was different, even though what Brownie did was irresponsible in a way," Torre said. "But he did it in the heat of competition.

"I think one thing happening on the field and one thing off the field has a different meaning for me."

The manager alluded to having people "committed in what we're doing," insinuating that the doughy Pavano was neither mentally nor physically preparing himself to participate in a championship season. Here he was, a multimillionaire who had become a laughingstock, a Cy Young contender two years earlier who was now persona non grata in the Bronx. Still, when Torre was asked at what point he would wash his hands of someone like Pavano, he hedged. It was all about fairness.

"As long as they're under contract, you've got to find a way to make it work," he said. "You can't really write somebody off as long as there's a reason for them to be here.

"And that's my job, to make sure that even though personally you feel one way because of the certain incident, you can't let it affect what's best for the team. You've gotta pretty much digest all the information and make that decision."

Finally, before walking away, Torre added this damning disclaimer: "I can't let the fact that I like somebody or hate somebody affect what decision I make."

Whereas everyone wearing a uniform saw Pavano as essentially a leper, Cashman saw an asset that was worth $20 million the next two seasons. Yes, it was clear to those who knew Cashman that he was frustrated at the pitcher's knuckleheaded actions. But in cold, calculating business terms, Cashman needed Pavano to pitch in order for Cashman to save face, and he'd do everything in his power to make sure that happened. At least publicly, Cashman was still trying to milk the final $20 million out of him, hoping it wouldn't be like drawing blood from a stone.

In many ways, Pavano was the egg on Cashman's face. The GM had taken over in 1998, traded for Chuck Knoblauch, and promptly won three straight World Series titles. But he wasn't a scout; his background was as an administrator, a person who was supposed to delegate authority and process information. Either the Yankee scouts had been duped on Pavano's makeup issues or Cashman (and Torre) had failed to consider them or had ignored them. Either way, they were paying the price. The Yankees' recent record with bringing in pitching from outside organizations was pockmarked with disappointments. For every find in Scott Proctor, there was a bust like Jeff Weaver or Kevin Brown. For every international gem in Chien-Ming Wang, there was a disappointment in Jose Contreras. For every acquisition of Roger Clemens, there was a Randy Johnson trade. If pitching was so crucial to success in the playoffs, if pitching was where teams win championships, then pitching was also the Yankees' Achilles heel. Cashman shouldn't be blamed for every failure, as a number of front office people had decision-making power for years. Now, though, it was on his watch.

By the end of 2006, Cashman still refused to believe that Pavano was willing to take unrelenting criticism by continually refusing to pitch. Pavano's family lived in Connecticut and they were huge Yankee fans. True, teammates had ratted out Pavano to management, griping that he'd been out late at the Blue Martini in Tampa or other places. But those complaints were dismissed, as players who were supposed to be playing in games the next day were engaging in the very same activities. In fact, in

2003, someone had written a letter to the front office saying that the Yan-kees players were running wild in south Florida the night before a World Series game against Florida when they should've been on lockdown. Pavano's contract was the envy of the team, from utility players to super-stars alike. And the sniping irritated the front office by the end of 2006, even though Cashman and others were also infuriated by the pitcher for withholding information about the car accident.

In previous generations, players would walk up to other players and tell them, in effect, to "cut the shit" if they were doing something coun-terproductive to the team. But in an era where the Players Association wields intimidating, overreaching clout run amok and every team's roster is populated not with players but with mini-corporations, that doesn't happen as often. Tony Womack was a perfect example. All indications were that Torre had grown sick of him and Cashman had spoken to him about his sulking attitude in 2005, but few players stood up and told him to act like a Yankee. That reflected on the Yankee captain, Derek Jeter, as well as other veterans who were supposed to proudly uphold the Yankee tradition.

The same went for Pavano: there were passive-aggressive actions, whether it was anonymous quotes in the papers or a poster of back pages from the *Daily News* and *Post* that someone hung in his corner locker at Yankee Stadium after the incident became public, but apparently nobody read him the riot act. Nobody told him to shape up. And to whatever extent anything was said to him player to player, it obviously didn't work.

By mid-September, Pavano was the laughingstock of not only the Yan-kee clubhouse but of others, too. When Boston was in town, Pavano's mother issued a front-page defense of her son in the *Daily News*. Red Sox players speculated that Pavano had been getting a blow job from his girl-friend, which caused the Porsche accident. The whole saga made for hilar-ious one-liners as Boston prepared for a baseball game.

One Yankee teammate said that when Pavano returned, he'd have trouble even getting his teammates to look him in the eye. The teammate said there was "borderline nothing wrong" with Pavano, and he felt Pavano was too scared to come back to the majors to earn his money. He thought the anxiety of pitching in the Yankee Fishbowl had completely overtaken his psyche. Although the teammate acknowledged that a marble-sized bone chip was nothing to scoff at, it was the rate of recovery that was so troubling. The teammate felt Pavano would rather go fishing or golfing than play baseball, and thought the pitcher had held the auto accident in his back pocket like a trump card to be pulled out when he was close to returning. Then he would "drop the kickstand," the teammate said.

Pavano visited with the team during a season-ending trip to play the Devil Rays, and Torre, pitching coach Ron Guidry, and a few players made him the butt of their jokes.

"This has been disappointing, frustrating, and humiliating," Pavano told reporters.

Someone asked if he thought he'd be better off elsewhere.

"That hasn't even crossed my mind. I'm a Yankee," he answered.

Guidry asked him if he'd gotten a new car and told him to buy a bicycle. Torre told reporters that he asked Pavano if it was OK to shake his hand, because he wasn't sure where the oft-injured pitcher was currently hurt.

"Baseball has to be his life and he's got to live his life that way," Torre said. "We thought it was important for him to come see his teammates—important to him, so he didn't have to wonder in spring training.

"He's here and whatever they choose to take from it or voice to him is up to them. There's been no meeting—'Here he is, have at him.' He's a member of the team. My feeling is he should mingle a little bit. He's got some work to do in that regard. He could've done a better job of helping himself."

Making matters worse, Pavano disagreed with Torre on the only thing that would make his life better in the Yankee Fishbowl.

"I don't feel like I have to address anything," Pavano said. "I don't expect anyone to feel sorry for me. There are a lot of things I can't control."

Over the course of his saga, he also issued completely oblivious statements such as this: "Me talking to them or trying to save face, that's not the type of guy I am. I'm going to go about my business. I'm not going to make excuses. I'm the type of guy who gives the benefit of the doubt. Not everyone is like me."

And: "This is something that was out of my control. I tried to deal with it the best that I could. Obviously that could be good enough for some people and then not for some others."

While some teammates shook his hand that day in St. Petersburg, most wouldn't talk to him. That certainly didn't bode well for 2007. Barring some sort of miraculous trade in the winter, or spring training, Pavano would be counted on more than ever.

"I don't care if he ever comes back," one teammate said at the end of the season.

CHAPTER FIFTEEN

CABRERA

In the summer of 2003, Jeff Karstens would constantly phone home from Staten Island to California raving about one of his teammates, showing all the enthusiasm of a young bird-dog scout. Karstens, born and raised in San Diego, was getting his first taste of professional ball with the team's short-season Class A team, his first taste of what potential major leaguers look like. He would inform his former high-school and junior college teammates of the sights and sounds of the Staten Island Yankees, but mostly he would rave about this one preternaturally calm teammate who was outstanding in the clutch.

Karstens, a lanky right-hander who played one season at Texas Tech before being drafted in the nineteenth round by the Bombers that summer, had seen the best players in the Big 12, had seen talent before. But he had never seen somebody as unique as the team's short, speedy center fielder. Karstens spoke Spanish, and he got to know the Santo Domingo, Dominican Republic, native, who was eighteen at the beginning of that season. He didn't act like it.

"He was very low-key, like he had been there before," Karstens said a few years later. "He was just different from everybody else. That kind of stuck out about him."

There was another thing that stuck out about him. He always seemed to perform, never seemed to act his age. He wasn't someone daunted by pressure situations.

"All he ever did was hit, hit, hit," Karstens said.

If Karstens' friends were wise, they would've remembered the odd-sounding name for their rotisserie baseball teams a few years later. They would've remembered the switch-hitting center fielder with the great arm and the quicksilver feet.

"This kid is really good," Karstens would tell them on his coast-to-coast phone calls. "He's going to make it someday."

Melky Cabrera did make it, but not the way it initially seemed. In the summer of 2005, when it became clear that Bernie Williams could no longer play every day, the Yankees "were grasping at straws" for a center fielder, as Joe Torre honestly put it. Hideki Matsui was no center fielder, and neither was Tony Womack.

So on July 7, 2005, Cabrera was promoted to the majors. He had never been with the major-league team during spring training and wasn't on the forty-man roster at the time, so his contract was purchased from Triple A Columbus, and he made his debut that night against Cleveland, going 1 for 4.

After starting 3 for 7 in his first two games, Cabrera went hitless in his next 11 at-bats. And on July 15, in the most hostile environment possible, he made a killer mistake. Playing in Fenway Park for the first time in his life, Cabrera charged a sinking liner from Trot Nixon, a slow-footed right fielder for the Red Sox. The ball bounced in front of him and eluded him, rolling to the green expanse near the mammoth wall in center. Nixon chugged around the bases for a three-run inside-the-park homer, the insulting exclamation point to Boston's 17-1 victory that day. The next day, Cabrera was demoted to Columbus, but the Yankee brass didn't think they had ruined their young prospect by rushing him.

"It just was six months too early, I guess," GM Brian Cashman said during the 2006 season. "'Nothing ventured, nothing gained' was my attitude. From what I understood of the player, it wasn't something that was going to hurt him.

"It was a huge compliment to his abilities to be put in a position that led me to believe he could help us at that point, and it didn't work out. So he goes back down, continues to work on what he needs to work on until he is a little more refined."

Although he was derided as a colossal failure and a non-prospect by some in the media, Cabrera didn't get down on himself, didn't let this spilled cup of coffee define who he was as a player that Cashman called "quiet but strong." In fact, in winter ball that season, he finished second in the MVP voting in the Dominican league, batting .315 with 18 RBIs in 40 games for the Las Aguilas team.

"He only got the experience for a few games," said his best friend, teammate Robinson Cano. "You know, when you're here and then you get sent down, you say, 'If I go up again, I want to stay up.' That's something you need to work hard [to accomplish]."

Cabrera's first major-league camp came at an opportune time: it coincided with the World Baseball Classic, and the Yankees had two outfielders, Johnny Damon and Williams, playing in it. That meant, at least for a few weeks, Cabrera could patrol center and get plenty of playing time.

Yankees officials met with him during the spring and talked about the importance of improving his defense. In 2005, Cabrera often seemed to get bad jumps on balls, and he needed to track balls better off the bat. The coaches, Torre, and Cashman all hammered this issue home with him.

"And the rest of the spring," Cashman said, "he busted his ass working on that.

"He's just someone who's very talented, who wants to be successful, and he's a hard worker. And so he's improved considerably and he continues to improve. And so I'm excited for him and for us.

"Because he's earned everything. He continues to work hard and earn it and is hungry and is happy and loves the game, and he plays it the right way."

Cabrera didn't make the team out of spring training, although he batted .349 in sixteen Grapefruit League games. But on May 9, he was called up from Triple A Columbus. He started that night in right field, and in another heated game against hated Boston, he dropped a fly ball Manny Ramirez hit down the right-field line. If the fans had stopped right there, if they hadn't given the twenty-one-year-old a longer second chance, they would've written him off for good. Also in that stretch, now playing left field in place of Matsui, Cabrera ran over to the line and stopped, letting a ball drop in for a double. Initially, Cabrera told Torre he was more comfortable in right field, but when Matsui broke his wrist, they needed his legs in Death Valley. Williams and other people could handle the smaller patrolling grounds in right, and the decision makers' move paid dividends for the rest of the season.

On June 6, Cabrera made one of the greatest catches of the year in the eighth inning of a 2-1 victory over Boston. Getting his revenge on Ramirez, whose ball he had dropped less than a month earlier, he sprinted back to the fence in left center (ironically, where a Japanese newspaper advertisement was) and leaped above the fence to take away a game-tying homer. Cabrera was knocked to the ground by the impact of the fence, but he had snow-coned the ball and held on to it. Johnny Damon, who had watched the play unfold from the best view in the house, put both arms up in jubilation, an incredibly raw display of excitement. Everyone wanted to congratulate Cabrera. Farnsworth hugged him as he came off the field. His teammates greeted him at the dugout. The Yankees held on to win that night, and opened up a one-and-a-half-game lead on Boston. It wasn't lost on Farnsworth that there was "no way [Matsui] makes that catch." The Japanese slugger simply didn't have the speed.

After the game, David Ortiz told Ramirez (while reporters listened), "That's why when I hit my shit, I hit it five hundred feet. I don't have to deal with that bullshit."

June was a pivotal month for Cabrera, who also went through his struggles. A 6-for-45 slump caused a one-game benching on June 21, but he ripped an RBI pinch-hit single in the eighth inning and recaptured his starting role. He was getting settled in the major leagues and making Yankee fans forget (or maybe not fixate on) the man they call Godzilla.

After batting .214 in June, he hit .313 in July and .311 in August. Torre judged his young rookie on what he saw against the Red Sox. On May 24 at Boston, the Yanks were without Damon, who was too battered to start. Torre put Cabrera atop the lineup, and he went 2 for 4 with four RBIs in the 8-6 victory that gave the Yanks the series. In the pivotal August series that sealed the AL East, he went 5 for 19 with seven runs scored in the sweep.

With one of the greatest regular-season triumphs in Yankees–Red Sox history, Torre had plenty of good moments and memories to savor. But the thing that made him the proudest, the thing that he said he'd always remember, was how Cabrera and Cano (8 for 24) contributed to the dismissal of the Sox.

"I had two young kids who went into that ballpark—which can be very intimidating—and performed the way Cabrera and Cano did in that five-game series. [That] was very memorable to me," Torre said.

"I don't think you can put a ceiling [on their talent], because you don't know. They're having so much fun playing the game, and putting themselves in pressure situations. And you look at the look in their face and they're just as calm as can be.

"At their age, you can only refer to yourself and think about how you would handle this situation. You don't know for sure, but you knew one thing: you weren't going to be as calm as they were, or what they seemed to betray, anyway."

Cabrera didn't speak any English, so he didn't demonstrate the humor that Cano said he possessed in spades, but he had an easy smile and took to the various nickname variations of "The Melkman." Cano did what he could to make his younger pal feel at ease in the big leagues, passing on the same lessons Alex Rodriguez and Derek Jeter had given him.

"They don't want me to be in trouble" on or off the field, Cano said. "That's what I do with him. Help him, keep him out of trouble.

"I'm just happy he's here and having fun."

No cliché: Matsui's long road back began with one step, and then another and another... At first, he wasn't even allowed to run, because the motion would jar the wrist. He did some walking and light workouts and kept his lower body in shape. On June 24, Torre reported that he was finally allowed to begin moving his fingers.

Next, he was cleared to run. He began returning to Yankee Stadium, and he was often seen after games jogging through the legendary outfield even in the rain, when the Japanese press corps took shelter in the dugout or went inside altogether. It was a tribute to his dedication to stay as sharp as possible. Soon after, he incorporated throwing into his routine— although he didn't catch the ball from his throwing partner. His interpreter, Rogelio Kahlon, and his Japanese media advisor, Isao Hirooka, would also be out there. Matsui would throw to one of them, who would throw to the other, who would give the ball back to Matsui.

By late July, Matsui was waiting on doctor's approval to field fly balls and swing with two hands. On July 17, he was hitting off the tee with one hand. He reported to Tampa on July 21, moving his rehab down there. He felt compelled to return by August 15, because his doctors told him it would be a minimum of three months from his surgery. He didn't want to waste one moment's time.

But on August 3, he underwent a check-up in Manhattan that revealed lingering tenderness in the wrist. He wasn't cleared to take BP. A week later, following another doctor's visit, he was put in a holding pattern for another week. His return became a bit murkier.

"If it's next year, it's next year," Torre said.

On August 22, though, he was finally cleared to hit off a tee, setting up a race against the end of the minor-league season. He was green-lighted to take batting practice beginning August 30. He had been doing only tee work and soft-toss drills before that.

"In terms of being pain-free, that's something I definitely feel good about," Matsui said. "I'm very satisfied.

"I'm still working on my mechanics and little things. That's kind of where I'm at right now. I'm definitely still being conscious about the wrist when I swing. Eventually I'll really move on to working on my mechanics thoroughly."

Matsui joined Double A Trenton for rehab games in the first week of September, which is when the Yankees began contemplating his role. The more it was discussed, the Yankees eventually came to the conclusion that Matsui should not return in the field so as to not reinjure his wrist.

"We see him as the DH because of the projection from the injury," Cashman said. "Him playing the outfield is something that may not happen, and Hideki knows it. I'm not saying it won't, but no one in the organization is counting on it."

Matsui had other ideas, but he bided his time. He told the reporters from Japan who cover his every move that he wanted to play defense so he could help the team on both ends of the game. But that would come later. Returning was the prime responsibility, as Matsui would put it. After four games for Trenton, in which he went 3 for 11 with five walks, a double, and an RBI, he returned on September 12 versus Tampa Bay.

At 7:31 P.M. that night at Yankee Stadium, Matsui received an uproarious ovation when he stepped into the batter's box in the first inning against righty Tim Corcoran. He dug his right foot into the batter's box with runners at the corners, and he dropped an RBI single into shallow center on a 1-and-2 pitch to put the Yanks up five runs. In the third inning, again cheered heartily, he lined a single to right on the second pitch.

Another bloop single followed in the fourth, and a sharp grounder up the middle in the sixth cleared the infield. Matsui was 4 for 4 in his first game back! The crowd of 52,265 was going bonkers, and the Yankees were laughing in the dugout over Matsui's remarkable return. After walking in the eighth and being replaced by a pinch-runner, he joked to them that he'd been sandbagging it the whole time, that he really wasn't injured but just wanted the attention. His teammates broke into hysterics. That would've made sense, considering how it looked as though he hadn't skipped a beat.

"Miss four months, get four hits, he made it look pretty easy," said Mike Mussina, that night's starter. "I hope they don't expect him to get four hits every night, that's a little too much. Maybe three."

"I never thought I'd have four hits," Matsui said after the game. "I was pleasantly surprised."

The surprise in the next few weeks was over the divide among Yankee fans who wanted Cabrera to remain in the lineup regularly. The thinking went that Cabrera, who had made 112 starts in left, 8 in right, and 1 in center, was simply a better defender. He was tied for second in the AL with 12 outfield assists, and his speed was more conducive to playing the field, especially in the cavernous area in Yankee Stadium. But Matsui was determined to prove he was all the way back, and another wrinkle was thrown into the mix: Gary Sheffield was on schedule to recover a few days after Matsui, which meant too many players for not enough positions.

If everyone was back healthy and was productive, the Yankees would have to bench someone for the playoffs, and Cabrera was the obvious choice despite finishing with a .280 average, 7 homers, and 50 RBIs. In fact, getting everyone on the playoff roster would seem like a challenge, although Sheffield remarked on the day of Matsui's return, "That's Joe Torre's problem."

You could argue Cabrera's postseason benching was one problem, albeit a minor one, that led to part of the inglorious ending.

CHAPTER SIXTEEN

JETER/A-ROD

On June 30, 2005, the Web site of *Radar* magazine posted an earth-shattering exposé. "New York Yankee stars Derek Jeter and Alex 'A-Rod' Rodriguez have stopped beating themselves up for their team's worst season in over a decade—and started beating on each other," the shocking scoop began.

Ten days earlier, Jeter had committed a costly throwing error early in a 5-4 loss to Tampa Bay. According to a witness claiming to be a TV producer doing an interview just after the game, "A-Rod walked past Jeter's locker and mumbled something about his throw, then Jeter told him to go fuck himself and all hell broke lose [*sic*]. Their teammates were pulling them away from each other."

The item went on to say that Jeter had never wanted A-Rod on the team, since their once-close friendship had turned frosty after Rodriguez cut down Jeter in an infamous 2001 *Esquire* interview. A PR man called the fight an "absolute fantasy" and denied any rift, but the item cited a "ballclub insider" who said the team was split right down the middle. Less than a year later, *GQ* picked up the item and ran with it, calling it one of "The Top Five Off-Field Sports Fights of the Decade."

The mainstream New York baseball media never reported on the event, or the non-event, depending on what you believe. As one longtime New York baseball writer mentioned early in the 2006 season, the Jeter-Rodriguez frostiness was one of the most underreported stories in New York. In a present-day culture where conspiracy theorists make fantastic movies and tabloids and blogs wield more clout than ever, the ultimate point probably isn't whether the fight actually happened. It's that it sounded totally and completely plausible—moreover, plausible enough for many to take the rumor seriously.

"Never. We've never had a scuffle since I've been here," Rodriguez said. "Not even close. No scuffle. That couldn't be further from the truth.

"We have a very good relationship. All you have to do is pay attention and see the way we interact. It's not hard to find out."

But Rodriguez and Jeter don't have a good relationship, using any number of barometers from any number of sources. Over the years, the two formerly tight buddies have drifted apart like continents breaking off from Pangaea.

Maybe the ultimate irony for the 2006 Yankees was that in a hellish year where Rodriguez, the 2005 AL MVP, was besieged by fans, media, opposing managers, and even his own teammates, Jeter was a leading candidate for winning the 2006 AL MVP. It was ironic because Jeter, who was cited for the award due to his leadership in steadying the ship after injuries to Hideki Matsui and Gary Sheffield, never lifted a finger publicly to take the heat off A-Rod. It was ironic because, other than Chuck Knoblauch's grotesque devolution into a Little League second baseman in 2001, it might have been the most necessary time in modern-day Yankee history for a captain to stand up in public support of a teammate during a season. And Jeter, literally, did nothing.

The way the season began, it looked as though A-Rod was going to be the hero, was going to be an MVP candidate again. When Hideki Matsui and Gary Sheffield went down within a few weeks' time in late April and May, Rodriguez picked up the slack. He smashed 8 homers in May with 28 RBIs and 25 runs, and he won the AL Player of the Month Award. His run-production numbers were better than Jeter's.

During that stretch, he said there was a sense of "not knowing where the hell this team was gonna go, where this ship was going to sail to. At the time, Boston was on fire. So that was probably the most questionable period of the year."

Then the season quickly turned hellish—not for the Yankees but for A-Rod. He started June 1 for 18 and went 1 for 10 against the Red Sox. He was coming up empty in the clutch and was subjected to boos virtually every night. It became so bad, fans were booing him *before* he came to the plate, not just when he made an out. He went hitless in 11 (of 24) games in June, the most of any month.

Rodriguez eventually admitted being bothered by the booing early in the season, more evidence about how sensitive he was. In May, he came up with his infamous Joe Carter quote.

"In my career, I've been hearing it for a long time," he told a group of reporters. "It will never stop until you win five or six World Series in a row, and hit a Joe Carter home run," referring to the three-run blast that brought Toronto its second straight World Series championship.

"I've done a lot of special things in this game, and for none of that to be considered clutch, it's an injustice. I don't take anything personally; I enjoy it, it motivates me, and I think it's comical. I think [for] anyone that drives in over 130 runs numerous times in his career, it's impossible not to be clutch."

Even when Rodriguez did something right, there was often an odor attached to it. On Wednesday, June 28, he hit a two-run homer off Atlanta's Jorge Sosa in the 12th inning for a 4-3 victory. He credited former manager Lou Piniella with helping him, telling radio broadcaster Suzyn Waldman that he'd worked with Piniella—his first manager in Seattle—until 3 A.M. that morning, and reportedly saying Piniella was "like an angel coming out of the sky." Joe Torre and Don Mattingly couldn't help but take note of that, which was a slap at the universally beloved hitting coach.

By a road trip in late July, after killing the club with a throwing error in one loss in Toronto, he had two hits and scored the go-ahead run in Texas. He then tried to compare his plight with that of Tiger Woods while speaking with beat reporters.

"You saw Tiger Woods three weeks ago, he didn't make the cut [at the U.S. Open], and he was thrown under every bus in the world. The same thing is going on with me. He just came back and won the British Open, so hopefully I can come back and shut some people up."

The difference was, Woods' father had died. Chalk up another misguided public statement.

On June 14, the legendary WFAN talk show hosts Mike and the Mad Dog argued that Jeter should stand up publicly and tell fans to stop booing, tell them they were making it worse. Jeter was apprised of the argument repeatedly, and he found it to be specious. He smiled wryly at the implications.

"You've got to realize one thing," Jeter said. "Everyone's been booed."

But would it have made it easier if he or Joe Torre had said something?

"Fans are going to do what they want to do," Jeter said. "It's not like I have some magic power to make people stop doing things.

"They're going to do what they want to do. It's something you've got to work yourself through. Like I said, if that was the case when they were booing me, I would've said, 'Hey, y'all stop booing me, please'? It doesn't happen like that."

With Jeter's silence, A-Rod slumped deeper and continued getting assailed in the press, taking body blow after body blow. Former Yankee David Justice pummeled him on the Yankee-owned YES Network on June 27 after previously telling people to be patient with Rodriguez, and at least one report stated the Yankee front-office handlers encouraged or ordered the hit.

"If the game is 9-2, he might make it 9-4," Justice said. "If the game is 7-1, he might make it 9-1. But when it is 2-2 late in the ball game and I need a base hit to score a run, the numbers show he has not been getting it done. . . .

"The one guy you need more than [Jeter, Johnny Damon, or Jason Giambi], just because of his sheer talent and ability to carry a ballclub on his back, is not answering the bell, and that is what is so frustrating to the fans. And I'm sure it is frustrating to him. . . .

"Everyone says he is going to come around, but if he comes around in two weeks, where will the Yankees be between now and two weeks?"

Number-one Yankee fan Rudy Giuliani respectfully disagreed with Jeter, and he was one of the few Yankee fans solidly in A-Rod's corner by late July. "America's Mayor" called up WFAN on July 24 and told Yankee fans exactly that. On the next homestand, it seemed as though they'd gotten the message. Rodriguez said the gesture "meant a lot to me."

"I thought it was a great, classy move, and very unexpected," Rodriguez said.

When asked about the notion that Jeter and/or Torre should've stood up and told the fans to knock off the booing, Rodriguez answered, "You've got to ask those guys about that. That's not me."

He disputed the notion that some teammates weren't supportive of him in his struggles, a theory that cemented into fact with the publishing of a cover story in *Sports Illustrated* on September 25 dubbing Rodriguez "The Lonely Yankee."

"Whoa, my teammates were very supportive," A-Rod said six days before the issue hit newsstands. "All of them. If you mention one or two, that's not my teammates. You've got to be specific. I had unbelievable support from my teammates."

Would Rodriguez ever go public in the press and say, "Don't boo this guy"?

"Would I ever do that? I don't know," he answered. "If the situation came up, I don't know how I would react. It's a hypothetical."

Jeter was a true student of the Yankees, falling in love with the team from the time his grandmother, Dorothy Connors, took him to his first game at the age of 6. By the time he was 8, he told his family he wanted to be a Yankee. According to his autobiography, *The Life You Imagine,* he hung a Yankee baseball cap and a uniform in his bedroom when he was an adolescent. There's a sense that with him, the awe has never completely worn off. During the first homestand of the year, Yankee players were given a copy of the 2006 team yearbook. Players are given so much free swag, from iPods to DVD players, it would astonish the average fan. Most of the giveaways go in the back of a player's locker, becoming clutter by the All-Star Game. And frankly, to see a player reading something other than *Field & Stream* or *Maxim* is quite astonishing.

But one day, before an afternoon game with Kansas City, Jeter leafed through the yearbook while sitting in front of his locker. He perused the glossy book, which was about half as thick as a phone book, studying the contents intently. Jeter was a Dave Winfield fan, oddly enough. Winfield had once been dubbed "Mr. May" by George Steinbrenner for a lack of clutch hitting, in direct contrast to Reggie Jackson. But Jeter also could rattle off the names Gehrig, Ruth, Munson, DiMaggio, and Mantle rat-a-tat-tat, and he understood their place in baseball lore. To the captain, there is a responsibility to wear the pinstripes with pride, to never embarrass a franchise steeped in grandeur.

"You're representing something more than yourself when you play for this team and play for this organization," he said. "You're representing all the players who have played here in the past, tradition, pride, excellence.

"Those are the things you have to take into consideration with how you carry yourself."

By coming through the organization, Jeter said, he learned about the qualities that make a Yankee great. But he also believed that it was innate, that he'd learned similar lessons growing up. He knew how to conduct himself in the most sacred clubhouse in professional sports. The notion that the clubhouse was more corporate in 2006 than it had been in 1996 isn't one that Jeter buys.

"I wouldn't necessarily say that," Jeter said. "People act a certain way when the media's in here. Because anything you do, people write about it and they run with stories. When the media's gone, people's personalities really come out."

OK, but is it as loose as any other clubhouse?

"I don't know, because this is the only clubhouse that I've been in," he said. "To be honest with you, I don't care about anyone's personality. As long as when they're on the field, they care about winning. As long as that's the case, you can act any way you want to act."

There have been changes since 1996, Jeter acknowledged, because the Yankees weren't expected to win that season. After they won once, the expectations were raised. He sees a difference between pressure and expectation level, although the unrelenting march to a world championship creates something unique in the Bronx. The Red Sox don't have the same mandate. Neither do the Mets.

Whether or not the Yankee dynasty is over is a matter of debate. Some thought it ended in 2001 after a Game 7 World Series loss to Arizona, when Paul O'Neill and Scott Brosius retired and Tino Martinez left the team. Others believe the run of nine straight AL East titles and twelve straight postseason appearances means the dynasty is still intact, pointing to the fact that after their last title, in 2000, the Yankees lost to the eventual world champions from 2001 through 2004.

"It may be kind of difficult to say a new era," he said. "Because [when] I think separate eras, the theory is maybe when you're rebuilding or things like that. In terms of making it to the playoffs and things, that pretty much has continued.

"I think when you say new era, you have to separate really going through some struggles. That's just my take on it. Someone else might have another take."

On June 3, 2003, Jeter was named the eleventh captain in club history. He thought that George Steinbrenner gave him the lofty title because of the way he always conducted himself, and he didn't think he needed to change. The only difference that he saw was that teammates came up to him a little bit more, asked him a few more questions. He already played with a responsibility to the Yankees, always carried himself well and played the game right because it was his responsibility to the fans. He tried to relate well to his teammates, although the A-Rod situation was an area where he fell short.

"Everyone's different, and everyone has different personalities, everyone has different demeanors," Jeter said. "Everyone handles things differently. So you can't say you treat everyone the same. You treat everyone fairly, but not the same."

Asked for an example, Jeter compared his longtime pal Jorge Posada with Miguel Cairo. Posada and Jeter were minor-league teammates back in 1992 in Greensboro, North Carolina. Cairo became a Yankee in 2004.

"Say for example hypothetically Miggy did something," Jeter said, declining to elaborate further. "Say Sado [Posada] did something. I know Sado better than I know Miggy, even though I know Miggy well.

"Say Miggy was very sensitive—*sensitivo*—so you know what I'm saying?" Jeter said as Cairo, tying his shoes, looked up for a moment a few lockers over. "You have to approach in different ways or handle situations. You have to know people's personalities."

Jeter then compared it to a friend from grade school versus a friend from college. You have more shared experiences with your grade-school buddy, so you're bound to interact in a different way.

As Jeter saw it, his role as the captain (or as a teammate) was to be supportive of the other Yankees, not to start handing down edicts to fans. When he was confronted with the idea that if he really cared about A-Rod, he would say something publicly, he countered with the evidence that he didn't tell the fans to stop booing Mariano Rivera in early 2005.

"That's just people trying to make up stories," Jeter summarized. "I mean, people try to put a twist in every story. But that's people trying to put a twist in a story any way they want to."

The twist to this story was this: when Jason Giambi became a pariah in the winter of 2004 because his grand jury testimony (in which he reportedly copped to steroid use) was leaked, Jeter called Giambi personally. He spoke out in support of Giambi with the media. He even visited Giambi in Las Vegas during the weekend of the Super Bowl. He went out on a limb for one of his teammates, and Giambi never forgot the gesture.

"Jason made a mistake, obviously," Jeter said during that period. "Everyone makes mistakes. He's got to deal with it. So it's an unfortunate situation, and you feel for him because he's going through it, but if he's back with us—he's on our team, so I would expect him to be back—you've got to support him."

For his part, Giambi couldn't thank Jeter enough and said he still would've considered Jeter a friend even if he'd kept his mouth shut ("He's Derek Jeter—he doesn't need to be getting into the stuff that was going on with me," was one Giambi quote from that period), but the captain was front and center alongside a teammate in need.

"I think it's pretty simple: When someone goes through struggles, that's when they need support," Jeter was quoted as saying about the Giambi situation. "So that's what you do."

That's what you do if a teammate allegedly, reportedly violates the drug laws of the country and the rules of the sport, but what about when another teammate is getting pilloried in the town square of public opinion for nothing worse than a fielding and hitting slump? Apparently, then, mum's the word.

The other twist was that while Jeter didn't think he had any extra obligation to A-Rod, Sheffield was feeling awful about the situation. Sheffield felt he could've made a difference if he'd been alongside Rodriguez in uniform. Instead, he was out after undergoing surgery on his left wrist in June. Sheffield has often been portrayed as selfish and cold-blooded, and rightly so. Meanwhile, tens of thousands of young ladies have fallen in love with a Jeter who's portrayed as warm and fuzzy to the MTV set (he has even dated an MTV VJ, Vanessa Minnillo). But in this instance, the roles were reversed. Sheffield was torn up that he couldn't help either A-Rod or starter Shawn Chacon, who lost his job and was traded in late July, and his face showed the anguish as he discussed the issue.

"It's hard for me to just see Alex going through what he's going through," Sheffield said. "I felt like if I was there, I could make a difference towards those guys. I could take the heat off those guys. Because so much attention is paid to me, on and off the field. I think it alleviates them having to deal with all the bulk of what they have to deal with."

While Jeter didn't betray any concern in the world about Rodriguez's struggles, other than saying, "It's something you've got to work yourself through," Sheffield was extremely worried about the long-term ramifications for A-Rod's psyche.

"I know it's going to make him stronger," Sheffield said, adding after a pause, "but I just hope that it doesn't hinder what he really could become. That's the only fear that I have—it will hinder what he truly is: probably the greatest player who ever lived. And he could be that. And I think the negative stuff, getting hit every day with that at this point in his life, I just hope it just doesn't hinder that."

Sheffield wasn't going to approach A-Rod, he said, because he wasn't the type of player to give unsolicited advice—"rush you," in Sheffield's vernacular. But he had developed a bond with Rodriguez where the two-time MVP could come to him the way a younger brother would. During the 2005 All-Star Game he'd called A-Rod "our jewel."

"I've been the best player on the team for a decade, I've been all of that," Sheffield said. "I've been where nobody torched nobody else on the team but me. I've been the highest-paid. So I don't know exactly everything he's been through, but I can kind of understand . . . because I've been there.

"I came into the league at eighteen years old, so I've got the bulk of that. I just think that our relationship has gotten so strong, he feels comfortable with approaching me about a lot of things now, as opposed to some things. He approaches me about most everything.

"And I can give him great advice because I've been through it. And to walk in the footsteps that I've walked, you had to be strong. And for me to be still standing, that's my testimony to him."

What was Jeter's testimony? On this topic, it's worth consulting the Book of Jeter, aka his 2000 autobiography, *The Life You Imagine* (written with *New York Times* scribe Jack Curry). On August 6, 1999, Jeter found himself in another controversy with a teammate—one that directly involved Rodriguez.

During the end of a bench-clearing brawl in Seattle, Jeter and Rodriguez found themselves next to each other as order was being restored. According to Jeter's book, A-Rod turned to him as the teams were heading back to the dugouts and said, "If we fight again, I'm coming after you." Jeter said he might've smiled or smirked at the comment, which was what TV cameras caught when they saw the two superstar shortstops chumming it up during an ugly altercation.

The scene looked bad to many, including Yankee bench player Chad Curtis, and he confronted Jeter about it on the field and again in the clubhouse with a host of reporters watching. According to the book, he told Jeter, "You're a good player, but you don't know how to play the game." Jeter disagreed with Curtis' way of handling the incident, said he didn't know what he was talking about, and unapologetically cut off Curtis—for life. Ironically, Rodriguez went to bat for Jeter, calling it "unfair criticism . . . to be knocking Derek, who is the ultimate team player and the ultimate professional, in any way, shape, or form." Seven years later, what kind of a difference could it have made to Yankee fans if Jeter had said those same few words about A-Rod?

But the incident revealed Jeter's own cold-blooded side, a side he hides from the general public because he admits he doesn't like showing his emotions. As he wrote, "I didn't have to deal with Chad anymore. That's the way I dealt with the situation. . . . He was my teammate and I wanted him to do well for the team, but I wasn't going to talk to the guy or go to dinner with him. No way, not after what he did. I didn't want to be bothered with Chad."

If Jeter was this upset about being called out by a journeyman backup in front of twelve reporters, how deep did his bitterness toward Rodriguez really go after the ballyhooed *Esquire* article? How long did he hold his grudge?

Keep in mind, in Jeter's autobiography, published before A-Rod's *Esquire* slip-up, he called A-Rod a role model and "my good friend" and published a full-color photograph of the then Seattle shortstop trying to complete a double play past a sliding Jeter. A-Rod similarly gushed about their friendship.

"At this point Derek has become like my brother," A-Rod said in the book. "I think the nice thing about it is we became good friends before we even made it to the big leagues. That makes it more of a healthy relationship."

When asked in 2006 if his friendship had changed with Rodriguez over the years, Jeter repeated the question and asked, "What do you mean?"

Had it changed from when they first met and hung out?

"Even when we hung out, Alex was in Seattle," he said. "I'm in New York. I'd see him a couple times a year. That's about it."

So it was fair to say he was always a guy Jeter was friendly with, but not necessarily a best friend?

"Well, I mean it would be impossible," Jeter said. "The geography."

Had being his teammate allowed them to get closer?

"Well, yeah, we're around each other every day now, so it's a little bit different," he said. "But he's got a family now. It's not like we're eighteen years old hanging out every single night."

As Jeter continued down a road he clearly had no desire to travel, his voice became low, almost hurt. "People are so concerned about our friendship and things like that," he said. "We're teammates, man. We're on the same team."

So you don't have to be best friends with everyone you work with?

"That's for everyone. In '98, '99, 2000, there are guys on that team that I never went out to eat with. After the game, that's why people have families. You do your own thing, but you're still a team. People are so concerned with what everybody does away from the field. It has no bearing on how you are as teammates."

Rodriguez's take on the friendship: "We have a good relationship. The relationship is good. It's good." Silence hung in the air as Rodriguez waited for the next question.

Perhaps the two most telling passive-aggressive exchanges of the year between Jeter and A-Rod came after the All-Star break, when the Yankees were fighting tooth and nail to stay in the playoff race. The Tigers were 59-29 after the first half, and the White Sox were 57-31 and leading the wild-card race. The Yanks, meanwhile, were 50-36, three games behind Boston and six games back in the wild-card standings. At the All-Star Game, Rodriguez said, "The wild card will not come out of the East. Period." When asked how confident he was in that statement, Rodriguez replied, "One hundred percent."

On July 15, after the Yanks had taken the first two games from the White Sox to start the second half, Jeter scoffed at the notion that the Bombers couldn't win the wild card.

"I don't know who's been saying it," he said derisively, a barb aimed across the clubhouse. "I haven't been saying it. I mean, we have seventy-something games left. You can't just punch a team's ticket with seventy-something games left.

"Why not [two playoff teams from the East]? Not saying that we're worried about a wild card. We're trying to win a division. Four games with seventy-something games left, I don't think that's that big of a lead . . . Four games, three games . . . that's a week, when you think about it."

A-Rod wasn't the only one in the Yankee clubhouse with that opinion. Johnny Damon sided with him, thinking that the Yanks needed to win the division to reach the playoffs.

"I'm a firm believer, I think the wild card is coming from the [Central] division," A-Rod said. "I really do. I don't think any of those teams is going to slow down.

"And I think it's best for us to think about the East. I don't think in mid-July we should be thinking about the wild card. . . . The thing about the White Sox is, they could go and leave this place and win eighteen out of twenty."

The incident was another window into the souls of the two men. Jeter was unable to concede anything to an opponent in the sphere of competition and was willing to make a teammate look bad with carefully chosen words to get his point across. Rodriguez, meanwhile, was the superstar apt to put his foot in his mouth by admitting something politically incorrect—something, incidentally, that many baseball observers believed at that point in the season. Of course, the Yankees played terrific baseball in the second half, passing both Chicago and Detroit in the standings. However, the Red Sox plummeted out of the playoff race. So while Minnesota won the AL Central, the Tigers hung on as the wild-card team. Technically, A-Rod ended up being right. He was vindicated by the truth. But Jeter's logic was Yankee logic.

On August 17, there was another infamous incident that the media jumped on. Right before the pivotal series of the season in Fenway, A-Rod and Jeter collided on a pop-up in the sixth inning of a 12-2 loss to Baltimore. Jeter knocked the ball out of Rodriguez's glove, and A-Rod was initially charged with the error before it was given to Jeter.

Jeter was shading his eyes from the sun with his glove and screaming, "I got it!" A-Rod, camped under the pop-up, didn't appear to yell anything (although he said he did). Jeter knocked the ball out of A-Rod's glove to the ground. Jeter began running off the field, thinking A-Rod had caught the ball for the final out of the inning. Some in the media thought Jeter was trying to show up A-Rod by running off the field, which the Yankee captain insisted wasn't the case. Upon looking at video replays, it simply appeared the shortstop and third baseman were not in synch—which any Yankee fan could've told you before the play. One report noted they both looked disgusted after the ball dropped.

A run scored on the play, and the subsequent hitter, Fernando Tatis, ripped a two-run homer. Jeter knew the issue would be blown up, much to his disdain.

"What happened?" Jeter asked. "It was dropped. It was hit, I was calling it, I guess he didn't hear me. I thought he had it. He said to me, 'Do you have it?' I said, 'You got it?' I thought he was playing around, so I started running off the field, because I didn't touch it. That's all the story you can do with a pop-up.

"The sun had nothing to do with it. I thought he caught it, so that's why I started running off the field. I don't know how big you can make this story. It's a pop-up that wasn't caught. That's about it."

A-Rod's take?

"Just a goofy play, that's all," he said. "He called it, I called it, we didn't hear each other. I'm not worried about it. No big deal. Just a stat. It's a goofy play all around. Kind of epitomizes the whole day."

Whom did Torre side with? The Yankee manager noted that the shortstop has jurisdiction on any pop-up in his range if he wants it. He bristled at the notion that it proved these two literally couldn't play side by side with one another.

"Oh, that's just evidence why they don't get along, right," Torre said sarcastically. "They're trying to catch the same fly ball."

Jeter, for his part, seemed surprised he was charged with an error, according to reports.

For those who followed the team and watched each player, it was, more than anything else, a matter of taste. What do you value? Coke or Pepsi? McDonald's or Burger King?

Rodriguez was the supremely talented shortstop who signed a ten-year, $252 million contract with Texas, the largest contract in North American sports. By the winter of 2003, A-Rod was miserable in Arlington and looking for a way out. At first, it looked as if Boston would acquire him, but the Players Association vetoed the deal because A-Rod was willing to cut his own salary too drastically ($28 to $30 million, according to one report), a no-no among the union hard-liners. Instead, just before spring training 2004, he was acquired by the Yankees after agreeing to switch to third base, an alien position. He jumped at the opportunity.

"It means everything to me," Rodriguez said of being a Yankee. "Out of all the things that I've accomplished in my career, the thing I'm most proud of is to be able to put this uniform on and be a part of the greatest franchise in sports history.

"See, I don't know if people just have it all wrong with me or whatnot. I don't care about myself. Everyone said, 'You're one home run shy of [Cal] Ripken [Jr.] and the [home-run] record [for shortstops].' It meant zero. It doesn't really matter.

"I think as a competitor, it's frustrating not being able to accomplish your goal every year, which is to go to the World Series and win the World Series. A team like this, we're fortunate every year we have an opportunity to win the World Series. And that's a tribute to our owner and our great manager."

Had Rodriguez been brought up through the Yankee organization, he conceded, it would've been "much easier" to adapt to the fans and media. But he cited other players who had initially established themselves in other cities before coming to New York, such as Reggie Jackson, Paul O'Neill, and David Cone, as role models. At one point he said he loved and admired them.

While Jeter received the lion's share of positive press, Rodriguez was often fed to the lions. Jeter would only rarely reveal the less savory side of his personality. Although he always watched what he'd say in front of the media, he didn't worry about criticizing a ball boy in full view in the clubhouse. Also, he occasionally upbraided a favorite whipping boy a few locker stalls over from him, Miguel Cairo. Perhaps it was a function of being the captain, or perhaps it was just his personality.

Jeter brought four World Series titles to New York before A-Rod agitated his way out of Texas, and naturally many people never considered Rodriguez a real Yankee even into his third season in pinstripes. Jeter was a homegrown kid who'd made good. Rodriguez was a carpetbagger.

Their interactions with the press may also reveal how they were portrayed. While A-Rod would arrogantly walk away from media members when he decided an interview was over, Jeter would stand at length but give bland, often contrarian answers to both biting and innocuous questions. Many reporters found A-Rod off-putting, even odious for the way he would nod, break eye contact, and leave a reporter standing in front of his locker with pen still in hand. Certainly, it was much ruder than Jeter's passive-aggressive attempts to throw a wet blanket over any line of questioning with some sizzle to it.

Rodriguez, it was said, also knew the names of every beat writer and columnist in the city, and he would unapologetically mete out time accordingly (Jeter often said, "Hey, buddy" to those who had been in the New York media for years). A-Rod gave those with the most clout the most time, the most honesty, and even the most latitude to rip him. He remained close with certain columnists who went after him unmercifully. Naturally, this rankled people on the low end of the press scale. Jeter might not give you anything, the thought went, but at least he sat by his locker and listened to your questions, whether you were Mike Lupica or Joe Shortwave, radio reporter for a 50-watt station on Staten Island.

Although Jeter was certainly fascinating in his own right, Rodriguez seemed the more complex character study. For someone who could act standoffish, A-Rod also acted more outwardly jovial to the fringe people who make up the Yankee Fishbowl, more inviting, more warm. His critics, of course, labeled him too phony, too polished.

Less than a week before *SI*'s "Lonely Yankee" story broke, the third baseman was amiably palling around with a number of people in the home clubhouse. When former major leaguer Jim Kaat, a broadcaster with the YES Network, walked through the clubhouse, Rodriguez asked him why he was retiring and chatted him up. Kaat discussed his first major-league victory as a Washington Senator in 1960, when he allowed four runs to the Yankees against Whitey Ford. Rodriguez, a student of the game, was enraptured.

Mariano Rivera, whom A-Rod had turned to for counsel and support, walked by A-Rod's locker on the way into the players' lounge.

"Hey, Mo," Rodriguez said, catching Rivera by his right arm.

The two momentarily spoke Spanish and Rodriguez gave a playful tug on the arm of Rivera, who was out in early September with a right forearm strain.

"Alex, don't pull his arm," Mike Myers said, his eyes fairly popping out of his skull. "Let go of his arm."

Later, when director of video operations Charlie Wonsowicz came over, Rodriguez let out a hearty "Hey, Charlie, what's up, my friend?" and gave him a solid handshake. When radio broadcaster Suzyn Waldman came over, he said, "I thought of you when I rounded first [the previous night], I swear."

On September 13, Rodriguez launched a homer into the black bleachers in center against Tampa Bay, a prodigious poke during a September in which he regained his stroke. Before the game that night, Waldman had instructed him, "Don't forget: right, right center." It was Waldman's contention that A-Rod was at his best when he was hitting the ball to the opposite field, and the slugger agreed.

"Not quite right center, but center," he told her with a smile.

Whether he was merely making Waldman feel good about their conversation or whether he'd actually had that thought, the effect was the same: A-Rod was thinking of someone besides himself, was reaching out, was making a connection at a human level.

In many ways, though, Rodriguez's 2006 journey was a solitary walk. From the time he waffled about picking a WBC team in the springtime (he was called a modern-day Hamlet), he was a man on an island. That's never the way he looked at it, though. Asked whom on the team he was really close to, whom he ate dinner with, Rodriguez asserted he was "close with everybody." He mentioned Johnny Damon, whom he'd first met when the two were high-school stars in the state of Florida. He mentioned that Rivera, a Yankee mentor of sorts, was "extremely close" with him. He mentioned Sheffield.

"All these guys," he said. "The way they've welcomed me in here has been incredible.

"I'm very blessed because of that. It's the best clubhouse I've ever been in in my career. It's a very tight, loose group. I think Johnny Damon has a lot to do with that. He's just brought an unbelievable dynamic to this team, along with many other guys. Mike [Myers]. There's been pieces that have fit like a glove in here."

Rodriguez felt it was difficult for him to comment on his stature in the Yankee Fishbowl, difficult for him to assess where he stood. He preferred to let others either defend or castigate him.

"You've got to ask my teammates about me," he said. "If you're an asshole, like some people might want me to be an asshole or portray, everyone knows you're an asshole. If you're phony, if you're fake, if you're this, if you're that, all these words have been used to describe me, you've got to ask my teammates.

"Ask the trainers. Ask the ball boys. I mean, those are the guys who are going to tell you the truth. And then you write the truth. You don't write what you think people want to read."

By July, the open rift between Rodriguez and some teammates was becoming apparent to anyone who was looking closely, especially regarding Giambi. The Central Park storyline was one example. On July 17, Rodriguez was photographed sunning himself shirtless in Central Park for over an hour when the temperature was 95 and the heat index was 102. That night, he committed his first three-error game in 1,680 major-league contests. The next day, though, he laughed off the suggestion that he might have been suffering from heatstroke or dehydration. My story in the next day's *New York Post* questioned whether there was a correlation and described teammates' amazed reactions to A-Rod's day in the sun.

The day a shirtless picture of A-Rod sunning in Central Park appeared in the *Post,* Giambi was aghast. He called the situation "unbelievable" and declared that Rodriguez brought some of this unwarranted and negative scrutiny upon himself. Giambi agreed with a reporter who joked that the rock Rodriguez was leaning against that blistering day was hot enough to spew lava. Rodriguez was, in Giambi's words, a "glutton for punishment."

Later in the season, the Yankee first baseman was quoted in *Sports Illustrated* as saying Rodriguez held "a false confidence." Another Giambi quote, on the *SI* cover, declared, "Alex doesn't know who he is. We're going to find out who he is in the next couple of months." The crux of the Giambi angle of the story was that the Yankee first baseman and third baseman were at odds because A-Rod wouldn't emotionally own up to his season-altering slump. Giambi had even asked manager Joe Torre to speak with A-Rod in August, the story revealed.

The revelation was troubling on a number of different levels. First, Giambi was immediately criticized as a hypocrite for the "false confidence" tag he slapped on A-Rod, considering there's strong anecdotal evidence that Giambi owes his confidence to illegal steroids, which would certainly fall into the false category. Use of such steroids turned Giambi into a different person, it could be argued, one who sacrificed his true, pre-bloated self on the altar of performance-enhancing drugs. It's easy to have confidence when you puff yourself up on juice the same way a barfly chugs liquid courage before starting a bar fight.

Maybe the most disconcerting notion was that Torre needed Giambi to inform him of A-Rod's delusions and needed a player to cajole him into action. True, by this time the sixty-six-year-old Torre delegated much to his coaches. And yes, it was reported that by 2006 Torre had tired of the high maintenance that Rodriguez required. But the fact that in August he'd be so obtuse (or else so numbed) to the maelstrom surrounding A-Rod was perplexing, if not outright disturbing.

Someone needed to attend to the care and nurturing of A-Rod's fragile ego, but Torre left A-Rod to his own devices. Then he and Giambi exposed him.

The *SI* story by Tom Verducci revealed a startling anecdote that described in perfect detail how polished Rodriguez truly tried to be. In December 2003, as the Red Sox were trying to acquire Rodriguez, they met him in a hotel suite at 1 A.M. A-Rod was still dressed in an expensive suit and tie, which the Boston execs found "odd" and "unsettling."

It's one criticism Rodriguez blanched at. His path is that of the American Dream. He was born into an impoverished background in the Washington Heights section of Manhattan, lived in the Dominican Republic, and came of age in Miami, always struggling to make ends meet after his father left his family. He recalled nights counting tip money with his mother after her waitress gig, and when $40 was a great night. From there, Rodriguez has become one of the most sharply dressed men in the world and one of the athletes most sought after for endorsements.

"Well, OK, if you're calling me too polished, OK, is one thing," he said. "But if you come out and say something like Big Papi, you get destroyed for that.

"So the thing is," Rodriguez said, "I make $25 million a year, and you can't get around that. . . . If I was a guy who was a utility player, I'd be a nice guy who was polished. Like Mike, there's no one more polished than Mike," Rodriguez said, pointing in the direction of Myers, the team's situational lefty.

"Guess what?" A-Rod said. "He's [the baseball equivalent of] a punter.

"I think people are jealous. There's a lot of that that goes on. Besides that, take away the contract, I'm a pretty likable guy. Accessible. I don't run, I don't hide. No one is going to go through a tougher time than I went through this summer. I never blamed anybody, I never said I wanted out. But yet no one writes that."

Earlier in that conversation Rodriguez referred to the media's reaction to something Boston slugger David Ortiz had said a few days earlier, and he had a great point. Ortiz had stuck his foot in his mouth during a conversation in which he criticized the MVP voting and, more specifically, Jeter's chances of winning the award.

"They're talking about Jeter a lot, right?" Ortiz asked a *Boston Globe* reporter late in the season. "He's done a great job, he's having a great season, but Jeter is not a 40-homer hitter or an RBI guy.

"It doesn't matter how much you've done for your ball club, the bottom line is, the guy who hits 40 home runs and knocks in 100, that's the guy you know helped your team win games.

"Don't get me wrong—he's a great player, having a great season, but he's got a lot of guys in that lineup. Top to bottom, you've got a guy who can hurt you. Come hit in this lineup, see how good you can be."

It was foolish of Ortiz to talk about personal goals, which someone like Jeter never does. Ironically, though, the comments were very similar to the ones a "polished" Rodriguez uttered in the infamous April 2001 *Esquire* article.

"The thing about [New York *Daily News* columnist] Mike Lupica that pisses me off is that he makes me look like the biggest [expletive] in the world, and then he takes a guy like Jeter and just puts him way up there," Rodriguez told *Esquire*. "Jeter's been blessed with great talent around him. He's never had to lead. He can just go and play and have fun. And he hits second—that's totally different than third and fourth in a lineup. You go into New York, you wanna stop Bernie [Williams] and [Paul] O'Neill. You never say, Don't let Derek beat you. He's never your concern."

Rodriguez learned the hard way, because many insiders believe Jeter never forgave him for those comments. And for a time in 2006, it looked as though Jeter might freeze Ortiz out or make him look bad in the same fashion.

"I'm not thinking about the MVP," Jeter initially told reporters. "No one's focus here is individual awards. We've still got something to play for this season."

Yet when Ortiz came to Yankee Stadium in September after his comments, he met with Jeter for about seven minutes outside the clubhouse and apologized for saying stupid stuff, in his words. Every time Ortiz batted that weekend, Ortiz was serenaded with "Derek Jeter!" chants from the crowd. But when he reached second base after doubling in his first at-bat in the first game, he made a joke to Jeter and the shortstop could be seen smiling. And at the end of the inning, with Ortiz still at second, Jeter slapped him on the butt with his glove before heading to the dugout. In the world of Jeter, where little gestures mean everything, the pat on the ass was a sign that all would be forgiven. Ortiz, it seemed, would escape a Jeter freeze-out, which people around him have said a person can never emerge from.

In July, former Met GM Steve Phillips banged the drum on ESPN's *Baseball Tonight* for the idea that the Yankees should trade Rodriguez in the off-season. Before the trade deadline, a rumor (that was circulating around Wall Street, according to the *New York Post*) had A-Rod headed to Philly. Rodriguez laughed at the rumor and said he'd veto the deal with his no-trade clause. Yet for someone who never wanted out, Rodriguez certainly had an excellent understanding of what it would take to acquire him in a deal.

"First of all, no one writes that I make $14 million a year with the Yankees," he said, noting that Texas was paying $10 million of his salary for 2006 and was on the hook for $41 million more until 2010. "And the fact that they say I'm . . . non-tradable. But I have ten teams out there that would take me for $14 million. And by the way, if the Yankees take $4, for $10 million . . . Eh? That's number one."

That quote, in a nutshell, sums up the thirty-one-year-old superstar. His intelligence and his awareness of a situation can be uncanny, but so can his ability to say the wrong thing. He can think like the shrewdest GM in the business, but he can also come off as overly calculating and entirely unlikable.

This was narcissism at its absolute worst. It wasn't enough that Rodriguez was playing for the most privileged franchise in baseball, wasn't enough that the Yankees were headed to the playoffs. He couldn't bear the idea that he was only in New York because of an onerous contract. More to the point, he couldn't bear the idea that nobody else wanted him. This was A-Rod's neediness coming out, his desire to be universally loved, and it was also something else, something more disturbing: the first sign of his escape hatch.

For someone who supposedly never wanted out, he certainly knew what it would take for a one-way ticket elsewhere. Would Jeter even think about what it would cost another team to acquire him, ever calculate the teams that might want him? Of course not. But here was A-Rod, weeks before the postseason, floating an exit strategy, albeit a hypothetical one. Still, so much of sports is mental, and how often did Rodriguez think of the math (14 minus 4) while he was going through a hellacious August? How often did he fantasize about playing in Chicago or Los Angeles (14 minus 4) or parts unknown? What, if any, effect did it have (14 minus 4) on his play? Was he selling the Yankees short in 2006, preparing to emotionally detach himself from them? It was a comment only somebody with wanderlust would make. Put it this way: it was at least as thought-out as the Bush administration's exit strategy in Iraq.

"Number two, nobody writes that this guy just kept going out there and out there," Rodriguez continued. "There's a lot to be said for that. 'This guy never ducked us.' But they'll just pound and pound and pound. I think that's just poor journalism, how the media has wanted to treat me. And I've never been resentful for that."

As far as playing every day, Rodriguez dropped a mention on August 13 to the *New York Post*'s Joel Sherman that he was fighting nonspecific physical issues that apparently hampered his hitting and fielding. It was another public misstep, because great players never blame poor performance on injuries, especially mysterious ones. It seemed another situation in which the hypersensitive Rodriguez wanted people to sympathize with him. One thing virtually everyone agrees on is that he's too sensitive, too eager to please people, too willing to try to quell the critics. It's something that at one time or another countless baseball columnists have touched upon, and it's become assumed as a fact by this point. It's one reason why, armchair psychologists have surmised, he works tirelessly at his craft, to the point of paralysis by analysis.

"The one thing I will tell you, and people don't write this, is they tell you, 'This guy's not sensitive.' Because I am not sensitive."

Alex Rodriguez is not sensitive?

"No one's ever written that. I've never heard that," he said a moment later. "Ever. I'm too sensitive? If I'm too sensitive, I'd be dead." He laughed. "Dead, I'd be fucking . . . Jesus Christ, I'd better not be sensitive, or else I never would've put myself in this situation," he said.

What other people see as sensitive, Rodriguez sees as the exact opposite. For example, when I approached him on September 13 to talk about the 2006 season, he immediately mentioned that he hadn't liked my line of questioning about Central Park back on July 18. He was polite but pointed. He told me it had been in "very poor taste" and indicated that he thought I'd made an attempt to embarrass him in a group setting— "fifteen to one," as he called it. He instructed me to ask him one on one about such matters in the future. It wasn't a wholly unreasonable request.

But A-Rod didn't say anything about my story in the *Post* until almost two months after the fact. When I asked him why he hadn't talked to me the day after the story appeared, Rodriguez said he hadn't had the "time or energy" to waste. But why bring it up two months later?

Rodriguez did say on September 14, "I didn't hold it against you. Some people, if you write one little thing, they won't talk to you for five years," he said. "I don't read anything. I've never read an article you've written.

"I think I'm the only guy on this team who doesn't read the paper. That's another big thing that people want to attack. Everybody reads the paper here."

It's worth noting that A-Rod said he was upset not at what I wrote (a possible correlation between sunning himself on a 95-degree day and three errors, and an amused reaction by teammates) but at the fact that I asked him about it in a group interview. In over six years in New York, I can recall only one other time when someone was angry about what was *asked* instead of what was *written*.

Rodriguez's protest seemed overcalculated, though. When an athlete admits he reads his own press clippings, that's often seen as proof that he's too sensitive or thin-skinned. Rodriguez wanted it to be known that he never read the paper (even though he learned every beat writer's name upon coming to New York). Moreover, that's not what various media outlets have been reporting for years. In fact, more than one writer has said Rodriguez reads *everything*. Seattle columnist Steve Kelley tells a story about A-Rod's time in Seattle when Kelley one day (ironically) wrote that Rodriguez should move to third base.

"He saw me the next day in a downtown clothing store and, without breaking stride, walked past me and said, 'I ain't playing third,'" Kelley later wrote.

To hear Rodriguez say he doesn't read the paper is like hearing Little Red Riding Hood declare that her favorite color is black. OK, if you say so . . .

Rodriguez was asked if someone—his agent, his spouse—reads the paper for him.

"No, it's natural that if somebody blasts you, you might have a friend say, 'Hey, so-and-so blasted you,'" he explained. "They blasted you in the paper, my question is, 'Who was the writer?' But I'm not going to go and read what the guy wrote, because what the hell . . . I know who my enemies are."

In 2006, the Bronx seemed a world away from Seattle, where Rodriguez was drafted and made a name for himself, and Texas, where he signed the biggest contract in baseball history. The two teams have fewer combined traveling beat writers than the New York media market.

"I knew this situation was going to be heaven or hell," he said. "There's nothing in between. You're also smart enough to know that when they blame something on you, like the five-game series last year [against the Angels], that's all garbage. Because it's a team sport, it's not tennis or golf, there's other guys on the team."

But if it's "garbage," why did he take the heat after the Yankees lost the Division Series in a fifth and deciding game in Anaheim in 2005? If it's garbage, why did he tell reporters he played like "a dog"?

"Because that's who I am," he answered. "I'm a stand-up guy. I don't hide. I also said I didn't do *my* part. Twenty-five-man team. The other guys . . . there's twenty-four other guys."

So much of what Rodriguez says seems to fit into one of two categories: disingenuous or disconcerting. Either he's telling you what he thinks you want to hear or you can't believe your ears. The "garbage" comment falls into the latter category, for obvious reasons.

Torre might have cut to the quick before Game 3 of the 2006 playoffs, might have figured out the essence of A-Rod. He told the beat reporters, "Maybe Alex, in trying to say the right things a lot of times, doesn't say the right things. [And that] sort of calls more attention to himself." But if the manager could be so astute an observer, that begs the question of why he didn't try to remedy the situation.

A-Rod has become a lightning rod in New York, perhaps more than any other player since Reggie Jackson. From the World Baseball Classic to Central Park to the booing that seems to follow him around like Pigpen's dirt cloud, Rodriguez has taken the hits. On that day in mid-September, he gave only one possible explanation.

"I think it's my contract," he said. "I think it all goes back there, unless you've got a better answer. Again, if I make $3 million a year, nobody's going to read what the fuck you're writing.

"The bottom line is that if you write something about me, people are going to read it. If you write something about Pete the ball boy here . . . So it's obviously a compelling story. I think people just like to read about me. I don't know."

He paused.

"What do you think?" he asked.

"I think you're an entertaining read," I replied.

"It really is," he agreed. "Good or bad."

Rodriguez professed confidence that Sheffield's fear wouldn't come to pass, that the New York media and fans wouldn't come to break him.

"For me personally, it's probably going to be the most productive year of my career from a sense of learning who you are, learning who those around you are—and really getting to appreciate how great this game is," he said. "Appreciate that you're able to accomplish great things in this game . . . [and] that it's not that easy. And if people take it for granted, I'm certainly not going to take it for granted."

When Rodriguez looked back at the 2006 regular season, he said his main problem was "not being able to get caught up in a rhythm. I can't point to one thing."

"I've been absolutely horseshit this year," Rodriguez told the New York *Daily News* on August 10. "In every facet of the game. I don't know why, but I think it's behind me. I'm not concerned with it because I'm in a good place now."

That night, he committed a throwing error in Chicago that led to a 5-4 loss. He also went 0 for 4 and twice failed to bring home a runner from third with less than two outs, a 2006 bugaboo for him. According to the Elias Sports Bureau, he had 49 chances in '06 in that spot and only came through 22 times (44.9 percent). The major-league average was 55.7 percent, according to Elias.

He was even more dismissive of his problems at third base. At one point, people were comparing him to Chuck Knoblauch. He settled down in the final six weeks before the playoffs, though, making only two errors in the team's final 42 games.

"It's a tough position," he said. "I've only played it for two years [before 2006]. I keep working at it. I've improved.

"I've been playing third for a couple of years. Sometimes you kind of cross your own feet and get confused a little bit. That's what people say. I don't know."

He knew how disappointed Yankee fans were about his season, but he reasoned that he couldn't control their reactions. He estimated the boobirds as "10–15 percent" of the people, another Pollyanna statement that seemed difficult for even him to believe.

"Throughout the city, I had unbelievable support," he said. "People coming up to me and telling me they were behind you and this or that. You can't take a certain amount of people or one writer and think, 'Oh, that's the general consensus.' It doesn't really matter what one writer thinks or a certain amount of people.

"I just focus always on who's on my side, who's supportive. Especially down times, you get to see who's who. So for me, it was productive.

"It's been a trial, but it's like the stock market. You can't get caught up every day in 'Is it hot? Is it cold?' I think you give any player six months, seven months, at least you'll get closer to the truth after seven months."

Whereas A-Rod's stock plummeted in 2006, Jeter's rose as high as it had ever been since he signed a ten-year, $189 million contract after the 2000 season, the Yanks' fourth world championship in five years. The captain was touted as an MVP candidate from midseason on, and his offensive numbers (.343, second in the AL; 14 homers, 97 RBIs, 118 runs in 154 games) were across the board his best output since 1999. He sprinted out to a terrific start, as punctuated by his go-ahead homer in the home opener. Jeter batted a career-best .398 (35 for 88) in the first month, where he hit safely in 20 of 23 games. In July, when A-Rod was weighing the team down, Jeter hit .412 (42 of 102). Although he went 189 at-bats without a homer in June and July, he batted .344 (65 for 189) in that span. By August, he was solidifying his MVP candidacy, although, strangely, neither Cashman nor Torre made any huge public proclamation that the captain was their most valuable player. Jeter hit in 25 straight games from August 20 to September 17, just after the Yankees had wrapped up the division with a five-game sweep of Boston. He scored 21 runs and drove in 25 during that time, and it was the longest Yankee hitting streak since Joe Gordon's 29-game streak in 1942. The shortstop reached base safely in 41 of his last 42 games. His numbers at the end of the regular season were highly impressive: he stole a career-high 34 bases. He was second in the AL with a .381 average with runners in scoring position. He was second in the league in runs and fourth in on-base percentage (.417).

To put his season into context, it's worth reviewing a statistic devised by the renowned Web site Baseball Prospectus called VORP, or value over replacement player. According to the Web site, it's defined as "the number of runs contributed beyond what a replacement-level player at the same position would contribute if given the same percentage of team plate appearances. VORP scores do not consider the quality of a player's defense." Jeter posted a 79.2 VORP, fourth in the majors. A-Rod was second on the Yankees (among hitters) with a 50.4, which was good for twenty-ninth in the majors.

And yet Jeter didn't completely counteract the notion that Rodriguez was still a better all-around player than he was. After the season, a *New York Times* article punctured the myth that Jeter was a more valuable Yankee than Rodriguez. The article cited a statistic that sabermetrician Bill James calls "win shares," which tries to determine how many victories a given player contributes to his team offensively and defensively. Rodriguez had collected 92 "win shares" in his three seasons in pinstripes, while Jeter had recorded 85 from 2004 to 2006. As the author of that article noted, that may seem like hair-splitting, but the Yanks won the division by three games in 2004 and won by a tie-breaker in '05 over the Red Sox.

Looking at a slightly more mainstream gauge, take OPS. Many people look at the combination of on-base percentage plus slugging percentage as the best measure of total offensive value, and Jeter has recorded only one season (1999) with a better mark than Rodriguez. In 2006, Jeter finished with a .900 OPS, but A-Rod—in what was deemed a failure of a season—was at .915. Despite two months of slumping, despite his worst year defensively, despite a spectacular year from Jeter, Rodriguez still proved himself valuable to the club, still proved he was better than almost everyone in the game.

Granted, Jeter was far more clutch in 2006. A-Rod batted only .302 with runners in scoring position, not bad but not Jeter-like. And Rodriguez batted a miserable .237 with 2 homers and 14 RBIs in "close and late" situations—Jeter was a .325 hitter with 2 home runs and 18 RBIs there.

Still, after all the hand-wringing, all the sports radio jabber, all the trade talk, and all the Knoblauch comparisons, A-Rod had survived, if not thrived. His numbers were strong compared to the rest of baseball, and he hit .358 in September with 8 homers and 25 RBIs. Even though he went 0 for 12 right after *SI*'s cover story came out, he ended the season 9 for 15 with three doubles, a homer, and five RBIs in his last five games. Yes, the postseason was going to be a litmus test, one that might determine whether Rodriguez would wear pinstripes in 2007 and beyond. Yes,

Yankee fans were on their last nerve when it came to the often self-delusional, often self-serving third baseman. Yes, Rodriguez couldn't repeat his 2005 playoff performance without harsh repercussions.

But when Hideki Matsui and Gary Sheffield came back from wrist injuries in September, it seemed as though it would serve as a kind of shield for A-Rod in the playoffs, take the pressure off him to come through with those two further down the lineup. And with Matsui and Sheffield back, the Yankee lineup was intimidating. On September 27 versus Baltimore, Torre wrote out a lineup of Damon, Jeter, Abreu, Rodriguez, Giambi, Sheffield, Matsui, Posada, and Cano. It was the first time all the regulars were back and playing with Abreu. The Yanks dropped 16 runs on Oriole pitching. The Yankees looked strong down the stretch, eventually earning home-field advantage throughout the playoffs. In a moment of foreshadowing, though, Torre made it a point to say after the rout that the aforementioned lineup wouldn't necessarily be the one he used in the playoffs. The only other time he played the same nine All-Stars down the stretch, on September 29, the team scored seven runs in a win over Toronto. Torre again made it a point to tell people that wouldn't necessarily be the Game 1 lineup. It seemed especially curious, given the club was 2 for 2 with that batting order.

Everything was clicking—and then Torre decided to move Rodriguez out of the cleanup spot for the playoffs. Torre, once so adept at handling the pressures of the Yankee Fishbowl and insulating his best players, didn't understand (or didn't care) that moving Rodriguez would make him a focal point of the playoffs, even more so than in the regular season.

The normally hands-off skipper revealed his stone hands. Torre decided to challenge his best player for no apparent reason, rather than protect him. And that was the beginning of the end for the Yankees in 2006.

CHAPTER SEVENTEEN

CASHMAN

Brian Cashman sat in the catbird's seat, literally and figuratively. As he perched over the field at Yankee Stadium in his private box behind home plate on the night of August 30, the team Cashman had constructed held a ten-game advantage in the loss column on the Boston Red Sox. Although there was still a month to go in the regular season, it was all over but the champagne.

"I think we need to take advantage of that and get some guys throughout the roster—not just the bullpen—some needed rest," Cashman said during the second game of a day-night doubleheader with Detroit. "Anybody that may have something that's a little bit of a concern, lose the battle to win the war.

"I think we have to approach that as we enter September without, obviously, fucking it up. Or screwing it up. I've talked to Joe, I've talked to our coaches. That's it."

As much as Cashman liked and appreciated Torre, he sometimes cringed at the way the manager overused his bullpen. He understood that his skipper would try to win each day's game to the best of his ability, but that didn't mean the GM agreed with the tactics. Which is why Cashman and his manager would need to discuss usage concerns more than once over a given season.

Cashman thought the placement of Mike Mussina on the DL in late August was a smart move, as Mussina was the team's most important pitcher in the first half, until Chien-Ming Wang rocketed to the top of the rotation. Reportedly, Mussina was even asked to be an All-Star at the last minute, but he declined. After tweaking his groin while pitching through the fifty-seven-minute rain delay in Boston on August 20, he was shelved. The GM was preaching a different approach heading into the final month, one that paired common sense with the final remaining goal: earning home-field advantage throughout the playoffs.

Although the Yanks were virtually assured of the AL East crown by the final day in August, they were still looking up at Detroit. Meanwhile, Minnesota was also on a tear, and they were a team to watch in the second half.

"Yeah, we'd like to have home-field advantage, but I'd like to have the strongest team possible as we enter the playoffs," Cashman said. "And some guys have done their fair share to get us to this point, so we need to back off certain guys. I could care less how we piece things together. We need to start protecting guys, letting them rejuvenate and get ready."

Nobody had been more important to the Yankees' run of championships than Mariano Rivera, and he was one player who seemed key to a long October run. This was the fourth straight year he had saved 30 or more games, and the ninth time in ten years.

"Superhuman, what he's done," Cashman said. "I'm not saying he's going to remain superhuman. He was the best of all time at what he does, and you will never be able to replace him. So the main question is going to be, whenever his time runs out, how big a drop-off will it be? Because you'll never replace somebody like that. How can you cushion the blow?"

And the workload, as always, was superhuman. Nine times Rivera made back-to-back appearances in '06, and he pitched in three straight games on three occasions. Once he even toiled in four straight games. He also worked at least two innings in eight games, including a game when he worked three innings (on May 30 at Detroit).

Having appeared in the opener of the doubleheader, saving a 2-0 victory for Wang, Rivera was not available in the nightcap. The next day, he requested an MRI on his right elbow. He had felt something in the elbow area for a few weeks, and told Torre about it, and Torre tried to manage around it. The test showed a mild muscle strain in the right forearm but no structural damage. Rivera told reporters that he wanted "peace of mind," which he received. But the Yankees wouldn't have peace of mind without a healthy closer, so after Rivera pitched on August 31, they shut him down until September 22. The same day Rivera was checked out with the MRI, Jason Giambi had an MRI on his left wrist. It was a problem area for the lefty slugger, and he'd require cortisone shots simply to get through the end of the year. Injuries were the great equalizer, the one uncontrollable wild card that could bring a team down in the blink of an eye.

"It's a slippery slope," Cashman admitted that week. "Look at what Boston's going through right now. They were a scary team not too long ago.

"That can happen to us with some unfortunate events. And we've already lived through some unfortunate events. So no, this is a very fragile sport, and things can change very quickly. And the worst thing you could be thinking is you're on top of the world, and things are going as good as they could possibly go. And all of a sudden the baseball gods will bring you to your knees.

"You've got to appreciate how difficult it is to stay healthy and stay on top of your game. There's examples all over. Alex is one, and Randy in the first half is one. Injuries to Matsui and Sheffield, all that stuff."

The Cashman who didn't concern himself about the rain back in April was long gone. That man had given way to someone who was a lot more agitated, a man who back in July was "mentally exhausted" and went a week without a good night's sleep. The guy who at the start had been Zen-like about the things out of his control in the final month of the season was saying things like, "You're always worried, you always feel like the fear of failure is always with me."

"I don't think you ever should be comfortable—because nothing ever is working perfect," Cashman argued. "So I'm just not a comfortable person by nature. I think if anybody's comfortable, they're the wrong people for the job. . . .

"When I've got a lot on my mind, I don't necessarily sleep as well. Just depends on circumstances. There's nights I toss and turn, there's other weeks I have great sleep.

"You get into a rut where there's a lot of things going you're wondering about, always looking to do the best thing you can possibly do. Always wondering if you're making mistakes, you don't want to make a mistake, and there's no guaranteed move you can make that will help, and you don't want to hurt. It's like a mental wrestling match."

In late 2006, Cashman wrestled with himself over the best plan for overhauling the baseball operations department. Part of the process meant letting some longtime employees go. Over the summer, he reportedly pink-slipped a number of scouts involved with the draft. National cross-checker Wayne Britton and east regional cross-checker Joe Arnold were two people in prominent positions who were kicked to the curb. He then told VP of international scouting Lin Garrett and coordinator of Pacific Rim scouting John Cox (who signed Wang) that their contracts wouldn't be renewed. More scouting firings came during the playoffs, when advance scouts Chuck Cottier and Wade Taylor were handed their walking papers. According to the *Post*, Taylor was told the club wanted to overhaul how it did its advance scouting, using more major-league scouts. The Yankees were also planning to increase their use of video scouting, in deference to bullpen coach Joe Kerrigan's expertise in that area.

During the Division Series, Cashman also axed the Double A Trenton manager Bill Masse, who angrily denied in the *New York Post* that he put winning ahead of development. In the off-season, Cashman fired the strength coach, Jeff Mangold, and the team's PR director, Rick Cerrone.

"It's not easy, but you've just got to make tough decisions," Cashman said in late August. "So you continue to move forward, you've got to continually evaluate yourselves, just as we have a lot of roster changes on the twenty-five-man roster.

"Every year we try to put the best out on the field. We want to try to put the best in the front office and scouting departments and player development side and cultivate that as we grow. So I have tough decisions to make. Some contracts are up and whether to decide to renew or not. And I've decided not to renew.

"Every day is a challenge to be the best you can possibly be at all levels. It sounds corny, but it's a fact. And we can have a real impact if we pursue that goal of excellence every day. Some of that means saying good-bye to good people."

During my hourlong conversation with Cashman, Billy Eppler stepped into the GM's box for a moment to check on the action. Eppler was an example of a good employee whom Cashman took a shine to, and one who enjoyed working for the demanding GM. When Cashman was summoned by president Randy Levine for a pressing business matter, Eppler discussed the pleasure of working for Cashman.

"You want to work hard and do your best because you like him so much and admire him," Eppler said. "He's the best."

Eppler came from the horrible Colorado Rockies organization, where he was once a scout. In 2005 for the Yanks, he was the assistant director of player development in charge of minor-league operations. A year later, he was the director of pro scouting, and Cashman moved him up to New York to work alongside him. The Yankee most closely tied to Eppler had an impact in the doubleheader finale versus the Tigers. Brian Bruney, a hulking right-handed reliever who reminded some New York reporters of the Gomer Pyle character in the movie *Full Metal Jacket,* pitched the end of the seventh inning, preserving a 3-2 lead for Jaret Wright. Bruney was 1-1 with an 0.87 ERA in 19 appearances for the Yanks.

Bruney had been a real thrift-store find during the summer. The 24-year-old righty began the year on Arizona's Triple A team, but after allowing 10 earned runs in 2⅔ innings, he was placed on the DL with a right elbow strain in mid-April and released a month later. Bruney rehabbed in the Phoenix area with Brett Fischer, who handled Randy Johnson's off-season workouts and improved his arm strength. When it came time for Bruney to work out in front of major-league scouts in late June, Eppler called Andy Stankiewicz, a former Yankee who was the club's southwest scout before taking an assistant coaching job at Arizona State. Stankiewicz arrived late on a Friday morning, however. The workout on an indoor mound began at 9 A.M., but Stankiewicz arrived around 9:30 A.M., in time to see only one pitch. Bruney really wanted to be a Yankee, and he and his agent offered to give him another private showing two days later. He was already throwing 92-94 mph without facing any hitters or getting the benefit of game-time adrenaline, and the Yanks liked what they saw. On July 1, the Yankees signed him to a minor-league deal. At the time, they weren't getting anything from righty reliever Octavio Dotel, who was recovering more slowly than anticipated from Tommy John surgery and never made a real 2006 impact. Bruney began in Triple A but was recalled by August 17, in time for the final stretch run. He struck out 25 batters in 20⅔ innings and allowed only one run over his final 16 appearances. Eppler really sold Cashman on the reliever throughout the process and earned cachet in Cashman's eyes because of it.

"He's done a good job," Cashman said of his protégé. "I just think sharp people stand out. Like I hired [assistant general manager] Jean Afterman, she was an agent. My dealings with Billy Eppler in Tampa, I really thought he was a guy who could be a huge asset and I'd love to have up here in New York to help me out in that capacity, and it opened up."

The Tigers-Yankees three-game set in August was one of those series that defines a season, because the Bombers were chasing Detroit despite taking three of four in Motown in late May and early June. The Tigers had avoided a sweep in that earlier series finale because Rivera was unavailable after working three innings the day before. Instead, Kyle Farnsworth, a $17 million setup man whom Cashman had signed for three years to replace Tom Gordon, blew that game on June 1. Now, two and a half months later, Cashman didn't know it as he was discussing the trials and travails of the season, but history was about to repeat itself.

In the eighth inning, as Cashman was talking about the physically and mentally draining nature of the Red Sox series, the Tigers were mounting a rally off Bruney and his successor, lefty Ron Villone. The GM wasn't happy that the Yankees had gone 2-4 on their West Coast road trip after sweeping the Red Sox in five games, but neither was he disappointed. Boston also went 2-4 during that time and didn't gain any ground.

"It's hard to maintain that type of energy level," he said. "We beat the Red Sox in Game 7 [of the ALCS] in '03 with a walk-off home run, and even our fans were drained in Game 1 against the Marlins in the World Series.

"It was probably the quietest game in World Series history. It was dead. And we lost, and I just think even the fans were drained. It's great for the sport—it's not good for the participants, but it's great for the sport."

With two outs and two on, Tigers first baseman Sean Casey hit a ball to the hole on the right side. Had it gone through, the game would've been tied. Second baseman Robinson Cano did well simply to get to it, but he then threw the ball to Aaron Guiel, an outfielder/first baseman. Cano's hasty throw put Guiel right in the path of Casey, who's listed at 237 pounds but probably is 10 pounds heavier. Guiel is listed at 5 foot 10 and 200 pounds but might be 2 inches shorter and 20 pounds lighter. A collision ensued, and Casey flattened Guiel the way an SUV would flatten a Corvette. But Guiel hung on to the ball, the Yankees were out of the inning, and Cashman was ebullient.

"Wow!" he screamed as the sellout crowd of 54,509 roared. "Wow, motherfuckers!"

Banging the table in front of him four times with both hands, he screamed out, "That's great! A lot of grinders out there! Whoa, fuck! Aaron Guiel. Another Billy Eppler guy." Indeed, Eppler had become acquainted with Guiel while they were both in Colorado, and he was claimed off waivers from Kansas City on July 5.

For all of the nice minor pickups that the Yankees grabbed during the season, though, the $194 million team's success would still revolve around how the stars would perform. And in 2006, Derek Jeter's star was ascending while Alex Rodriguez's was plummeting to earth. Cashman struck an uneasy but unapologetic tone when asked about A-Rod, who was in the midst of an 0-for-7 twin bill.

"The big thing, if you have a team, the concept is you pick people up when they're down," Cashman said. "So what we can do for Alex is make sure he knows we're there for him and we've got his back every step of the way and he'll figure it out eventually.

"We've afforded him in every step of the process with coaching and instructing and patting on the back. And he'll be there eventually, just like Randy Johnson earlier in the year was struggling, we needed for other guys to pick up the slack and you knew Randy would eventually get going. Eventually, he has.

"Alex was the Player of the Month in May, where Randy Johnson might've been the anti–Player of the Month in May in the American League. Now Randy's on line and Alex is struggling. It's all about picking each other up. Right now, it's time for everybody to pick Alex up, and there will be a time for Alex to pick us up."

But by late August, A-Rod was getting booed again by the home fans. If the objective was to pick people up and let people know who was there for him, shouldn't there have been more public support? Shouldn't Jeter have come forward?

"I said a lot, I can't make people say things," Cashman said. "I think people say what they feel they should say. . . . Derek can't fake Derek and I'm not going to fake me. I said what I thought was right. Derek said what he felt was right and leave it at that."

Whether it was because of the A-Rod situation, because he didn't worry about individual honors, or because of something else entirely, Cashman didn't jump out in front and champion his shortstop's MVP bid.

While he noted that he hadn't even looked at the competition and dismissed the race as something that would be figured out when the dust settled, he knew that Jeter was a strong candidate. By this time, the drum was being beaten in New York that the Yankee captain should win the award.

When Jason Giambi batted late in the eighth inning, though, Cashman pointed down to the field at him and noted, "But this guy's a candidate for me, too. Johnny Damon I think should be a candidate, too.

"I think individually we've had some guys step up like Proctor and Melky. We've had a lot of team MVPs to me to get us where we're going, but Jeter's been awesome, no doubt about it."

While Scott Proctor may have stepped up in the 2006 season, he didn't step up in the doubleheader finale. Proctor, who was acquired along with outfielder Bubba Crosby at the 2003 trade deadline for Robin Ventura, had become a reliable eighth-inning setup man, one who could start innings or jump into trouble. With Rivera not available, he was summoned to save what would've been a 3-2 victory, but he issued a one-out walk to Brandon Inge and a two-out walk to Curtis Granderson, names that would become very familiar to Yankee fans in October. Proctor was one strike away on three pitches to the pesky Granderson, who worked a walk in a nine-pitch at-bat.

The Tigers were one of those teams that nobody expected to do anything at the beginning of the year but became baseball's annual surprise in 2006. They quickly took on the countenance of their feisty first-year manager, Jim Leyland, and they left baseball observers with a positive impression even during losses because they fought relentlessly. At the end of a long day's journey into night, they fought tooth and nail.

Craig Monroe, another name that held no meaning to Yankee fans prior to October 2006, stepped to the plate after Granderson and crushed Proctor's first pitch—a slider—onto the netting in left center field for a three-run homer. A half inning later, a pretty sure thing had turned into a 5-3 loss, and a sweep attempt had been squandered. The Yanks would win the next day when Rivera returned to his role, meaning that the team took five of the seven games in which he pitched—and blowing the two in which he hadn't. A month later, everyone from Yankee fans to pro scouts thought the Bombers were catching a break in the playoffs by drawing Detroit instead of Minnesota, but playing the Tigers was no break.

As the ball carried and carried off Monroe's bat, disappearing into the night, there was no animated display in the GM's box this time. There was no screaming or yelling. There were no F-bombs. There was only one word from Cashman, and maybe a harbinger of doom in that word.

"Good-bye," Cashman said.

CHAPTER EIGHTEEN
DIVISION SERIES

Fresh paint. You could see it, you could smell it, and you could even get it on your shoes if you ventured too close to the walls of Yankee Stadium on the workout day before the Division Series against Detroit began. On October 2, "Wet Paint" signs lined the stairway where the players walked down into the bowels of the stadium, and a new blue and white coat was laid all the way to the edge of the venerable clubhouse and the historic field.

Every day, Yankee players came to work through the same press gate entrance, then headed down the stairs and passed by an unmistakably large metal sign proclaiming the Yankees' twenty-six world championships. The thorough paint job—even the trash cans were painted—signaled the obvious hope that the Yankees would be playing deep into October, would be claiming championship number 27. In the beginning of the year, "One Team, One Mission" T-shirts were handed out with that number on the shirts. But what couldn't be painted over, what couldn't be dressed up, was a putrid effort over the following week.

The Yankees were heavy favorites to beat the Tigers, who fell out of the AL Central by losing five straight, including a season-ending sweep at home versus Kansas City. In fact, the Yankees were so strong that Gary Sheffield cautioned on the workout day that the Yankees better not think they could take Detroit for granted, better not believe that they could roll out of bed and beat them. Apparently, Joe Torre delivered a similar message in his team meeting that morning. But those words were lost in the perfect storm developing over at another locker.

Torre announced his batting order for the first game, and Alex Rodriguez was dropped to sixth. It was the worst decision, with very little logic behind the move, and it came at the worst time. Understand, in the times at the end of the year when the entire offense was healthy, A-Rod never batted sixth. Never. He hadn't batted sixth since June 22, 1995, and his numbers against Detroit's Game 1 starter, Nate Robertson (6 for 19 with a homer and five RBIs in the regular season), were better than those of Sheffield, who was being moved up to cleanup after hitting sixth at the end of the year. Apparently, the two homers Sheff hit in the final nine games coming back from left wrist surgery made him worthy of a promotion. Either that, or the 1-for-8 mark he had managed in previous confrontations against Robertson was the reason.

"I told the players this morning when I held—when I read it to them, I said I can hold it this way, this way, this way, this way, it doesn't bother me," Torre said during his press conference on the workout day before Game 1. "But you have to put them in order and . . . we basically separated the lefties and you know, we let it fly."

When asked about A-Rod's comfort level over the weekend and the importance of his work in the next week, the manager said, "Alex is one of the nine guys in the lineup." He noted that A-Rod seemed to be having more fun in the last week or two and seemed very comfortable, and agreed that it was important for him to hit.

"But hopefully Alex will just allow his ability to talk and if that's the case, then we feel pretty good," he said. "We all know, Alex is very conscientious, he would like to do tons of things and we feel that just to sort of allow things to happen more so than just trying to do too much is probably a better way to approach it."

Well, if Torre wanted Rodriguez's ability to talk, this was a strange way of making it happen. Rodriguez was swarmed by about fifty media members when he came off the field during BP that day, forced to downplay the suddenly glaring issue of his demotion. When he came into the clubhouse, many reporters weren't aware that he'd already addressed the issue, and they cornered him again.

"It doesn't make a difference," Rodriguez said. "Joe talked to me and it's no big deal. Robinson [Cano] is hitting ninth and for 99 percent of the teams he would be hitting third. Anywhere in our lineup is a good place to be and [Hideki] Matsui is hitting behind me."

The third baseman, who had weathered awful slumps throughout the 2006 season only to put up respectable All-Star numbers at the end, was treated like a detriment before the series even started. And this after hitting .358 with 8 homers and 25 RBIs in September.

Torre was sending a message to his club that no man was too important to be moved down in the lineup, but the manager reportedly had refused to make such a move in late August on the West Coast, after the Yanks had won five straight from Boston without much pop from Rodriguez. He moved him up to second instead. Others thought Torre was rewarding Sheffield, who'd batted .250 (7 for 28) with two homers and six RBIs down the stretch. If so, Sheffield had a strange way of returning the favor, mentioning how Tigers manager Jim Leyland was at the top of his favorite-managers list because of a hard-core attitude that included wearing spikes in the dugout.

So, to recap, Torre—the supposed master of keeping brush fires from turning into forest fires in the New York media—moved the number-four hitter he'd stuck with through thick and thin virtually the entire season down to sixth. In the cleanup spot he put someone with only twenty-eight September at-bats under his belt, a player who admittedly wasn't swinging with his usual terrifying force. And he was doing this even though A-Rod had a better history against the opposing starter. The move recalled a famous scene in *The Shawshank Redemption* where Andy Dufresne said to the warden, "How can you be so obtuse?"

Rodriguez, who was often guilty of "trying to do too much," as Torre put it (a euphemism for pressing to the point of choking in the clutch), was about to have one of the worst series of his life. And oh, by the way, so were the Yankees. When asked if he would be able to use the sixth spot to relax, A-Rod answered, "We'll see."

Things started off on the right foot, mainly because Chien-Ming Wang was wisely inserted into the number-one starter's role. Wang cracked up the assembled press corps in his workout day interview by telling them he wouldn't be nervous on the field but was rattled in the press conference setting with more limited weapons (his grasp of English was spotty, although his attempts were earnest). Wang was 11-3 with a 3.03 ERA in 17 starts at Yankee Stadium. His June 1 start against Detroit hadn't been good, but the second-year righty allowed only three hits and two walks during 7⅔ innings of shutout ball on August 30 in the Bronx against them, earning one of his 19 victories.

"You get to the high-profile games because you earn it, because the manager and the organization know you can handle the situations," Game 2 starter Mike Mussina noted of Wang before the series began.

The 26-year-old made the people in Taiwan proud, pitching into the seventh inning of an 8-4 victory in the opener. The Yanks handled Robertson, batting around during a five-run third that cinched the game. Jason Giambi, who endured multiple cortisone shots in an ailing left wrist that would need surgery after the season, smashed a two-run bomb to cap the Yanks' biggest rally in the Division Series. Sheffield's RBI single was a key factor in the rally, and A-Rod went 1 for 4 but hit lineouts to the second baseman and right fielder.

For one playoff game, at least, all was right in the Yankee Fishbowl.

Jim Leyland was aware of the perception. Before the series began, the Detroit manager knew a lot of people thought this matchup would be the varsity scrimmaging with the freshman team. But he knew his team hadn't snuck into the playoffs. Leyland's team was far and away the best club in the AL for much of the season.

What made it tough for the Tigers skipper was that he respected the Yankees . . . and he feared them. He knew what they were capable of doing, and although his club had the best ERA in baseball during the regular season, this series was expected to break them. Leyland was a Yankee fan, too, though, because he admired players such as Derek Jeter and described Torre as a "close friend." He lamented that he couldn't dig up a grudge to use for his team.

"I wish we had some extra motivation to hate the Yankees, but we don't," he said. "We respect them and we like them."

Detroit's season, in many ways, was defined on April 17, when the Tigers embarked on a West Coast trip after a 10-2 matinee loss at home against Cleveland. It was defined by a Leyland tirade after the game, a calculated move to shake his team up—one that showed him to be the antithesis of Torre.

The back story to the April 17 explosion was this: Detroit had won two of the first three games of the series, and a split wasn't good enough for the manager.

"We stunk, period," Leyland said that day, blasting his team in the media. "Stunk, and it's not good enough. It's been going on here before, and it's not going to happen here [now]. It's not going to go on here."

In 2003, the Tigers were the laughingstock of baseball, losing 119 games. They even needed a miracle rally in the season finale to avoid the infamy of tying the 1962 Mets, who most believe were the worst team of the modern era. Leyland was hired after longtime Detroit shortstop Alan Trammell was fired following three lackluster seasons, charged to turn things around immediately.

"I'm not talking about anybody in particular," Leyland continued during his infamous April rant. "I'm talking about the team—myself, the coaches, and everybody else included.

"It's my responsibility to have the team ready to play today. They weren't ready to play. They were ready to get on the plane and go to Oakland. If we won, it was OK. If we lost, it was OK. And that's not good enough."

After dropping to 7-6 that day and losing the next game to fall to .500, the Tigers went 88-60 the rest of the way, although a collapse in the final week prevented the joy of a division title and ensured a seemingly dangerous matchup with the Yankees. Those managerial blowups often make a manager look, frankly, like a clown—until they work, that is.

Sometimes what gets a team fired up is not what's said but something that's just a matter of circumstance. And when downpours forced a cancellation of Game 2 on Wednesday, October 4, the Tigers had their bit of adversity to stare down.

On that night, a forecast of torrential rain—not the rain itself—prevented the game from starting on time. It was initially unclear when the teams would try to play. The rationale Major League Baseball gave after the fact was that playing two or three innings before a downpour was senseless, because the stoppage was expected to be for ninety minutes to two hours—too long for a starter to come back out to pitch. What galled the Tigers, however, was that at 9:30 P.M., when the tarp was removed from the field and an announcement was made that the game would start at 10 P.M., some Detroit players began stretching (including starter Justin Verlander, who played a little catch), while the Yanks were still in the clubhouse.

"We were informed the game time was at ten o'clock," Verlander said. "Obviously, I got out there and Mussina's not out there. Nobody's out there."

In fact, Mussina might've been the impetus for the cancellation. Mussina, who was the team's player representative, tracked the storm system on Intellicast.com and Weather.com and realized there was a more ominous band of showers on the way than the one that had just exited the Bronx. Along with a few of his teammates, he went to Torre and pitching coach Ron Guidry and informed them.

"Quite a few of us said this is crazy," Mussina said. "You're gonna mess up the whole series, play a couple innings and get rained out.

"It's just better this way. Even if it stopped raining ten minutes from now, it's just better this way."

Once Yankee officials began asking questions of MLB officials, they were told the window was about an hour—way too short to get a regulation game in, and nobody wanted to play a truncated playoff game. The game was canceled soon after, which is what some Yankee officials thought should've happened hours earlier. Mussina said it actually wasn't that big a deal and he would be fine for the rescheduled game the next afternoon.

Torre was bothered by it, though, and actually left the ballpark without talking to reporters that night. He wasn't the only person peeved—the Tigers had a much bigger bone to pick.

"I want to make sure that everybody knows that this was not the Yankees' fault," Leyland said the next day. "I don't think the Yankees had anything to do with it. But I've got to give Joe Torre credit," he quipped. "This is the first time in my life that I was ever outmanaged on an off day."

The Tigers had checked out of their hotel rooms at the Hyatt on the afternoon Game 2 was scheduled, planning to take a charter to Michigan after the game. Instead, they were stuck in the Big Apple for another night, forced to scurry for rooms in various inns and lodges. Some stayed at the Hyatt, while others were in the Hilton. *Detroit Free Press* columnist Michael Rosenberg chronicled the inconveniences that might have sparked a turnaround. GM Dave Dombrowski told him it helped "galvanize the team" when they came to Yankee Stadium for the makeup game the next day.

"There wasn't a specific incident in the clubhouse that day," Dombrowski told Rosenberg. "But I just sensed a little different feeling than I had sensed before.

"I do think that the rainout . . . it seemed to really bring our group together again. It was really a rallying cry. People felt—and rightfully so—that we didn't get the same information. Our guys weren't happy about it—staff and players."

Although a bit weary and cranky, the Tigers seized momentum the next afternoon. Although Yankee Stadium announced a sellout of 56,252, there were plenty of fans masquerading as blue seats. In other words, fans with tickets for the night before couldn't come to the game because of something called work. The atmosphere in the ballpark was mundane, and so was Mussina. In the fourth inning, Johnny Damon ripped a three-run homer into the upper deck in right to give the home team a 3-1 edge. Given a two-run lead for the fifth inning, it was up to Mussina to make it stick. Instead, he bled it back run by run—one in the fifth, one in the sixth, and one in the seventh—never putting away the pesky Tiger hitters.

"It's frustrating," Mussina told reporters afterward. "I felt like I had control, and then I'd get into a bad count, or the leadoff guy would swing at the first pitch and get one down the line.

"It was just strange and frustrating. It was tough. I felt better than that, and I felt like I threw the ball better than that. Every time they had a chance to score, they scored."

In the fifth, he allowed a leadoff double to Marcus Thames, the number-eight hitter, and wild-pitched him to third. In the sixth, Carlos Guillen whacked a 2-and-0 fastball over the fence to tie the game. And in the seventh, Mussina allowed a leadoff single to Thames and then a passed ball moved him to second. Some observers lamented that Thames' bloop would've been run down by the speedy Melky Cabrera, who was benched when Matsui returned from injury.

Thames was sacrificed to third, and Curtis Granderson's triple to left center on an 0-and-2 pitch plated the go-ahead run. Granderson fouled off two pitches before stroking the winning hit. It was there, GM Brian Cashman decided later, that the momentum in the series changed for good.

Mussina turned out to be one of the biggest goats in the series, but he was pointing fingers and downplaying the loss immediately after the game. He noted that Rodriguez's failure to get a hit with the bases loaded and two outs in the first was a turning point, as was getting two on with nobody out in the second.

"You need to get runs once in a while there," he said. "The postseason is low-scoring."

He noted Posada's passed ball in the seventh was critical, but so was his own wild pitch two innings earlier. The veteran, who was getting closer and closer to retiring without a championship ring, claimed the loss in Game 5 against the Angels in 2005 was "more frustrating" and that this one wouldn't gnaw at him. Perspective aside, he came up short on an afternoon when the Yanks needed him.

As the shadows moved over the field in late afternoon, the Tigers brought in flamethrower Joel Zumaya, who struck out three in 1⅔ innings. Zumaya hit 103 mph on the radar gun when striking out Jason Giambi in the eighth, and he whiffed A-Rod on 101 mph heat to end the frame. Rodriguez turned to plate umpire Laz Diaz and asked him if he'd seen any of the pitches, because A-Rod admittedly hadn't.

Leyland was as classy as he could possibly be after the game.

"To be honest with you, I think we caught a big break, and I don't want to take anything away from our club," he said. "But if you look, the shadows were pretty tough as it got late in the game.

"And you've got a guy throwing 98, 99, 100 miles an hour with shadows that make the hitting conditions very tough for both teams. I tip my hat to Zumaya and our team, but we also caught a break with the time of day it was."

With the 0-for-4 collar, the slump was officially on for Rodriguez. Still, he was one of eight other players—besides Damon—who didn't hit in the desultory 4-3 loss that tied the series up. There were plenty of explanations—the lackluster crowd following the rainout, the shadows late in the game, the fact that the club probably expected Mussina to take a two-run fifth-inning lead to the bank. That's why it was so odd what Torre did next with the lineup.

It was supposed to be a simple two-block walk to the doctor's office. As Randy Johnson found out quickly, nothing in the Yankee Fishbowl was simple. On January 10, 2005, Johnson's foray out of the Four Seasons Hotel on 58th Street became front-page tabloid fodder known as the "Madison

Avenue meltdown." He attacked a cameraman whom he deemed too close to his personal space, turning an innocuous stroll into a national story. And so his tenure in pinstripes began.

The reverberations, Torre believed, were felt throughout the turbulent 2005 season, in which he went 17-8 with a 3.79 ERA but never seemed comfortable. And like a stone skipped across a pond, nobody could predict or even visualize where the ripple effect would end.

"I think when he started here, he probably won't admit this, but in the back of his mind is what went on in Manhattan," Torre said in early 2006. "Everybody thought he was this ogre, and he wasn't the aggressive guy we had watched across the field."

In 2005, Johnson butted heads repeatedly with Posada to the point the two couldn't work together. He got himself tossed from a critical late-season game in Toronto for arguing with an umpire and then asked the Yankee Stadium crowd to boo him if they wished before Game 3 of the Division Series. When he stank up the joint over three-plus innings, they unhappily complied.

The Yankees bent over backward acquiring the Big Unit, trading the disappointing Javier Vázquez and two prospects for him and signing him to a two-year, $32 million extension. Although it was a hefty ransom for a man who was already forty-one years old by the end of the 2004 season, Johnson was a five-time Cy Young Award winner. He was also someone with a creaky knee and a creaking back, something the organization downplayed at the time.

In July 2005, they made another move that showed they were willing to do what it took to make Johnson comfortable. Joe Kerrigan, Johnson's Double A and Triple A pitching coach in the Montreal farm system in the late 1980s, was hired as a special advisor to GM Brian Cashman. In the off-season, the Yankees catered to Johnson again. They hired Kerrigan as the bullpen coach. Catcher Kelly Stinnett, who worked with Johnson in Arizona in 1998 and 1999, was signed to replace John Flaherty as the backup.

Johnson was an enigma to teammates, even those such as Flaherty, who worked with him the most. And media members were irked by his disdain for them and even their most innocuous questions.

In 2006, Johnson seemed to act more relaxed during spring training, even joking about the Madison Avenue meltdown.

"In retrospect, I probably should have handled that differently," he told the Westchester *Journal News'* Peter Abraham. "You think?"

Things were supposed to be better in 2006, but the intensely private Johnson was spread on the front page of tabloids in late March when it was learned he was suing the mother of a sixteen-year-old daughter he fathered out of wedlock to get back $71,000 in child support payments he'd made after the girl was too old for day care. For those who thought Johnson was—when you get down to the brass tacks—just a bad guy, this was their evidence, their smoking gun. Johnson's daughter told the *New York Post* that he treated her coldly and she couldn't bear to watch him pitch anymore. He would sign cards "Randy" instead of "Dad," even though he reportedly demanded a paternity test that proved he was the father.

"It's a situation my family knew the whole time. It's a family matter. I want to keep it private," Johnson told the *Post.*

Eventually Johnson dropped the suit, but it got another season off to a bad start and reiterated how different life was in New York. Even when he improved to 5-2 in early May, his ERA was 5.02. And it was that kind of year for Johnson, who turned forty-three in September and lost virtually all aura of invincibility.

Although he finished 17-11, Johnson posted a 5.00 ERA and was constantly battling his mechanics. There was a longish stretch early in the year when he couldn't keep his arm angle up, and some people thought he was done. Johnson soldiered through in stoic form and eventually managed to be fairly successful. He was also fairly lucky, however, as the club scored nine or more runs in seven of his victories.

Right before the playoffs began, his body finally broke down. An MRI during the last week of the regular season revealed a herniated disk in his lower back, something the Big Unit had been pitching with during his last three starts of the regular season, when he allowed 24 hits and 15 earned runs for a 7.64 ERA. His status put the Yankees' World Series hopes in peril. He took an epidural for the back pain, though, and vowed to try to make his Game 3 start.

"My main objective is . . . I could win 17 games anywhere," he said on the last weekend of the regular season. "But my better chances of going to the playoffs were coming to the Yankees. That's why I'm here. So I'll do whatever it takes.

"I've pitched through pain and discomfort before and I'm forty-three years old, got an arthritic [right] knee, probably need knee replacement when I'm done. I'm a candidate for that. I've had one back surgery and another one, probably, that I may need. I'm not going to complain about my health. I'm here to pitch in the postseason and I'll do whatever I can. Obviously I don't want to put the team in jeopardy by not being effective."

Even though Johnson was pitching with the back of an eighty-year-old as the series shifted to Detroit, the Game 3 matchup still appeared to favor the Yankees at first glance. The Tigers were starting Kenny Rogers, an ex-Yankee who had always choked in the playoffs and earned the eternal hatred of New York fans because of that fact. Rogers didn't like pitching anywhere in New York. As a Met in 1999, he'd walked in the winning run in Game 6 of the NLCS versus Atlanta. He was a prime example of someone who shrank from the Big Apple spotlight, someone who flinched when times got toughest. The Yankees batted a collective .365 versus Rogers lifetime.

If there was a picture next to the word *choker* in the dictionary, it would've been of Rogers. He had allowed 20 earned runs over 20⅓ innings entering the 2006 postseason, and Leyland wouldn't even pitch him in the Bronx because he knew the predictable outcome. Instead, he saved him for Detroit's home playoff opener, and it was a master stroke.

Torre, meanwhile, tried his own bit of managerial sleight of hand, but it blew up in his face. The Yankee manager moved A-Rod up to fourth, a place he hadn't been deemed good enough to occupy at the beginning of the series. He benched Gary Sheffield, who was 3 for 17 lifetime against Rogers. He installed Bernie Williams as the DH and batted him eighth, and he put Jason Giambi—sore wrist and all—out at first base. Meanwhile, Cabrera—the spark plug for most of the season—was still mired on the bench.

The Williams move was not so much an ode to the good old days as an ode to the good old numbers: the former championship cornerstone was .353 (12 for 34, two homers) lifetime against Rogers.

"Their lineup is just going to be what the PlayStation 3 comes out with," Rogers quipped before the start. "That's the lineup that's going to be there. Everybody's hitting .350 [against Rogers] with 40 homers and whatever.

"It will rival any lineup that's ever been out there. I know they are great. I know they have fantastic players."

The game, really, turned in the second at-bat between the two former teammates. In the fifth, Williams just missed a two-run homer by inches down the left-field line that would've cut a deficit to 3-2, and he eventually struck out on a pitch in the dirt. In the bottom of that inning, Detroit tacked on two runs to put the game away.

Giambi was 0 for 3 off Rogers with a K and failed to complete a pick-off of Curtis Granderson by making a late, inaccurate throw to second base in the second, which led to the third Detroit run. That was all Rogers needed, as many believed he pitched the game of his life—an even more impressive outing than his perfect game in 1994. He allowed five hits over 7⅔ shutout innings of a 6-0 victory that put the Bombers' season on the edge of a cliff.

Utilizing a 93-mph fastball the Yankees said they had never seen before and a knee-buckling curveball that the overaggressive offense flailed away at, the forty-one-year-old Rogers earned his revenge. Rogers had always been known as a high-strung individual, but he yelled and hopped around and pumped his fist throughout his shutdown of the Yankees, mainlining his adrenaline from his heart out to his left arm.

"Whether anyone else believed I could go out there and beat these guys, to tell you the truth, I knew that if I wasn't determined and matching any kind of intensity that was put back to me, then I would have been in the same boat that I always have been in with these guys," he said. "They have beat me, but I think it was because maybe I was passive and maybe a little too cautious.

"Today I tried not to be that. If I was going to get beat, I was leaving it all out there. I wanted this game as much as I ever wanted any in my life."

Leyland summarized it perfectly: "For this one night, he got it all together. And he was probably as determined as you'll ever see anybody pitch a ball game."

In the World Series, Rogers was suspected of using pine tar that he rubbed on his pitching palm to get a great grip on his curveball. He washed it off before the second inning of his Game 2 Fall Classic start after being spotted by TV cameras, so the accusation could never be proven. After the fact, it was reported that Rogers had the same brown "dirt" on his left palm during all three of his playoff starts, although Torre took the high road when asked about it and declined to use that as an excuse.

Every time the Yankees put a runner on in Game 3, they failed. They were 0 for 18 with runners on base, a staggering statistic that showed how Rogers elevated his game and/or how the Bombers squeezed the sawdust out of their bats. After the game, Torre got angry enough to tell his team to "wake up," according to reports, but the proclamation fell on deaf ears, as it turned out. With two odd lineup shifts in the first three games, the Bombers were a team in turmoil.

"I think there's some tension," Rodriguez admitted.

And what of Johnson? That's exactly the point: he was an afterthought. That didn't absolve him of responsibility, though. And bad back or not, it didn't exclude him from being a goat or deny the fact that the Yankees had allowed themselves to be put in this untenable predicament by their own choices.

Johnson—who allowed eight hits and five earned runs over 5⅔ innings—deserved some praise for gutting out the start, although Posada overstated the case when he said the Big Unit's pitching was "outstanding."

Nobody expected Johnson to throw a perfect game, but he needed to be the ace the Yankees had thought they were acquiring. He needed to summon the skill and guile that had helped him earn five Cy Young Awards, and somehow get the game into the late innings while still giving his club a chance. He didn't come close. Four well-timed, well-placed hits in the second gave Detroit a three-run edge, with the key being a Sean Casey RBI single that Robinson Cano didn't dive for. Cano had a horrible series, and that lack of effort cost Johnson.

But the Big Unit wasn't sharp, wasn't intimidating, wasn't pitching like someone who wanted the game as badly as Rogers did. Johnson needed an epidural simply to make the start, and if you want to absolve Johnson of the loss for pitching in that condition, that's fine. But then, you have to blame the Yankees for being in that position.

Really, how healthy did the club expect Johnson to be in the 2006 playoffs at age forty-three? When they'd acquired him two years earlier, they knew that he had back woes (including surgery to repair a different herniated disk in 1996) and needed injections of synthetic material in his right knee because of a lack of cartilage. Nevertheless, they were banking on him being their ace, so it was either a failure of organizational thinking or a failure of execution on Johnson's part.

Time and time again over two years, the Yankees had seen the Big Unit come up small, seen him be booed off the Yankee Stadium mound, seen him only occasionally tease them with his dominant slider and eye-popping fastball of yesteryear. More often, he simply produced the type of mediocre pitching that they could've gotten anywhere from anyone for a far lower price. More often, he showed he was no longer an ace—never more, though, than on that hill in the middle of downtown Detroit.

"I think we're getting away from what happened tonight," Johnson protested at one point following Game 3. "Kenny Rogers pitched an outstanding ball game."

Exactly. One ornery geriatric pitcher raised his game to a transcendent level, while the other looked like he was ready for the glue factory.

Up two games to one, Leyland wouldn't allow himself to get overconfident, wouldn't allow himself to get ahead of himself, wouldn't allow himself to truly believe what he was seeing: the Yankees were disintegrating in front of his very eyes, were being toppled by his upstart band.

"The Yankees, in my opinion, are the most patient-hitting team in baseball," Leyland said after Game 3. "It's also one of the reasons they are the best-hitting team. . . .

"As the game went on tonight and we added on a couple of runs, it was really the first time that they became a little bit impatient. But I can promise you, that won't happen tomorrow."

When Saturday morning arrived, Detroit was in a state of delirium. The Tigers were one win away from knocking off the vaunted Yankees, who had been expected—by their owner on down—to run roughshod over every opponent in the playoffs. The lineup was too good, the pitching too adequate, for any other result. Detroit had limped into the playoffs, had too many question marks, had too little experience. Instead, the Tigers began playing loose and fast, and the Yankees tightened up.

Leyland, though, didn't sleep well at all after Friday's win. His family was in town with him, and he was lying in bed talking with his wife and son about how he'd have to find another way to shut down the Yankees' lineup in a matter of hours. He was still up at 4:00 A.M. eating M&Ms, he told reporters during his pregame press conference.

"I kept closing my eyes and all I could see was Abreu and Giambi and Jeter, and I mean that sincerely," Leyland said. "The toughest part about that, it was such an enjoyable win for me, but I didn't get to enjoy it for long. It's never-ending."

With the rest of Michigan on party alert, Leyland was sounding downright pessimistic.

"I mean, I guess this sounds terrible, but one way or the other, in the next two days, it's going to be over," he said, "and I'll be glad not to have to look at Jeter and Abreu and Johnny Damon and Giambi. And

I love Sheffield, he's my buddy, but I'll be glad I don't have to look at them until next spring, and that's a compliment. I mean, you can have nightmares."

Leyland was concerned because he felt the Yanks would be right back into their patience mode, but he'd noticed something during garbage time of Game 3. In the last two innings, with the exasperation setting in, the visitors had expanded their strike zone uncharacteristically. It was very rare to see them get frustrated, the longtime baseball man noted, and he was certain it wouldn't happen again in Game 4. They were the most patient team the Tigers had pitched against. Leyland was as impressed with the lineup's combined intelligence and approach as he was with their collective power or ability.

But if patience was the key, the Yankee example was set by Torre—who was suddenly uncharacteristically impatient. The Yankee manager, so highly esteemed for his grace under pressure, rejiggered the lineup for the third time in four games from what it initially had been once all nine regulars returned in September. This was a Yankee lineup that didn't need much maneuvering; it wasn't because of constant flip-flopping that the team led the majors in runs scored. It was because of talent. That talent was now essentially reassembled willy-nilly.

A-Rod was moved from cleanup to eighth. Sheffield went from the bench to the cleanup spot. Giambi was benched, and Cabrera—who had inspired the team throughout the season—was finally given a start. It was a flat-out panic move, Sheffield hinted later, and the players on both teams seemed to know it.

"I think that affected the morale and psyche of the entire team, not just A-Rod," Sheffield told USA Today's Bob Nightengale after the series ended. "I'm not making any excuses, but everyone was wondering what was going on. It made it a real weird day.

"You would like to be treated with a little respect, I don't care who you play for. We were worrying about all of that stuff, and we still had a game to play.

"If I'm on the other side, and all of a sudden they're putting Rodriguez eighth and putting me or Jason on the bench, you wonder what's going on. Those guys [from Detroit] were asking me about it. I think it boosted their morale. It gave them confidence they didn't have.

"Jim Leyland took advantage of that. He can make you believe anything. He can put a fire under your belt like you never had before in your life. Not to make excuses, but we didn't have that."

While an astute journalist later pointed out that Sheffield had to be told that A-Rod was batting eighth and Giambi wasn't playing—and thus couldn't have been too consumed too far in advance—Sheff's other premise was accurate: how could the Tigers not notice that the Yankees were scrambling for the winning formula? How could they not become emboldened by that? And, Sheffield's initial surprise aside, how could the Yankees relax knowing that their boss was less impressed with his lineup than the other manager across the field, that he was still searching for the right mix like an amateur cook frantically piling ingredients into a pot?

Torre was highly concerned about the perception of the moves, because when the beat writers asked him an initial question about A-Rod's demotion before the game, he mentioned that the line of questioning was unfair. Giambi was being benched outright, but still the focus was on A-Rod. Who was partly to blame for that, though, at least over the past week? Torre.

Still, the manager was on the defensive during his pregame televised press conference, when A-Rod was again part of the first question. (By the way, the Associated Press wittily called Rodriguez "8-Rod.")

"You found that A-Rod hitting eighth is more important than Giambi not playing. See, that's not fair," Torre said. "That's not fair. I think the first question should've been why isn't Giambi playing."

Giambi was devastated by the news. Even though he had a torn tendon in his left wrist that would need surgery after the season and was mostly ineffective, he did homer in Game 1.

"It'll be miserable, but I'm not going to let it take away from my teammates," Giambi said before the game. "The more important thing is it's not about me, it's about winning games."

Unfortunately for Giambi, he watched the Yankees' final game of 2006 from the bench. Jeremy Bonderman, one of the Tigers' dynamic young fireballers, dominated the Yankee lineup the way few pitchers had during the regular season. And the offense, as it did most of the series, helped him out. Bonderman needed only twenty-three pitches to get through the first three innings. He had thrown only eight balls through the first five frames. And at that point, Bonderman was still working on a perfect game.

Afterward, there was talk about how—true to Leyland's prediction— the Yankees were more patient. Twelve of the first nineteen hitters took the first pitch, but that wasn't the statistic that mattered. In fact, the Yankees looked like they couldn't wait to get the series over with. Bonderman was dealing, but wasn't that why this super-lineup had been constructed in the first place—to beat even the best of pitchers on even the best of days? Wasn't that why the Bombers overemphasized offense?

Keith Law of ESPN.com pointed out that the Yanks swung at 41 of the first 66 pitches through the first seven innings. Four hitters made first-pitch outs, and seven more were retired on the second pitch, Law noted. The Yankees were letting Bonderman get them out on his pitch, refusing to tangle deep in the count with him, and it was a costly gamble. They began the series with a great game plan against Robertson and ended it with a lackadaisical, halfhearted approach against Bonderman—who'd pitched poorly in his final regular-season start against crummy Kansas City.

Of course, for the second day in a row, it really was a moot point. Jaret Wright, the former rookie phenom who pitched the seventh game of the World Series for the 1997 Indians, was handed the ball for the do-or-die start against Detroit. Wright, the number-four starter who took twenty-three starts to work his way into the seventh inning of a ballgame in 2006, was the only thing standing between Detroit and destiny. Again, who in the Yankee organization thought this was a championship strategy? He didn't make it out of the third inning.

Wright had signed a three-year, $21 million contract during part of the mistake-laden 2004 off-season despite having failed a physical between the initial agreement and the ink drying on the final one. He was one of the people, along with Johnson and Pavano, who were expected to help bring another world championship up the Canyon of Heroes, were expected to carry their fair share of the load. After a perfect first inning, though, Wright allowed a solo bomb to Magglio Ordoñez in the second followed by a two-run jack to Craig Monroe—the spoiler in the double-header finale a little more than a month earlier—and the rout was on.

In the third, a Rodriguez throwing error led to another run, as A-Rod made a throw that Sheffield simply would not go into the baseline to try to corral. Wright was given the hook for Cory Lidle, the Abreu throw-in who was 4-3 with a 5.16 ERA in ten appearances (nine starts). Lidle got out of the third and fourth without damage, but when he allowed four straight hits to open the fifth, the Yankees' fate was sealed. Lidle's appearance became an afterthought, though it would turn out to be the last time he would ever pitch in his life.

There was nothing that the Yankees were doing right as the innings and outs ticked down to the off-season, although they finally managed to get a hit in the sixth—a Cano single—and score three runs before the 8-3 drubbing was complete. With two outs in the ninth and two runs in, Rodriguez came out to the on-deck circle as Cano batted against Jamie Walker. Cano took a called strike, then drove the next pitch into the ground toward second baseman Plácido Polanco. When Polanco threw to Sean Casey for the final out, one of the most ecstatic celebrations ever witnessed on a baseball field erupted. Rodriguez, who went 1 for 14 in the series without an RBI, lingered on the field.

He dropped the donut off his bat and knocked the bat against both cleats. He watched the impromptu party gather in the middle infield, letting the defeat soak in. Once again, he would be a goat. Once again, he would be denied a World Series ring. Once again, the usual questions would start up. Once again, he would be forced to defend his desire to stay in New York.

The mood in the visitors' clubhouse was resigned. Even now, the Yankees hadn't awoken from their somnambulant stroll to an ignominious defeat. They were detached. Across living rooms all over the greater New York area, a visceral anger was likely unleashed on TV sets and the occasional unsuspecting canine, if the ensuing talk-show calls can be believed. Yet the mood inside the cramped, poorly designed clubhouse was cold, as if this was predictable. Jeter, revealing a rare show of testiness, was the most emotional player in the clubhouse. Although his season had been extinguished, his competitive fire wasn't out yet. As soon as the media were allowed in the room, questions began about making wholesale changes for 2007.

"I'm not worried about changes right now, man," Jeter snapped. "We just lost ten, fifteen minutes ago."

Someone else asked him how the loss ranked, and baseball observers would come to believe that it was one of the worst series defeats in the drought years that had begun in 2001. Nothing would ever overtake the colossal choke job of the 2004 squad, which surrendered a three-games-to-none lead to Boston. But this was nearly as bad, and it was worse than 2005, was worse than Series losses in 2001 and 2003.

"I don't sit around and rank them," Jeter said, his words clipped. "I mean, you lose, you go home. They all don't feel good. So I don't think you say this one ranks any worse than another one."

Everyone had thought the Yankees would somehow turn it around, somehow right the ship.

"You think so," Jeter said, "but it didn't happen. Now we're out of games. That's what you would expect, that's what we thought. But it just didn't happen. We just didn't get too many things going."

Just to Jeter's right, Bernie Williams was swarmed. The former cornerstone to four world championships was asked for the secret to the recent failures. Why had the dynasty ended? Where had it gone wrong? Williams, perhaps in his final moments as a Yankee, was asked what was missing.

"The only thing missing is we didn't win," he said. "We had a very good team coming into this series and we liked our chances. But we got outplayed. They got the best of us. They played their game, and they did a great job of keeping us off balance. We just couldn't score any runs. . . .

"It's very frustrating, because obviously you have teams that are very capable of going all the way. And the fact that we didn't is obviously disappointing, but you've obviously still got to give credit to the opposition, in this case the Tigers. They pitched well, they hit well, they were taking first and third all the time."

It seemed to many within the organization to be the type of year that was supposed to end in a parade, a year for the ages. As unrealistic as even Williams knew it was to win every year (something he said at the beginning of the season), the Yankees were not supposed to go out this way. Not like this.

"If it was all on paper, it would've been a lot easier," Williams said. "That's why you play this game, because you never know what's going to happen. You prove what you're made of. They played good.

"Baseball's so unpredictable. We have a team of All-Stars out there and we have all the resources we want. And that's exactly why we play these games, because you never know what's going to happen."

Eventually, frustration became evident in Williams' voice as he was asked to analyze similarities and differences, cohesion and distractions, success and failure.

"I think we had a lot of distractions in the clubhouse, but nothing like we haven't handled in the past," he said. "We had sickness in the past, we had people coming up with cancer and things like that. And we were able to overcome those situations, too. I think it really didn't have anything to do with the outcome. We played our hardest and came up short."

Ultimately, Williams decided, the only difference between his championship teams and this imposter was the breaks: the key hits, runs, and outs that Paul O'Neill and David Cone and Tino Martinez always managed to unearth were nowhere to be found here. Giambi echoed Williams' belief in the difficulty of winning eleven postseason games, echoed the realization—which he too made during the season—that a championship wasn't a Yankee birthright after all, but a precious gift that was bought only by finishing a grueling gauntlet.

"That's what makes what they did that special," Giambi said of the 1996 and 1998–2000 teams. "It's not as easy as everybody thinks.

"It's not just a guarantee, 'Oh, God, they're this, they're that.' There's a lot that goes into a five-game series. One swing is a big-game swing."

Giambi, red-faced and emotionally shaken, never saw a pitch in the final game, while Sheffield went 0 for 3 and committed an error. Sheffield admitted in November that he'd probably rushed back too soon and wasn't able to help the team. It was the toughest of the four playoff losses Giambi had endured in his four seasons as a Yankee.

"We've been through a lot of adversity," he said. "That's what makes it even harder than any other year. The adversity we went through to get into those playoffs, missing those guys. And that's probably why it hurts a little bit more than any other year."

Questions about Torre's job security were already being chucked like hand grenades, and Mariano Rivera was one of the first players to field one. Rivera had watched the final three games from the bullpen, helpless to make any mark on the series. Now, some shrewdly suspected, Torre would be on the firing line.

"I don't worry at all," Rivera said, dismissing such talk. "He did tremendous this year. He did real good. But the manager cannot do the job that we have to do. We had to do our job. It's simple. We didn't do it."

But there was something more than that, something that could be described as a general malaise. Johnny Damon, once the leader of the free-spirited Red Sox, attributed it to the Tigers beating the Yanks all over the field. But if Damon was being honest with himself, he would concede that the corporate attitude the Yankees often display hadn't played well now for six postseasons.

"We were expected to win a world championship from spring training," Damon said. "A couple days ago, we were talking about how great our offense was rolling after that first game. Three days later, it's all . . . it's gone."

For his media bloodletting, A-Rod stood in the center of the clubhouse still wearing his uniform pants. Now 4 for 41 with no RBIs over his last twelve playoff games for the Yankees, he was forced to own up to his shortcomings, the way he had a year before in Anaheim after a 2-for-15 series. Of course, by September 2006 he'd said it was "garbage" that he was blamed for the 2005 flameout, so who knew how he really felt at this moment? He was certainly saying all the right things.

"I got no one to blame but myself," he said. "You kind of get tired of giving the other team credit. At some point you've got to look in the mirror and say, 'I sucked.' I don't know how to explain it. I could have been better."

As it was with Torre, speculation was that A-Rod had forced his own exit with the execrable series. He hedged slightly when asked about the notion that he had played his final game as a Yankee, saying he'd consider waiving his no-trade clause if the club was "dying to get rid of" him. Rodriguez had coldly and calculatingly sized up his own trade value not a month earlier with his "ten teams" and "if the Yankees take four [million]" comments, so he certainly knew what the market would be.

But mostly he expressed a desire to bring a world championship to the city in 2007 and end his career in New York.

"I don't want out," Rodriguez said. "If they would want to get rid of me, I hope that's not the case. I think I'm part of the solution."

There was a decided lack of emotion inside the clubhouse, a decided lack of sorrow, but Cashman and Torre more than made up for that. In his postgame press conference, the Yankee manager was choked up. His team—a team that, along with the Mets, was the best in baseball in 2006—was ushered out of the first round. For Torre, it was the third time in five years he hadn't even sniffed the ALCS. After five World Series trips in his first six seasons, this must've been like an oenophile being served prune juice.

"You know, as I said before, we felt pretty good about ourselves," Torre said. "But right now, it's just—it's just tough."

A few minutes later, Cashman seemed like a man in shock. Wearing a suede jacket and leaning against a tan brick wall in the clubhouse, he was admittedly stunned by the turn of events.

"It all happened so fast," he told reporters. "I don't know what happened. It wasn't pretty. They played great baseball and we didn't.

"They earned it and we certainly deserved what we got by the way we played, too. You've got to play your best baseball in October. You cannot make any mistakes and expect to go forward."

Asked about both Rodriguez and Torre, Cashman answered, "Why wouldn't they be coming back? That's not something that I'm even thinking about."

Cashman, the man who had wrested control of the baseball operations department from George Steinbrenner's lackeys, minions, and insidious forces who helped speed the downfall of the dynasty, was crestfallen himself. Moreover, he admittedly had a blind spot about the team's inherent weaknesses.

"This team fooled me to some degree," Cashman said.

As Leyland was carried off the field like a triumphant general, Torre composed himself in the manager's office, dressed for the ensuing plane trip, and set out for one final order of business.

Torre walked down the long, narrow hallway out of the visitors' clubhouse area and stopped at a set of metal double doors, the kind you would see inside a high-school gymnasium. For a moment, there was some confusion. Torre, now in a snappy dress coat and carrying his bags, was looking for his wife, Ali, who had come down to the clubhouse but was waiting for him somewhere else.

They finally found each other, and both stood by the doors for what seemed like an eternity—for what, it wasn't immediately clear. Torre hung his head, the mark of a defeated man. He couldn't find many words for his wife, and so he waited. She stared at him with a slight, loving smile, the look only a woman can give when she's proud of her man, regardless of defeat.

Torre, as it turned out, had asked a clubhouse attendant for a favor, and the attendant complied as soon as he could, bringing Leyland through the double doors. The Tigers manager, in celebratory mode, was in full uniform and fully doused by champagne. Upon seeing Mrs. Torre, he removed his cap, hugged her, and embraced Torre. A handshake turned into a hug.

Jeter and Jorge Posada had come out by then, dressed in suits and toting rolling luggage. Jeter made a detour just in time to congratulate

Leyland and then Pudge Rodriguez, who had also come to pay his respects and patted the Yankee captain on the shoulder, saying, "It's all right."

Following behind Jeter and Posada, A-Rod also walked out of the club-house, alone, "the Lonely Yankee" headed to the bus that would take the disappointing club to the airport. He didn't have any luggage with him, which was laughably ironic: the Yankee who now carried more metaphor-ical baggage than a 767 was momentarily unencumbered. But then again, it made sense: someone else was doing the heavy lifting somewhere.

Torre's congratulatory moment with Leyland was very nearly his last meaningful moment as Yankee manager. Because as the team took a dreary flight home to New York, George Steinbrenner was in a firing kind of mood.

CHAPTER NINETEEN

FALLOUT

"I am deeply disappointed at our being eliminated so early
in the playoffs. This result is absolutely not acceptable to me nor
to our great and loyal Yankee fans. I want to congratulate the
Detroit Tigers organization and wish them well. Rest assured,
we will go back to work immediately and try to right this
sad failure and provide a championship for the Yankees,
as is our goal every year."

YANKEES OWNER GEORGE STEINBRENNER,
OCTOBER 8, 2006

Anger was the emotion of the day, and for many days. From George
Steinbrenner on down, a first-round defeat in the Division Series
was simply unacceptable. The Yankee players shrugged it off as a hot
team getting good pitching and timely hitting at the right time. They
washed the defeat away in the shower jets in Detroit's visitors' clubhouse.
But that wasn't going to cut it for George Michael Steinbrenner III. He
might've been seventy-six, he might've been in failing health, but the man
knew good baseball, and he knew failure when he saw it. The Bombers
had made Steinbrenner, who proclaimed, "We haven't won it in a while.
We are going to win it this year," lose some credibility with the fans.

As Joe Torre and his players packed up after the defeat and headed
back to New York, one voice from the past spoke up. One of the cornerstones of the last four championships had been watching, scrutinizing the
series, and hated what he saw. Despised it. It made him sick.

Nobody was more apoplectic than Paul O'Neill, the former Yankee
right fielder doing commentary for the YES Network after Game 4.

O'Neill laid into his former team, and *Newsday*'s Neil Best chronicled it in the next day's paper.

"Today was absolutely ridiculous," O'Neill said from the YES studio. "It looked like a young team that was hungry against a veteran team that figured it would win easily."

At perhaps the same moment his former teammates Bernie Williams and Mariano Rivera were saying that nothing was absent and nothing was different from those championship teams of yesteryear, O'Neill was claiming there was "something missing," live on the franchise's network.

"You watch the other series and you see so much energy from the other teams," O'Neill noted.

It was a common refrain, a common rebuke. The Yankees, for all their talent, lacked a certain joie de vivre. They were mercenaries. They were less than the sum of their parts. Growing mustaches in August in homage to Don Mattingly—as some guys on the club did—didn't change that. Neither did Sal Fasano's chess games, which drew the C-list players and helped them pass the time until the playoffs. Sure, there was better chemistry than the past few seasons, but you were talking about a club that expected Kevin Brown, Kenny Lofton, Tony Womack, and Carl Pavano to be good teammates.

The Yankees flew home Saturday night and, according to one report, Torre walked through the airplane and thanked each player personally. The next day, Sunday, October 8, the *New York Post* had a back page that read "Disgrace"—with an Old English *D*, of course.

The *New York Daily News* had something different. On the front page, the paper blared that Torre was out. The story left more wiggle room than that, but Bill Madden and T. J. Quinn wrote, "Unless other team officials can talk The Boss out of it, or unless Torre, 66, agrees to resign in order to save face, sources said principal owner George Steinbrenner will replace the manager who was credited with returning the team to its fabled glory." The story mentioned that The Boss would love to hire Lou Piniella, a former Yankee manager and Alex Rodriguez's first skipper in Seattle.

The *Daily News* was ahead of the pack, and it was as big and juicy a story as it gets. But by the next day, other outlets were reporting that Steinbrenner, while angry enough to make a move, was undecided. The more time that passed, the more likely Steinbrenner was to waver or be talked out of the move. If Torre's firing didn't happen, the *Daily News* wouldn't be able to trumpet its exclusive as loudly. And that, in the tabloid wars, was no small thing.

Piniella was actually close with Madden, the top-bylined writer of the Torre firing exclusive. Piniella had managed the Yankees for the entire 1986 and 1987 seasons and parts of the 1988 season after playing in the Bronx from 1974 to 1984. Madden had been the *Daily News'* Yankee beat writer from 1980 to 1988, so he and Piniella went back more than twenty-five years. The two men had dined together during the 2004 winter meetings in the Marriott hotel in Anaheim, California, one example of their friendly relationship.

That's not to claim Madden's relationship with Piniella was driving the coverage, or that this was a one-source story. Madden was an acclaimed columnist and author who also went way back with Steinbrenner and reportedly admitted on the radio that The Boss was one of his sources for the original story.

But other reporters from competing papers were concerned about the potential Piniella hiring because they knew he was tight with Madden, and they feared that both New York baseball teams would be leaking stories to the *Daily News* on a regular basis if Torre was canned. One New York writer, clearly bothered by the predicament, told me that it would be disastrous if Piniella became the next manager for that very reason.

Torre's foibles were never more apparent than in the 2006 Division Series; his weaknesses had never shone through more than in the just-completed travesty. But he didn't appear to play favorites with the media. He'd go toe to toe with ESPN and even YES Network commentator Michael Kay if he didn't see something he'd like; in contrast, he'd be respectful to the smallest small-timers who showed up at Yankee Stadium. That's why some newspapermen felt a Torre firing would be a nightmare. The playing field, they believed, would've been tilted like a broken pinball machine.

As the heretofore Teflon Torre sat home in his Westchester County, New York, house and the media gathered outside of it waiting in vain for comment, different columnists offered contrasting views on the direction the Yankees must go.

Over the next two days, various Yankees came in to clean out their lockers, discuss why it all went wrong, and support Torre in various ways. None of the true superstars came in, though, so it was left to people such as Ron Villone, Jaret Wright . . . and Cory Lidle.

Lidle was a bit player in the grand scope of the 2006 season, although he did have an impact on the division-winning team. When he was dealt, a Philadelphia writer told me Lidle was usually a good quote. He didn't disappoint on the day he packed up his baseball gear, it turned out, for the final time of his life.

"We got taken by surprise," Lidle told reporters. "We got matched up with a team that was a little bit more ready to play than we were. We were all pretty surprised at how not ready we were for that series. I don't think we took the Tigers for granted, I just think they were up for it a little more than we were.

"They were fighting tooth and nail down to the last game of the season. We clinched pretty early. Maybe we were just in cruise control a little bit too much. It was kind of surprising, but they came out—they threw the ball exceptionally well. They hit the ball well. They did everything right."

Steinbrenner was staying at his hotel, the Regency, which had the Yankees flag up for all of New York to see. It was a wonder there weren't black or white plumes of smoke coming from the chimneys of the hotel.

It was believed Derek Jeter phoned Steinbrenner during this time, but the captain engaged in his standard non-denial semantics when he met with reporters at the World Series and the topic was broached. On that Sunday, though, Jeter publicly issued a statement through his agent that said, "By no means was Mr. Torre part of the problem. The bottom line is that we didn't get it done on the field. As a matter of fact, it was the best job he has done since he has been here."

Also, GM Brian Cashman and general partner Steve Swindal, The Boss' son-in-law, were said to be lobbying hard for Torre. The GM was Torre's biggest fan, even if Cashman had to occasionally cajole him to play youngsters such as Andy Phillips and Melky Cabrera, and even if he occasionally winced while Torre overused the bullpen during the course of a full-throttle season. Monday afternoon. The Boss bumped into reporters on his way out of town and said he hadn't made up his mind yet. He left for Tampa and left Yankee fans waiting in the breach.

In a bizarre coincidence during a bizarre week, A-Rod walked right by the Regency on the way to lunch with his wife, Cynthia, on that Monday, which was Columbus Day. When the writers staking out Steinbrenner saw Rodriguez walk by, they frantically called their sports editors, who pulled some of their men out of the Yankee Stadium clubhouse and into midtown Manhattan.

As A-Rod came out of Serafina restaurant on East 61st Street a while later, he was asked if he could spare a moment to talk. He answered, "No chance. Zero." But he pleasantly made small talk with fans who wanted autographs, though, momentarily losing his wife in the ensuing throng of media and supporters. The reporters were undaunted, and they pursued him regarding Torre's job status. A-Rod was silent.

In all fairness, Rodriguez had answered a slew of questions in Detroit, refusing to point a finger at Torre for his 1-for-14 series, saying he's "been incredible to me." By now, though, shrewd inquisitors knew not to take many of Rodriguez's words at face value. Especially when his actions spoke louder.

"Alex, are you going to be a Yankee next year?" one reporter yelled.

"Alex, what do you think of news Joe might be fired?" another hollered.

"If you could talk to Mr. Steinbrenner, what would you say?" someone inquired, telling A-Rod that The Boss was less than a block away.

"If Lou [Piniella] came, would you be psyched?" someone else asked.

A-Rod continued to give the reporters—and the referendum on Torre—the silent treatment, a stark contrast to the release Jeter issued on his skipper's behalf. Police officers actually escorted Rodriguez around the block to ward off reporters, although a TV cameraman momentarily stopped him.

"Guys, I'm with my wife," he said at the corner of Park and 61st. "I would like a little private time. I'd really appreciate it. Thank you, guys."

Oddly, Rodriguez and his wife went around an entire block after finishing lunch at approximately 3:20 P.M. The couple went east on 61st, south on Park, west on 60th, and north on Madison until they went into Barney's department store. Right before they entered the store, he stopped and chatted up an acquaintance he'd run into on Madison and 60th. Rodriguez told the man, "God is too good and we're too blessed."

When Rodriguez disappeared into the store, either for a shopping spree or as a way to lose the tailing reporters, the story seemed finished. But it wasn't. Hours later, after Rodriguez had had a chance to think the issue through, he called the New York Post's excellent beat writer, George King, and said, "Myself—and to my knowledge all of my teammates—support and enjoy playing for Joe Torre."

Shortly thereafter, King got a much bigger scoop. He broke the story for Tuesday's editions that Torre was indeed coming back, which was proven true when Steinbrenner called the manager fifteen minutes before a scheduled press conference to tell him he was still employed. It was sweet vindication for the *Post* . . . and the ultimate "up yours" to the *Daily News*. The next day, the *Post* riffed a *Daily News* logo that had said the *Daily News* had the best playoff coverage in town, saying that the *Post*'s was the most accurate.

"Keep your head down, because there is much crossfire in the tabloid wars," wrote ESPN.com's Buster Olney, who authored *The Last Night of the Yankee Dynasty* and kept the premier blog on baseball on the ESPN Web site.

"There is much speculation among New York journalists about who may have been the sources for the *Post* story Tuesday, and one popular theory is that the *Post* scoop was fueled by particular members of the Yankees' family as payback for the *News'* stories Sunday."

On October 30, the *Post* received the ultimate payoff: the newest circulation figures indicated that it had overtaken both the *Daily News* and the *Washington Post* and was now the fifth-biggest newspaper in the country. It listed ten snarky reasons it had triumphed in the latest circulation battle. The number-three reason was, "We didn't fire Joe Torre."

In the end, Steinbrenner realized he could live with Torre for another year. Nearly everyone who knew him or knew of him figured that The Boss would've canned Torre without a second thought a few decades ago. Perhaps, with age, he took heed of the saying "The devil you know is better than the devil you don't." He recognized that a lot of good was done in 2006 and throughout Torre's tenure, and he decided to let him finish out the final year of his three-year contract. General partner Steve Swindal and Cashman were reported to be the voices of reason in protecting Torre, and the cost of eating Torre's contract and then paying Piniella millions was also reportedly a critical factor.

Steinbrenner released his second statement in three days, saying, "I spoke to Joe Torre today and I told him, 'You're back for the year. I expect a great deal from you and the entire team. I have high expectations and I want to see enthusiasm, a fighting spirit and a team that works together. The responsibility is yours, Joe, and all of the Yankees.' Yes, I am deeply disappointed about our loss this year, we have to do better. And I deeply want a championship. It's about time."

Steinbrenner keyed in on a couple of important themes of the 2006 debacle. "A team that works together" could indicate a lack of cohesion in the clubhouse; it could particularly refer to Jeter's refusal to thaw out his relationship with A-Rod. "Enthusiasm" and "a fighting spirit" obviously referred to the team's sleepwalk through the Division Series. The fact that Steinbrenner said he deeply wanted a championship could speak to his own mortality in addition to his exacting standards. George wasn't getting any younger, and the Yankees were seemingly farther than they'd ever been from a World Series triumph.

Torre, though, seemed vindicated.

"I'm very excited about it," he said. "This has been the best job of my life. . . .

"Knowing what this organization expects from its people, especially its manager, it's something that on the heels of not being able to get through the first round, it's just something that you understand goes with the territory.

"Unfortunately, this year ended all too abruptly, but the season itself was very gratifying for me. I'm glad I get a chance to do it again."

Torre took issue with a media member who said that it has been six ringless years in the Bronx. He noted that it had been eighteen when he first got there. And he was right. Torre's four championships in five years will never be sullied by panicky managing in the 2006 playoffs or an inability to motivate his best player.

The exchange, however, illustrated that there were plenty of those in the media who were no longer blinded by Torre's aura of invincibility. There were even some who thought he was the principal problem that needed to be fixed, and it now seemed as if the Yankees were preparing for life beyond him when Don Mattingly was installed as bench coach and Lee Mazzilli was fired. Brian Cashman liked Mattingly almost as much as he liked Torre, and he was putting his people in place to move the organization forward. Torre, who once envisioned managing into his seventies, was grateful now just to get one more year.

Torre's mistakes couldn't be rectified unless the Bombers earned their twenty-seventh world championship and unless A-Rod was a signature piece of that title. One of the manager's shortcomings was in hanging Rodriguez out to dry, and the superstar knew it. A friend of A-Rod told SI's Jon Heyman that winter that A-Rod could live with Torre "for a year" if he had to, but he much preferred Piniella—who landed on his feet as the Cubs manager.

The day of Torre's press conference, Cashman said, "I fully expect [Alex Rodriguez] to stay here," silencing many people who thought one or the other must ship out before 2007. With Cashman's strong statement, it appeared that the Yankees' off-season would at least temporarily return to normal.

Cory Lidle was just happy to be here. Really. In the final weekend of the regular season, Lidle knew he probably wasn't going to be assigned a start in the Division Series. He hadn't done enough to usurp Jaret Wright's rule as the number-four starter, and the writing was on the clubhouse wall.

By all indications, that didn't seem to depress the thirty-four-year-old righty, kill his mood, or get him to question the decision makers in the organization. If he had to, the journeyman would pitch out of the bullpen—gladly. Now with his seventh organization, he was thrilled simply to get a chance for a World Series ring. As he stood by his locker for a conversation before a meaningless game against Toronto on September 30, he spoke of how being a Yankee was the best thing that had happened in his career.

"It means more to put on pinstripes than any other pair of pants, to me," he said. "There's a lot more pride in this clubhouse than other clubhouses that I've been in, and it's pretty special to be part of that."

Eleven days later, Lidle was dead. In an accident that made national news and had New Yorkers momentarily fearful of another terrorist attack, the budding pilot crashed into the thirtieth floor of a Manhattan apartment building called the Belaire during a flight in his single-engine, four-seat Cirrus SR20. He was traveling with Tyler Stanger, a flight instructor and friend. The two planned to fly to Nashville that night, and Lidle planned to fly eventually to his off-season home in California.

According to a report, fifteen firefighters, five civilians, and one police officer were taken to New York Presbyterian Hospital / Weill Cornell Medical Center with injuries from the crash. Nobody but Lidle and Stanger died. It was a particularly frightening and harrowing incident because of the terrorist attacks on September 11, 2001, in New York, although word broke by midafternoon that it was a private plane accident unconnected to terrorism. Still, it was particularly painful to the Yankees despite the fact that Lidle had been with them only a short time, because it evoked memories of former captain Thurman Munson's death in a small-airplane accident on August 2, 1979. In early September, Lidle had discussed his budding hobby with *New York Times* Yankee beat writer Tyler Kepner, who published perhaps the definitive piece on the pitcher's love of flying. In the 948-word profile, Lidle pooh-poohed the dangers of flying, and Stanger extolled his pupil's prowess.

"The whole plane has a parachute on it," Lidle told Kepner. "Ninety-nine percent of pilots that go up never have engine failure, and the one percent that do usually land it. But if you're up in the air and something goes wrong, you pull that parachute, and the whole plane goes down slowly."

Lidle was a controversial figure in the majors, even as a Yankee. He was a replacement player for Milwaukee during the strike in 1995, when it was clear that was his best chance at getting a legitimate look, and union hard-liners denounced him as a scab for many years afterward. When Lidle was traded to the Yankees on July 30, he criticized the Phillies on the way out, earning former teammate Arthur Rhodes' wrath.

"He is a scab," Rhodes told the Post's George King. "When he started, he would go 5⅓ innings and [the bullpen] would have to win the game for him. The only thing Cory Lidle wants to do is fly around in his airplane and gamble."

Rhodes was irate because Lidle said the Phillies weren't committed to winning, a frank admission that most major leaguers stay away from for obvious reasons. But Lidle seemed to have an addiction to truth-telling, or at least an addiction to being brutally honest about his own feelings.

"When he pitched, we busted our tails for him," Rhodes said. "He shouldn't say that, he shouldn't say anything like that because he is a scab. He crossed the line when guys like me, Flash [Tom Gordon], and [Mike] Lieberthal were playing. He is a replacement player.

"He doesn't have a work ethic. After every start, he didn't run or lift weights. He would sit in the clubhouse and eat ice cream."

For someone who was a throw-in to a deal for a superstar [Bobby Abreu], Lidle had an unusual amount of baggage. That's why when he made the "taken by surprise" comments about the Yankees after the 2006 season ended in embarrassment, none of the reporters was, well, taken by surprise.

On October 9, WFAN radio hosts Mike and the Mad Dog blasted Lidle for what they felt was criticism of Torre's lack of leadership and the Yankees' lack of overall preparation. Lidle attempted to backtrack and tried to claim he had been misquoted during a radio interview, although he hadn't read newspaper reports about his comments. He called Torre "a first-class manager."

"You know, we had quite a few meetings in the short time I was here. More meetings this year in the last two months than I've had on all my other teams put together," Lidle said. "Joe keeps them short, knows what to say. He gets respect from all of his players. His job is to keep players ready and I thought he did a really good job with it. . . .

"It's a team effort. There's no one that you can point a finger at. It's a team effort. You win as a team, you lose as a team. And we got beat."

Finally, he said, "On the record, I think Joe Torre is the man for this job and I'll leave it at that."

Lidle held out an olive branch to the radio hosts near the end of the interview, saying he'd like to sit down and meet with them so they could get a better understanding of who he really was rather than who they thought he was. It was another glimpse of his humanity, another example of his uniqueness. Another peer into the soul of an uncommon man.

The reality was, many media members appreciated his candor and good humor, and they enjoyed his worldview—which extended significantly beyond an outfield fence in a ballpark. Although Lidle spoke with reporters in the aftermath of the Division Series loss as he cleaned out his locker, his comments on September 30 were almost certainly his final at-length, one-on-one interview on the pleasure of being a Yankee.

His graciousness and humility should be remembered as part of a complete portrait, rather than just the harried phone conversation on WFAN or the broadsides in the daily papers. Lidle, for too short a period, was a Yankee. He knew how unique it was that he was walking in hallowed footsteps.

"How can you tell?" he asked. "Just how people carry themselves around here, the respect that the veterans give to the younger players. You can see it.

"And then on the field, the way the younger players are treated, they perform better when they get a shot—because they're more comfortable. It's just from top to bottom, it's run very professionally."

Growing up outside Los Angeles, Lidle didn't know much about the Yankee tradition. If it wasn't connected with the Dodgers or Angels, he said, he didn't know much about it. When asked why other teams didn't follow the Yankee blueprint, he didn't think they knew how.

"It really isn't complicated," he said. "It's just a sense of pride that starts at the top. For everyone that's not around here, you always hear the name George Steinbrenner. Well, it's his pride that filters through this organization—that makes the Yankees the Yankees."

Lidle, though, refused to attack the Phillies when given an opening, saying that they had a young core that was going to be good for a long time. He cited Cole Hamels as one of a few young pitchers who could help them immediately. There appeared to be no lingering animosity on his part.

"I just think once they made a change with the general manager, Pat Gillick took over, I think Gillick's going to put together a good team," he said. "I think they will win."

Although he was a key trade-deadline component, Lidle didn't feel any anxiety about having to produce in pinstripes.

"I haven't felt any different kind of pressure because the team wants to win," he said. "In fact, it's almost easier for a starting pitcher to pitch for this team. You know we're going to score runs, we have a good defense. They make the plays they're supposed to make. It almost makes it seem easier to pitch for this team.

"Everyone's got everyone's back."

One of Lidle's most vivid memories of the Yankees came in his first game against them, a Subway Series clash in his rookie year of 1997 while he was a Met. Lidle had finally made the major leagues on May 8 of that season, culminating a long journey that included outright releases from a couple of organizations. On the night of June 17 at The House That Ruth Built, Lidle answered an early call out of the bullpen when Met starter Armando Reynoso took a Luis Sojo one-hopper off his shin during the second inning.

"Yeah," he said wistfully, "I remember that day perfectly."

Four runs were already in, and the first hitter Lidle faced, O'Neill, hit an infield single that moved Sojo to third. Lidle walked Cecil Fielder, and the bases were suddenly loaded for Tino Martinez, who was having an outstanding season. Martinez had hit 12 homers in his first 30 games, and he had 28 homers by the end of June. Clearly, this was not a hitter you wanted to face.

"I'll never forget that day," Lidle said almost a decade later. "Tino Martinez was hot as could be."

Suddenly, Lidle couldn't find the strike zone. Ball one. Ball two. Ball three, and 56,253 were screaming at the top of their lungs.

"[I] stepped off the mound and told myself, 'This is not me. I've gotta throw strikes,'" Lidle said.

Lidle chucked a fastball for a called strike one. He got the count full. And then Martinez ripped a hard-hit one-hopper to the Mets' defensively stellar first baseman, John Olerud, who took care of the third out of the inning.

Emboldened, the Mets scored three times in the top of the third, but it wasn't enough. Lidle worked 4⅓ innings, allowing five hits and two unearned runs in the seventh, his final inning of work in the 6-3 loss. Lidle remembered Mets manager Bobby Valentine saying after the game that "he liked how I pitched and he thought I was fearless out there."

"I'll never forget that," Lidle said. "I got it done against this team."

In his other memorable clash against the Yankees, Lidle didn't get it done. In 2001, Lidle had become Oakland's fourth starter, and his 13-6 record and 3.59 ERA in 29 starts constituted his best season in the bigs. In the first postseason start of his career, though, he went up against a blood-ied but unbowed dynasty. By then, the Yankees had won three straight World Series and four in five years, but they had fallen behind two games to none to the A's in the Division Series. People who were ready for a new world champion were giddy over the Yanks' possibly early demise.

"They had different plans," Lidle said. "The Yankees had different plans."

In Game 3, Mike Mussina pitched one of the best games of his career but was overshadowed by Derek Jeter's terrific "flip play" at home plate to preserve a 1-0 victory over Oakland. Lidle had the unfortunate task of pitching the next night, and he was shelled for five hits and six runs (four earned) over 3⅓ innings of the 9-2 loss. The Yanks won the series in New York the next night.

"We all thought, especially after we won the first two games, we had it," Lidle said. "But basically we learned very quickly not to take anything for granted in sports, especially when you're dealing with a team that has as much pride as this team.

"I think if we got up 2-0 against other teams, the Twins or something like that, we probably would've walked over them in the next two games. But not here."

Entering the 2006 postseason, Lidle felt wearing pinstripes gave the Yankees an advantage, because the players could draw upon their experience.

"The core of this team has fallen behind in the playoffs," he said. "And when that happened, you know how not to quit—as opposed to say a younger team, like the Tigers or something. If they fall behind 0 and 2, they might not know how to fight back."

As it turned out, Lidle was mistaken. The Yankees seemed drained of their magical comeback abilities by 2006, squandering series leads in *every* playoff series that they lost over the last five years. They were up three games to two on Arizona in '01, a game on Anaheim in '02, two games to one on Florida in '03, three games on Boston in '04, and one game on the Tigers in '05.

Lidle couldn't do much about the last Division Series loss, pitching in relief in Game 4 for a horrible Wright. He retired the first four men he faced and allowed hits to his next four.

However, if there was a high-water mark in 2006, it came on the afternoon of August 21 at Fenway Park. And Lidle was front and center in it. The Yankees had won the first four games of the series, and Lidle started against Boston's David Wells, who was trying to prevent a season-killing sweep. Ironically enough, Wells was the winning pitcher for the Yankees when Lidle made that first appearance against them in 1997. This time, his team was triumphant. This time, Lidle's effort wasn't squandered. He tossed six scoreless innings of three-hit ball, and the bullpen preserved a 2-1 victory that sewed up the AL East six weeks early.

He had missed the first few games of the series while attending a funeral for his grandmother in California, so this was admittedly a very emotional start for him. He was able to analyze his own performance proudly but in the proper perspective. If anything, he downplayed his own role.

"I hadn't been around to see or be a part of that rivalry before, but I felt like I was right in the middle of it," he said. "Getting the ball in [the fifth game] was huge for me. And to come up on the winning side, I think it opened a lot of people's eyes to what I can do in a pressure situation.

"Yeah, I threw the ball well. [But] Wells threw the ball well, we only scored two runs that game. It's one of those things where it went our way and I made good pitches, got into trouble a couple times but got out of it."

Lidle's status as a replacement player obviously dogged him everywhere he went, including Philadelphia. Up until his death, it was the issue that most people identified him with. At least those who knew him and liked him can know that he sensed it wasn't an issue with the Yankees.

"The first five minutes you walk in this clubhouse," he said, "you know it's a different atmosphere."

When the Yankees won Lidle's first start in early August, Fasano—a former teammate of his in Philly—put ice cream bars on the chair of his locker. It was just another fond memory of his time in New York, another anecdote to cherish.

"Everybody over here has made it very easy," he said. "Like, Mariano is easy to talk to, Jeter and [Jorge] Posada. Bernie. I've known Jason for a long time.

"All those guys are very easy to talk to. They make you feel comfortable, make you feel like part of the team right away. And that's another reason why this team does so good year in and year out, because the core group of these guys know how to make everyone in the clubhouse feel like they're part of the team."

As Lidle spoke, it was easy to view a picture that he displayed prominently in his locker. It was of himself, his wife, Melanie, and his six-year-old son, Christopher, smiling widely with Yankee Stadium in the background. Good times, cut way too short.

About the only thing that went right for the Yankees in October was that the Mets lost in the NLCS in a thrilling but heartbreaking seven games to St. Louis. Had they reached the Fall Classic for the fifth time in their franchise's history, it might've turned New York into a Mets town again. And a World Series title, in all likelihood, would've tipped the balance among the casual fans—the undecideds, if you will—the way the war on Iraq tipped the scale on the 2006 elections that November.

Instead, the Mets didn't eclipse the Yankees, at least not in 2006. But that didn't mean they weren't about to. It didn't mean that for the first time in a while, there was an argument that could be made about which club was stronger, which club was going in the right direction faster.

The Yankees began their off-season by subtraction, and Gary Sheffield was the first casualty—but not until he had agitated and infuriated members of the organization, and not until he had cast a blinding light on the perceived shortcomings of the venerable franchise.

The ironic part of the Sheffield saga that played out in October and early November was this: Sheffield refused to talk after the Game 4 loss, refused to face the music and answer the questions about the stunning embarrassment. And he was as much to blame as anyone. He admitted during the winter that he'd rushed back after the injury and wasn't at his best, so in effect he created a logjam and forced the Yankees' hand.

Of course, they also should be blamed for the disastrous experiment. In the organization's arrogance, it was decided that someone who hadn't played more than two games in the infield since 1993 was capable of making a move to first. The Mets made the same dumb decision with catcher Mike Piazza in 2003, and Piazza was an utter failure there. Sheffield committed an error in the final game and began catching balls underhanded, because his wrist hurt from the constant twisting and pounding that he took fielding practice throws. It's worth noting Jason Giambi had a similar wrist injury in September, and his doctor told him it would be better on the hinge if he didn't play first. Now Sheffield, off surgery that season, was being put there.

To clarify the issue, it wasn't that Sheffield's poor defense caused a Division Series flameout. Rather, his impotent bat (he had an opposite-field RBI single in Game 1 and finished 1 for 12 in the series) helped kill the lineup's momentum. His bat kept Melky Cabrera out of the starting lineup, because had he been relegated to a bench role, Cabrera could've played left, Giambi could've played first, and Matsui could've been the DH.

"Nobody was asked to change positions but me," Sheffield was glad to point out. "I was put in the toughest situation. I tried to do what I could to help the team, but unfortunately I didn't have enough time."

Right after the series ended, he expressed surprise that it was Torre's head on the chopping block. In an interview with *USA Today*, he said he predicted he and A-Rod would be the first two run out of town, and—as usual—he was half right. The Yankees decided to exercise Sheffield's option for the sole purpose of trading him. They didn't want Boston or Toronto to get their hands on him, and he was hopping mad when he found out. Yes, the man who was infuriated in the spring when he found out the club might not exercise his contract was now irate that they would.

"This will not work, this will not work at all," Sheffield told *USA Today*. "I don't want to play first base a year for them. I will not do that.

"I don't know what they're [Yankees] going to do. Maybe they picked it up just to trade me. If they do that, if I just go to a team for one year, there's going to be a problem. A big problem. I will not do this."

Sheffield found sympathetic ears in the media and continued to pound his message home. In at least one case, he called a media member unsolicited. He said he would not play first base and DH for one year with the Yankees.

"It ain't going to work," he told YESNetwork.com. "I ain't going down this easily.

"If you don't think much of me, somebody else will. I can be a fit with someone else. Here's some friendly advice. If you want to trade for me, you have to deal with me directly. Trust me, you won't want me there if I'm not happy.

"I don't care if I love the owner, if I love the GM, if I love the city. I'm going on my terms. . . . I was excited to be a free agent. But I've been playing too long to be put in these situations. I shouldn't have these negotiation problems. All I've done is produce for eighteen years."

By November 5, though, his tone had changed. He told the very same Web site, "I'm good. Everything is good. I've been talking to Brian a lot and we've worked things out. I just have to end up in the right place."

It was dizzying trying to keep up with Sheffield's moods. On Wednesday, November 8, Sheffield appeared at the opening of a diner in Times Square, ostensibly to pick up a $25,000 check for his charitable foundation. Unbeknownst at the time, the Yankees had traded him to Detroit the day before, on Tuesday afternoon. The Tigers requested a seventy-two-hour window to negotiate an extension, which turned out to be for two years and $28 million.

So even though Sheffield was a goner, he attacked the Yankees with a staggering vigor. After sounding respectful at the beginning, he dropped numerous bombs on the organization that he'd said he loved, and threatened to make them pay in the end.

"Everybody knows when I come to another team, I'm coming back looking for you," he said. "That's just the way it is. For the Dodgers it happened, for the Marlins it happened.

"When you let me go, I've got a chip on my shoulder, and I'm coming with it."

Sheffield's biggest gripe was that he was sent packing because of Bobby Abreu, whom he deemed an inferior player but Cashman didn't.

"He's a good player," Sheffield said. "But like I say, you can draw it up any kind of way: he ain't me. And that's the bottom line.

"I understood them having to make this move for the remainder of the season. But to sit there and I'm leaving because of [him], I was always told you leave because somebody's better than you. I don't think that's the case here."

The veteran slugger's other contention was that he was blocked by "middlemen" from speaking with Steinbrenner. He insisted that if Steinbrenner was in better health, he would've been a Yankee in 2007.

"I know I would be here," he said. "Because when you have middlemen blocking him and won't let you do certain things, they get in the way and their personal feelings get in the way, that's what happens.

"You know who the middleman is. You all talk to him every day."

Sheffield waited outside an International House of Pancakes that The Boss frequented in Tampa for two hours, but he never talked with the man he negotiated the original contract with. From the moment he arrived as a Yankee, Sheffield wanted a world championship ring with the famous NY logo on it. He had said it was his mission, but now he said he had come to grips with the fact that it now was *Mission: Impossible*.

"If I was fully appreciated like I should be, then it would've mattered to me," he said. "But I know I only came to the Yankees because of George Steinbrenner. And if one guy only wants you here, and that's the reason why you're here, then it becomes a thing where you let bygones be bygones. And that's what I've done."

After insinuating Cashman was one of the nefarious "middlemen" and again blasting Torre for his lineup shuffling in the playoffs, Sheffield admitted he wished he had a better relationship with those two. It was Sheffield at his hypocritical best—or worst—depending on your vantage point. The reporters assembled at the diner that night couldn't hold back their glee, knowing the disgruntled outfielder's comments would be blown up on the back page the next morning.

"My situation, honestly, I never was comfortable," he said. "I was always feeling a little insecure with where I fit here and where I belonged. Do they want me here?

"And I had to play on those terms. And I was being a man about it and going out and trying to do my job under the conditions. I'm not going to complain about it. I didn't complain about it then, and I'm not gonna complain about it now."

Although he knew he was a goner, Sheffield acknowledged he was Alex Rodriguez's sounding board in 2006. Asked who would take his place, he answered, "Nobody," a perceived shot at Derek Jeter and other team leaders.

"You all better get ready," he said. "There's nobody."

With one more incendiary comment to the *New York Times* that night, Sheffield issued a disturbing warning for 2007.

"I will tell you that not everything is rosy in Yankeeland," he said. "It's all a façade—it ain't real."

Sheffield was revealed, when the trade became official two days later, as an ingrate. His comments were as inconsistent and contradictory as always. Cashman, one of the "middlemen," had dealt him to a team that promised not to play him at first, to a contender, to a club that gladly was willing to negotiate a two-year option. And the GM sent the slugger to the manager he loved playing for. And yet, knowing all this, Sheffield still left town with guns blazing.

Despite what he said briefly about the Yankees in his teleconference with the Tigers, there was rancor in the air. Although he justified his actions by saying he'd acted as his own agent and was forced into saying and doing things he didn't want to do, it was a hollow rationalization. And he crowed that he received his extension in the end, so he wasn't that broken up about his harsh words. The whole situation was hypocritical.

With that disclaimer, it doesn't mean that his words had no truth to them. Police officers and law enforcement officials often get their most important evidence from stool pigeons, from whistle-blowers, from malcontents. Even though those people have an axe to grind, they often have seen the truth. And they often have nothing to lose.

Sheffield was the Yankees' agitator, and he was churning plenty of dirty laundry. Many thought Steinbrenner to be in failing health, and he fainted during his granddaughter's play on October 29 in North Carolina and was rushed to the hospital. It was the second time in three years Steinbrenner had fainted in public, since, as previously noted, he also passed out during Otto Graham's funeral in December 2003. He also had a rough time moving around during the groundbreaking in August and mentioned the heat at the time.

If The Boss was losing his battle with age, if he was finally succumbing to the passage of time, he certainly deserved to do so with dignity. Nevertheless, it affected the decisions in the organization, because The Boss would've never let Torre keep his job years ago, many baseball observers believed.

The A-Rod/Jeter issue was perhaps more disconcerting, though, because it affected what happened on the field. There's nothing you can do about a man growing old, but there was something to be done about the two infielders' uneasy relationship.

When Jeter picked up the Hank Aaron Award at Game 4 of the World Series in St. Louis, he was deluged by questions about the 2006 team's failings. Specifically, he was asked about Rodriguez. Although the Yankees had said A-Rod wouldn't be traded and the third baseman expressed a desire to remain with the Yankees through the end of his career, few people were naive enough to think a deal was an impossibility.

"Do I expect him back?" Jeter asked. "Yeah, why wouldn't I expect him to be back?

"You never sit around trying to figure out with our organization, but Alex has what, a few more years left on his deal? So yeah, I would expect him to be back."

Jeter denied there was any tension in the clubhouse, something Rodriguez specifically mentioned after Game 3.

"What tension?" Jeter asked.

The captain was then buttonholed about whether he could make a better show of public support for Rodriguez, and he made it sound like nothing would change in 2007.

"What would you like me to do?" he asked. "You're there, everyone supports all your teammates all the time. I don't know if there's anything else I can do. I'm not that smart."

Jeter has always been cited as the ultimate team player and one of the ultimate winners in the history of professional sports. But in being intractable on the issue of Rodriguez, some observers felt his own human weaknesses got in the way of his club's success. He couldn't drop his grudge, even at the expense of Rodriguez's—and by extension the team's—performance, these observers felt.

Until a rapprochement happened, these observers believed, he and Rodriguez would never win a world championship together. And both men were so supremely talented, neither might win a championship without the other if they were to part company. They were in this together, like it or not.

The day after Sheffield's most inflammatory comments, top Yankees officials were in Staten Island to unveil a new business partnership regarding their Class A club. Swindal and Levine disputed the notion that Steinbrenner's health was more fragile than ever. They refused to concede that The Boss' latest incident was more evidence that the team's principal owner was in a delicate, precarious state. He had passed out during a performance of *Cabaret* in which his granddaughter, Haley Swindal, was playing the lead role. His spokesman called the venue "a Revolutionary War [era] auditorium with no air-conditioning and the windows closed tight."

"I was at my daughter's play," Swindal said. "It was so hot and miserable, I could've fallen down just as easily. It was a very tough environment for somebody to sit in, much less somebody seventy-six years old.

"He was awake and alert when they took him away."

After Steinbrenner's latest scare became public, his publicist, Howard Rubenstein, claimed he was doing well and "raising hell." The Boss went back to work in his Legends Field office in Tampa, but that didn't mean he wasn't more fragile than ever physically.

"I think it's a nice thing for [Sheffield] to be concerned about The Boss' health," Levine said, probably facetiously. "But [Steinbrenner] is in perfect health.

"I talked to him three times this morning. I talked to him well into the night. He's working very, very hard. We have very, very sophisticated issues we're dealing with on the business side. Putting a team together. Intricate financial and other arrangements. He's on top of the game."

Levine felt the issue remained in the public spotlight because the media wouldn't back off it, but the truth was that Steinbrenner had two extremely public health scares within a three-year period. Many thought he might've had a mini-stroke at the Graham funeral, which he vehemently denied.

Other than the Sheffield saga, the front-burner issue at the beginning of the off-season was the bidding war on Japanese righty Daisuke Matsuzaka. The Seibu Lions were posting their number-one starter, who was the MVP of the World Baseball Classic back in March. The posting process occurs when a Japanese player is not yet eligible for free agency but the team he's under contract with wants to get a financial reward for allowing him to go to Major League Baseball. At the time, the thought was that the winning post could reach $30 million.

"He's definitely a top-of-the-rotation starter," one general manager said. "He's one of those guys that never really throws the same pitch twice in the same sequence.

"He's a guy who should have tremendous success in the States. He's probably like [Greg] Maddux early in his prime—probably with a little more fastball."

The posting process ended at 5:00 P.M. on November 8, and Seibu had four business days to reject or accept the bid after that. As the Yankees gathered in Staten Island the day after that, they still had no knowledge of whether they'd submitted the winning bid.

For the Yankees to move forward in 2007, for them to legitimately fix their weaknesses and build a team meant for the playoffs, they absolutely needed someone like Matsuzaka. And because two of their primary foes, the Mets and Red Sox, were expected to bid competitively on him, they needed to win the negotiating rights to keep him out of their hands. If Matsuzaka landed with the Mets, they might finally eclipse the Yankees in New York from a popularity standpoint. But if Boston landed him, it would reshape the AL East. It had a chance to affect the Bombers the way the Johnny Damon signing affected the Red Sox in 2006.

The twenty-six-year-old won three games during the World Baseball Classic and was 17-5 with a 2.13 ERA for Seibu, whiffing 200 in 186⅓ innings. Speculation was that the bidding would be furious, and there were reportedly back-channel negotiation attempts by three unnamed teams. His agent, Scott Boras, compared his fastball to Tom Seaver's and his slider to Steve Carlton's. Boras was looking for a minimum of a four-year deal.

Meanwhile, the Yankees were in a real pitching bind. Other than Chien-Ming Wang, there were question marks regarding every established starter. After the club refused the $17 million option on Mike Mussina for 2007, however, they negotiated a two-year deal with the thirty-seven-year-old righty fairly quickly. Nearly every baseball observer believed keeping Mussina was a good idea because of his dependability, fairly good health record, and budding role as an elder statesman for the staff. One of the most established columnists in the city—the *New York Times'* Murray Chass—didn't seem to agree, though.

The day of Torre's press conference, while nearly everybody else in the city was sizing up the manager's job status, Chass used his column to take more shots at Mussina, who seemed to be his primary target.

"Nothing against Mike Mussina," Chass began, "but he is the symbol of the Yankees' failure to win the World Series the last six years. If George Steinbrenner is seeking a scapegoat, make it Mussina."

Actually, of the four established starters acquired or signed from outside the organization who were still with the team at the time, Mussina was the best of the bunch. If anybody symbolized the Yankees' mistakes, their arrogance to throw money at pitching, it was Randy Johnson, Jaret Wright, or Carl Pavano. Although Mussina coughed up a two-run lead in the fifth inning of Game 2, an egregious failure, he still pitched far better than Johnson or Wright, in both the short term and the long term.

But of Johnson, Chass wrote, "Johnson has become an aging and aching pitcher, not to mention an inconsistent one. As a postseason pitcher, he reached his zenith in 2001 with Arizona. That was a lot of innings ago. In Game 3 last week, he allowed five runs in five and two-thirds innings."

Then, although Mussina was markedly better than that, Chass wrote, "Mussina pitched his division series game against the Tigers just well enough to lose. A genuinely top-notch pitcher finds a way to win. Mussina finds a way to lose."

Chass' axe grinding aside, Johnson's status was far more worrisome heading into 2007. He underwent surgery to repair a herniated disk after the season, and Cashman wasn't counting on him for Opening Day.

"Because of his age, I don't think anybody should make any representations that he's going to be ready for spring training," the GM said. "I suspect we'll take him along slowly. And does that jeopardize him being ready for Opening Day?

"The time frame could allow him to be ready for Opening Day, but we just want to make sure we get it right so we have him for the long haul. So if it takes a little extra time, so be it. Because we want to have a full, healthy Randy the whole season. So if it costs us the beginning of April, that's fine."

A death in Johnson's family changed the Yankees' plans, however, The sudden passing of Johnson's brother over the winter led to a condolence phone call by Cashman. When the Big Unit and Cashman spoke, Johnson expressed a strong desire to be traded west, so he could be closer to family. Although he owned a no-trade clause, he told the Yankee GM that wouldn't be a problem.

On January 9, the Yankees announced that a trade with Arizona was official. The Bombers received right-handed pitchers Luis Vizcaíno, Steven Jackson, Ross Ohlendorf, and infielder Alberto Gonzalez from Arizona. All but Vizcaíno were expected to start the 2007 season in the minors, but the GM jettisoned an underperformer, grabbed three promising minor leaguers, and had to pay only $2 million of Johnson's $16 million salary. It was considered addition by subtraction for the many fans and media members who loathed the Big Unit, but it was also another move forward in Cashman's master plan of getting younger, cheaper, and deeper in the farm system.

Since the club also traded Wright to Baltimore a few days after the Staten Island function, Pavano's role in 2007 loomed larger than ever. Pavano was emblematic of the Yanks' problems following their championship years.

The pitcher was a critical player for Cashman and Torre, who both enthusiastically supported his signing. For two years, Pavano seemed to treat his employment with the Yankees like a mobster who has been given a no-show job. Now, Pavano would be the key pitching figure in 2007, if Cashman stood by his proclamation that he wouldn't trade him. Pavano is a prime example of why the NFL doesn't have guaranteed contracts. If he was a malingering quarterback, he would've been cut long ago.

The GM went way out on a limb by 2006, remaining the right-hander's only public supporter after everyone else turned away. Although even he gave up on Pavano at the time of the car accident, Cashman knew he still needed a return for his investment in 2007.

"I'm not going to say I'm looking at it as a bonus, but I'm not going to also say I can count on him, either, because maybe I've jinxed myself the last two years," Cashman said. "But when you come up with the back and the shoulder strain he had the first year and the car accident, he's had some incredibly bad, unfortunate luck—as have we because of it—the first two years.

"When he's healthy, I have no doubt what he's capable of doing. I know there's a lot of people out there that seem to doubt that. I do not. He's a quality major-league starter when healthy. Physically, he's not been able to get to the post. If physically he's able to get to the post, I have no doubt he'll be successful.

"And I want him to be with us, because I'm not going to sell—I have no intention of selling—him off short and buying out just because of the bad taste in my mouth the first two years because of injuries."

When Cashman was reminded of the dire need to improve the rotation, he dropped the names of righty prospects Darrell Rasner and Jeff Karstens and mentioned how youngsters Philip Hughes and Tyler Clippard were getting closer to the majors. For fans who watched Cashman trade for Roger Clemens coming off a world championship, this could be considered a shock to the system. But Cashman is proud of his farm system, and he spent considerable time and energy rebuilding it after it was carpet-bombed in the aftermath of the dynasty years. Still, he knew his rotation would be scrutinized more than ever the following season.

"It's all talk, it's all noise until you're taking the ball every five days and you're being productive," he said. "So obviously this is going to be an area of concern. . . .

"This question's not going to go away. When we get to camp, our starting rotation will obviously be under a lot of scrutiny because of the injuries and surgeries and stuff of that nature."

While the GM appeared to have a strong grip on the reins of the franchise, turning the Yankees away from their dysfunction of a few years ago was not an easy task. He even helped turn Steinbrenner away from firing Torre, and he'd be vindicated if the manager won in the final year of his contract.

The reality was, even if lackeys such as Billy Connors and Bill Emslie no longer wielded any significant power in the Yankee Fishbowl, people such as Pavano were still walking, talking evidence of past mistakes. From that standpoint, the winter of 2004 was a low-water mark, because that's when Pavano and Wright were signed and Johnson was acquired. The GM couldn't wash his hands totally of the last few years, even if he often wasn't the decision-making figure in key moves such as signing Sheffield and Wright. Since winning the last World Series, the Yankees had brought in pitching from all over the world, and Jeff Weaver, Ted Lilly, Javier Vázquez, Kevin Brown, Jose Contreras, and Esteban Loaiza mostly failed on the biggest stage in baseball.

The reality was, even with Cashman leading the baseball operations with a strong hand and a clear vision, the 2006 season was a failure of epic proportions. The 2006 club looked beautiful on a lineup card but wretched in the playoffs, much like a foreign sports car that appears gorgeous in the showroom but keeps breaking down. Although it wasn't his job to assimilate new Yankees into the clubhouse, Cashman was charged with building a team that could work together and break the drought in 2007.

The intense scrutiny and sometimes unrealistic expectations of the media and fans were a reality that no Yankee could avoid, and the Jeter/ A-Rod dynamic was the prime example of that. But the Yankees also shot themselves in the foot with their own arrogance, and anointing Sheffield as the starting first baseman for the playoffs was a foolhardy move.

During a quiet aside at the end of the day in Staten Island, though, Cashman tried to put the situation in perspective.

"Should've been a world championship season," he said inside the St. George Theater. "I did everything I could do. I can live with [the ultimate outcome]."

Both he and Torre tried to reason out the playoff loss, especially in the aftermath of St. Louis' staggering championship following an 83-victory regular season. The Cardinals very nearly blew the NL Central with a terrifying September collapse, but they instead won the World Series. Of the five teams Cards manager Tony La Russa had brought to the Fall Classic, this was hands down his weakest team. Yet he won. It was all a crapshoot, Torre, Cashman, and many other baseball observers believed.

"This past year and the last five years have shown whoever is the best on paper doesn't necessarily translate in the postseason anyway," Cashman said.

Given a choice between redemption and bread, the great Russian novelist Fyodor Dostoevsky once wrote, human beings will choose bread. In that vein, given a choice between perspective and lust, Yankee fans were conditioned for the latter. They wanted a championship, not explanations. Blame it on eight decades of unparalleled success.

On November 10, the team heard unofficial word that Matsuzaka would be an enemy combatant, not a Yankee. On the night of Torre's Safe at Home Foundation dinner, ESPN's Olney reported that the Red Sox appeared to win the bidding with a staggering posting of $38–$45 million. (It turned out to be $51.1 million.) It looked as though the Yankees would be forced to face the Japanese Maddux, the guy who had Seaver's fastball and Carlton's slider. It was another kick in the stomach in a year that had begun with such promise.

"We've come up short, evidently," Torre said, citing the report. "It's one of those blind draws you just have to deal with. I don't know a great deal about him, other than he was of great interest to us."

That night at Pier 60 of Chelsea Piers, Torre welcomed back members of the 1996 world championship team, the team that resurrected the Yankee dynasty, the club that broke the drought—as Torre had pointed out a month earlier—of eighteen years. Some of the men, such as Jimmy Key, looked older than their years; others, such as Andy Pettitte and Jeter, looked like they had another decade of baseball in them if they so desired. Indeed, after flirting with retirement, Pettitte decided to keep pitching, and he agreed to a one-year $16 million contract on December 8 with a player option for 2008. It was a "Back to the Future" move by the Yanks, who also hoped to bring Clemens back for part of 2007.

So as the calendar prepared to turn on another ringless year in the Bronx, this is where the Yankees were. Once again, they promised to have an amazing stew of individuals on the 2007 roster, a veritable All-Star lineup. They promised to have at least a handful of players with past World Series rings on board. Their tradition remained unmatched, their resources were second to none, and their owner and their front office remained dedicated to doing everything possible to win a world championship.

But there's no such thing as stacking the deck in baseball, the Yankees have learned the hard way. With the pride of playing in pinstripes comes an unfathomable, unrelenting pressure. Competition is the ultimate equalizing factor. You can't buy a World Series; there has to be an element of chemistry that goes beyond skill. Still more, there has to be an element of luck—or call it magic, if you're supernaturally inclined. And that was one thing, ultimately, that has been missing in the Bronx for years.

On the night of his Safe at Home Foundation dinner, Torre was in a jovial mood, using the 1996 team's appearance to make a point about soaring expectations, to make a point about what's lost when playoff perfection becomes a demand.

"There was a certain innocence about this '96 team," Torre said. "We were underdogs. And if we had not gotten to the World Series in '96, I sensed that everybody would've been proud of what we'd done."

It was a quaint thought.

INDEX